Sea of Marmara

Thásos

Samothrace

Imbroz

Dardanelles

Lemnos

A E G E A N

S E A

Skiros

Psará

Chios

Smyrna

Lesbos

Ándros

Sámos

Tinos

Ikaria

River Menderes

Cyclades

Páros

Náxos

Amorgós

Kos

Bodrum

Milos

Astipália

Thira

Rhodes

Karpáthos

Kásos

| 0 | 20 | 40 | 60 | 80 | 100 Miles |

| 0 | 40 | 80 | 120 | 160 Kilometres |

The Greek Adventure

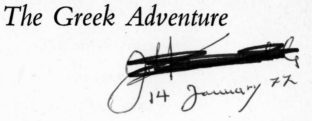

14 January 77

The Greek Adventure

Lord Byron and Other Eccentrics
in the War of Independence

David Howarth

COLLINS
St James's Place, London
1976

William Collins Sons & Co Ltd
London · Glasgow · Sydney . Auckland
Toronto · Johannesburg

First published 1976
© David Howarth 1976

ISBN 0 00 216058 7

Set in Monotype Bembo
Made and printed in Great Britain by
William Collins Sons & Co Ltd Glasgow

Contents

Illustrations

The author thanks the owners for their kind permission
to reproduce these pictures, and Sue Ullstein and Marian
Berman for their help in collecting them.

8

Prologue

A few summers ago I sailed my small yacht into Missalonghi on the west coast of Greece. We had come across from Italy, and south by way of Corfu and some of the other Ionian Islands, Paxos, Lefkas, Ithaca and Cephalonia; and we were on our way to the Corinth Canal, which leads to the Aegean.

The Ionian Sea and the islands are blessed by warmth and light. On most summer days there is a breeze, enough to exercise whatever skill in sailing you may have, and not often enough to alarm you. The sea scintillates, and when the sun is too hot you heave to and jump overboard and swim round the boat, and then sail on again, still wet and salty. Usually in the afternoon it is calm; and then, however long you sit and look down into the water, its colour is always unbelievable, sometimes a luminous turquoise and sometimes the deepest cobalt blue. It is so clean and clear you can see the bottom of it at forty feet. At nightfall you make for a village harbour or an empty anchorage you have chosen from the chart, where the only sound is the bells of the herds of goats, and the Mediterranean scent comes off the land, of the spiky aromatic bushes that mottle the hills.

All round like painted backdrops on a stage are landmarks that remind you of things you learned at school, however long ago you began to forget them. Ahead, a gap in the hills is the narrow entrance of the Gulf of Corinth: the Emperor Nero must have known it well. Astern is the island where Homer lived; to the south, the mountains of the Peloponnese, with Olympia among them and Argos and Sparta beyond them; and to the north, the Acarnanian mountains which rise farther east to the summit of Parnassus.

The entrance to Missalonghi from this Elysian sea is not very easy to find, especially in the agreeable torpor of a summer after-

noon. The part of the coast where it lies is unlike any other in Greece.
For miles and miles, it is straight and flat and uninhabited, without
any landmark you can identify, and the sea is so shallow you cannot
come close inshore. Indeed, what you can see is scarcely a coast at
all. It is only a narrow line of muddy dunes, and behind it is a wide
inaccessible marsh where the British Admiralty chart has some rare
inscriptions: 'Fisheries covered with a few inches of water' and
'Mudbanks barely covered' – things that could only exist on the
edge of a tideless sea. Beyond the marsh on the chart (which is
based on a survey made by HMS *Hydra* in 1864) are words that are
even less alluring: 'Extensive plains flooded during the winter.'
That is where Missalonghi is. But you cannot see the town from the
sea in a boat as small as mine.

At last, when you think you must have gone too far, you find
two buoys about half a mile off shore, and between them a channel,
hopefully dredged, which leads to a gap in the dunes. You sail
through the gap, and the scene is abruptly transformed. The water
is no longer blue, it is thick and brown; you can see the dirt in it
swirling in your wake. To port is a bare bank of mud cracking
open in the sun, to starboard a modern causeway, and beyond it
the surface the naval surveyor described so long ago; it is certainly
not solid, yet hardly seems to deserve to be called a liquid. For two
miles the channel goes straight through this melancholy swamp,
and then it opens into a large harbour, also dredged from the mud.
It was empty when we sailed in, and looked as though it always had
been. There was no crane or warehouse on its quays, and no sign
that anything had ever been shipped or landed; and there were
none of the cheerful taverns that line most waterfronts in Greece.
A few small boys were sitting by their bicycles fishing, and on the
waste land behind, stray dogs were hunting garbage.

The town is ten minutes' walk from the harbour, and it had the
same air of hopeless resignation, as if it had just survived a pestil-
ence or was expecting one. Most of the men drinking ouzo in the
square were soldiers; obviously they did not belong there and wished
they were somewhere else. It was all un-Greek. Most Greek towns

are built on a steep hillside or round an acropolis, but Missalonghi is flat; its narrow streets, intersecting at drab right-angles, are only a little higher than the bog around the town, and in winter only a little drier. And most Greek people, on the whole, are optimistic and carry lightly whatever cares they have; but the Missalonghiotes seem glum, at least on a superficial acquaintance, as if the agues of the swamp were always in their bones, and the residue of past generations of malaria in their blood. Looking back from the harbour you can still see the mountains, but the marshes of Missalonghi are a sad unique enclave in the radiant land, and even the sun seems dimmer.

*

On this sombre shore, in the morning of the 5th of January 1824, there was a bizarre event. Two ships had come to anchor in the offing, and after breakfast a party of foreign visitors with a vast amount of baggage climbed down into boats and were rowed through one of the gaps in the sodden dunes and across the miles of shallows to the town: there was no dredged channel and no harbour then.

Everyone in the town turned out to look at them and cheer; somebody fired a salvo of artillery, and muskets were discharged above the heads of the crowd. The welcome was led by a party of Greek captains of bandits and guerillas, a bishop, a score or so of foreign army officers, French, German and Italian, all in gallant uniforms, and one English colonel; and at the head of them all, a very small portly man with a face like an amiable rodent, who wore a formal European morning dress, a flat cap and thick pebble glasses. This was Prince Alexander Mavrocordato, who was not really a prince in any normal sense of the word, but at that moment was the President of the Greek Senate. He and the officers were the survivors of a recent disaster in battle, and Greece was involved in a blood-thirsty war to win freedom from the Turks.

The first man ashore was also in a magnificent scarlet uniform, although he had never worn a uniform before. This was Lord

Byron, already famous as a poet and notorious as a libertine. The
rest of the party was his personal entourage: Count Pietro Gamba,
the young brother of the last of his mistresses; his valet Fletcher,
who had shared all his travels and remained, whatever happened,
unalterably English; Tita Falcieri the Venetian gondolier, who
believed rightly or wrongly that his father had sold him to Byron;
Lega Zambelli the steward, who in moments of crisis lay coiled like
a viper on his master's money chest; a black American groom whose
name was never recorded; Loukas Chalandritsanos, a beautiful
Greek boy dressed as a page, the object of Byron's last and most
poignant love-poem; Francesco Bruno, the personal physician, only
just qualified; a Newfoundland dog, a bulldog and five horses.
Each of the men in his way was devoted to Byron, except perhaps
Loukas, whose feelings were enigmatic; and all of them were afraid
of him, especially Dr Bruno, who was terrified not only of Byron
but also of Tita and the dogs.

Of all the Greeks in Missalonghi, Mavrocordato was probably the
only one who knew that Byron was a poet, and if any of the rest
had known they would not have cared. They believed he was a
famous English general who had come to lead them against the
Turks. They could not have been more mistaken. He had a half-
hidden ambition to be a military hero, but he laughed at it whenever
he felt that anyone else might laugh at it, and his only possible
qualification was that he was a good shot with a pistol. But what
most excited the people of Missalonghi was that they heard he was
rich. They were all poor and many were destitute, and Mavrocordato's government was bankrupt. Every single one of them was
hoping and planning to put his own hand on a share of the money
the English milord had brought with him. Nobody can blame them,
but that was why they cheered.

*

When I first sailed in to Missalonghi, I knew of that weird event;
so does anyone else who has read a biography of Byron. But I
knew of it as an episode in his life, not as an episode in the war the

Greeks were fighting. The night I arrived, an unseasonable gale blew up and we had to haul off from the quay and anchor on the far side of the harbour; and sitting out there in the dark, and watching the marks to see if the anchor was holding, I made up my mind with unaccustomed speed to find out all I could about that distant war: who were the people who fought it, and what they thought they were fighting for, and what Byron achieved, if anything, by his visit to this dismal place and his lonely death. Since then, I have sailed much more in Greece and read much more in Athens and in London, and talked to many people; and this book is the result.

It was a war, I found, that was even more barbarous than most, and barbarities are no pleasure to write or read about. But it had a peculiar charm: among its ghastly massacres there were often moments of the purest farce, as if a gothic tragedy were being played by the cast of a comic opera. For its leaders included Greeks and Albanians, Turks and Egyptians, so shamelessly villainous that their wickedness, at this safe distance, seems endearing; and among the many foreigners who went before and after Byron, to give the leaders advice they did not want, were the most diverse, eccentric, quarrelsome, vain and unconsciously comical men who ever assembled anywhere to do heroic deeds or to boast about doing them.

The war was a very complicated affair that went on for years, and the apparition of Byron was only an incident in the middle of it. So I have picked a way of my own through the complications. Scores of the foreigners and a few of the Greeks wrote reminiscences, and two of them, Thomas Gordon and George Finlay, wrote complete histories. Recently William St Clair has written an excellent and very thorough study of the parts the foreigners played, which is called *That Greece Might Still Be Free*. Anyone who wants to know more than I have written will find it in these three books, and in the complete bibliography William St. Clair has compiled.

Within the limits I chose, I have made the story as accurate and truthful as I can. But of all its characters, there were not much more than half a dozen that none of the others spoke ill of, and I doubt if anyone ever has or ever will be sure he has sorted all the truth from all the tall stories they told about their own adventures, or the slanderous stories they told about each other.

About spelling: I do not think anyone need be pedantic in spelling names that are properly written in a different alphabet. I may have been inconsistent, but mainly I have used the spelling the foreigners used at the time of the war, because I think it still looks more familiar to English-speaking people. Missalonghi, for example, seems more natural than the modern Mesolongion, Nauplia than Nafplion, Piraeus than Pireefs, Corinth than Korinthos. Some place-names have changed completely, mostly because a Venetian name has been dropped and an older Hellenic name revived. Lepanto is now called Nafpaktos, Modon is Methoni, Zante is Zakinthos, and Corfu is known to the Greeks but to few other people as Kerkyra. I have noted these where they first appear in the story, and the modern names are marked in brackets on the maps.

PART ONE

Greeks and Philhellenes
1821-1822

CHAPTER ONE

Revolt
January—June 1821

Ali Pasha · Archbishop Germanos · Petrobey
Theodore Colocotrones
Prince Demetrius Hypsilantes

At the time of the Battle of Waterloo, Greece was a wild, remote and primitive place, where life revolved round the church, the meagre crops and the flocks of sheep and goats. The great events of Europe had scarcely any effect on it. Most of the people were simple peasants, who knew very little of what was happening beyond the arid mountains that enclosed their villages, and nothing at all of what was happening in the wider world. Life was precarious, much as it had been all over Europe in the middle ages, and travel was dangerous. Once in a while, on certain routes, strange foreigners might be seen, but they openly despised the peasantry; their only interest, pedantic and academic, was in the ancient ruins, which the peasants themselves regarded as shameful relics of a pagan age.

In some parts of the country, most of the people were Greek, although even among the Greeks there were separate tribes and communities hostile to each other. In some parts, most were Albanians who had come as settlers in earlier generations. In some, most were Turkish; and many of the Turkish families had been there so long they had forgotten their own language. On all the suitable rocks and hilltops there were fortresses, as there still are, which had been built by invaders in the past, Romans, Venetians, and the western people known collectively as Franks; and the strongest of these fortresses were manned in a desultory way by Turkish soldiers.

For three and a half centuries, the country had been ruled by Turks, a part of the Ottoman Empire, paying tribute to the Sultan in Constantinople. Foreign rule is normally unhappy, especially when the rulers and ruled have different religions; and the Greeks, of course, were Christians while the Turks were Mohammedans. But the Turkish dominion might have been worse. It would be an injustice to say the Greeks were contented with it: when the time came, they certainly showed they were not. They always grumbled about taxes, and about the amount of land the Turks possessed, which left too little for the Greeks to live on. But what they suffered from was not the strictness of the rule, it was its laxity, corruption and inefficiency. Even that had lasted so long that it seemed a natural state of affairs; and left to themselves they might never have felt resentful enough to do anything about it.

One compensation of the Turkish rule was that an enterprising Christian, one way or another, always had a chance to dig himself up out of poverty and win a position of power. Some inherited power as tribal chiefs, and if they were powerful enough the Turks left them to their own devices. Failing that, a Greek could be a successful brigand: there were swarms of them in the mountains. They were called klephts. Greek ballads made heroes of them, not unlike the ballads of Robin Hood, and they were proud of their calling – although the word klepht means simply thief, as in kleptomania. Or he could join the armatoli, who were a kind of guerilla police force the Turks had organized for the hopeless task of putting down the klephts. The two were not always easy to distinguish. Both ravaged the countryside from time to time, and even joined forces to do it; and some men became klephts in the summer and armatoli in the winter, when life in the mountains was harsh. Or a Greek could become a seaman. The Greeks were always better seamen than the Turks, and most of the seaborne trade of the empire was run by them, especially by the men of the islands of Hydra, Spetsai and Psara. They were pirates too, and sea captains and ship owners could make a handsome fortune.

Even within the Turkish administration, Greeks could rise to power. The Turks had never attempted a mass conversion of Christians; they used Christians to control their Christian minorities. In Greece, every village had a Greek official who collected the taxes and saw or tried to see that the law was obeyed. These men were called archontes, which is usually translated as primates, although the words mayor or magistrate would give a better idea of their status. They were not always popular figures, but they did well for themselves. There were also Greeks in even the highest ranks of government, with the titles of Grand Vizier, Grand Dragoman or Hospodar; but these heights were only reached by the sons of a few Greek families who were known as Phanariots, because they had lived for generations in the district of Constantinople which was called Phanar. Mavrocordato was a Phanariot, and the title of Prince which he used among Europeans was a very free translation of his Turkish rank.

Finally, as a road to power open to any Greek, there was the hierarchy of the Orthodox Church, the only institution that bound all Greeks together. Its priests and bishops and archbishops were Greek, and so was the Patriarch himself in Constantinople. Most Sultans of Turkey had guaranteed the freedom of the Church and treated its Patriarch with respect; and that, if nothing more, was a shrewd political move. The Greek Church had often showed it preferred the tolerance of the Moslem rulers to the heresies of the Roman Catholic Church, which it detested; and so the Sultans insured themselves against a crusading attack from the west, like the crusade which disrupted the Byzantine Empire in 1204, or the incursions of Venice and other Catholic powers which shook the Turkish rule in later centuries.

When suddenly, in 1821, revolt broke out and the peasants took to arms, men of all these various kinds of power laid claims to be leaders of it – brigand klephts, armatoli, primates, tribal chiefs, bishops, sea captains and phanariots. Of course, they all tried to lead it in different directions of their own.

*

There was one other kind of Greek distinct from all the rest. This was the kind that had emigrated to other parts of Europe, or been born to families that were established there. Most of them lived in Greek communities in Russia, Italy, Austria and France; and they were different from the Greeks in Greece because they were outside the isolation of the Turkish world and knew what was happening in Europe and America. They knew about the Napoleonic Wars which had only just ended, and had some conception, if only second-hand, of what could be achieved by modern military power. They knew also about the American War of Independence, and the French Revolution, and Bolivar's campaigns to free the Spanish colonies. They were full of the new ideas of freedom and equality.

And they had absorbed another idea that did not exist at all in Greece itself, except among a few Phanariots and seamen who had also had glimpses of the outside world. This was the European concept of a sovereign independent nation, self-contained within specific frontiers. In all its history, Greece had never been a nation of that kind. In classical times, it was a collection of separate city states, Athens, Sparta, Corinth, Argos and Thebes, which were often at war with each other. Then it became a part of the empire of Alexander, and then of Rome. It came nearest to nationhood in the Byzantine Empire, which was predominantly Greek; but even then, the capital was Constantinople, and the homeland of Greece was only a province, which was overrun from time to time by Slavs and other uncouth people from the north and east. The crusade of 1204 detached it from that empire and divided it in pieces, owned and governed by feudal counts and barons from almost every part of Europe; and it was still in pieces when the Turks took Constantinople in 1453 and gradually conquered all of Greece except the Ionian Islands, which remained a Venetian colony.

So the Greeks who lived in Greece had no thoughts of themselves as citizens of a united independent nation. Their ancestors never had been. It is true they had a very strong sense of their Greekness, but it was religious rather than national or racial; they would have defined a Greek as a member of the Greek Church, the only true church in their eyes. National patriotism was a virtue outside their experience, if indeed it is a virtue: they had never had anything to be patriotic about. But the Greeks in other countries acutely felt the need of a recognizable country of their own. Many of them, perhaps most, had never been to Greece. But these were the people who began to think and talk about revolt against the Turks.

What they did, in the fashion of the age, was to found a secret society. It was called Philiki Hetairia, the Friendly Society, and it began in Russia, probably soon after Napoleon's retreat from Moscow and before the battle of Waterloo.

It was the essence of a secret society that nobody knew who was running it, and therefore that nobody had any clear idea of its aims. But revolution and freedom were seeds that found plenty of fertile ground. Every member had the responsibility of recruiting more, who were admitted with fearsome oaths of secrecy; and the Hetairia spread, between 1815 and 1820, through all the Greek communities in Europe and into Constantinople and Greece itself, where bishops, klephts, shipowners and primates took the oath. As it grew wider, so did its members' conception of what it was all about. Some of the Greeks abroad had the great and naïve ambition of recapturing Constantinople and recreating the Christian glory of Byzantium, and they believed quite wrongly that the Czar of Russia and other powers would support them. All of them hoped to establish in Greece a national homeland like other European nations. But none of them understood that this was a totally foreign idea to the Greeks who already lived there. Klephts and primates, secretly discussing the oath they had taken, shared only two ideas. One was to get rid of the Turks in the small part of Greece they knew, and then rule it themselves. The other, some centuries out of date, was that the Greeks abroad, together with the Church, were asking for a holy war, a new crusade to exterminate infidels.

Nothing much might have happened, but for a fortuitous event. A local ruler named Ali Pasha, at Joannina in the north-west of what is now the mainland of Greece, was declared a rebel by the Sultan, and a powerful Turkish army was sent to subdue him. That was the match that lit the fuse the secret society laid.

*

Joannina nowadays is a large unremarkable city. But it stands on a pretty lake among mountains, and down on a promontory are the walls of a smaller, older town. They are so massive that the road that leads in through an archway has room to make an S-bend inside the thickness of the wall, an ingenious though expensive kind of defence. Within, there are narrow old winding streets, and in the highest corner, looking out over the lake, are the bleak remains of a citadel, thoroughly demolished, and a sight that is seldom seen in Greece: two mosques with their minarets. One is a municipal museum; the other is derelict, and is said to be the burial place of Ali Pasha's body – only his body, because his head finished up on a dish in Constantinople.

Ali, who held court in this castle for thirty-five years, was a fascinating character: a little fat old man, grey-bearded, charming, hospitable, and quite preposterously wicked. He was neither Greek nor Turk, he was Albanian; and his forebears were Christian but he was a Moslem – though a Moslem with ideas that were all his own. The people under his dominion were of all three races and both religions, and his rule was a good though extreme example of what life could be like for the Sultan's distant subjects.

For several generations, Ali's family had been brigands of varying distinction, and his father achieved a position of power by poisoning his two elder brothers. But he also died young – perhaps, some people said, by inadvertently poisoning himself – and when Ali was a child his mother took over command of her husband's gang. This was not an exceptional event: there were to be other formidable widows in the War of Independence. In due course she was ambushed and beaten by rivals from a neighbouring town, and she and Ali's sister were imprisoned and insulted in ways that history does not tell. They escaped alive, and Ali's education after that was solely in the duty of revenge. It seems he grew up with firm ideas of such things as truth and morality; but by most people's standards

22

they were inside out. Truth was to be avoided, and morality to be exploited as a weakness. He sincerely believed that cunning was the height of human achievement; his conversation was normally intended to mislead. He was immensely proud to claim that he could deceive anybody, and nobody could deceive him. So by turns he was audacious and wary, affectionate and cruel, tolerant and tyrannical, and nobody ever knew which mood was coming next. They only knew his affection and tolerance were danger signals that meant he was probably plotting some new enormity.

It is hard to imagine a system of government entirely based on deceit, but Ali's undoubtedly was; and it was so successful that in the end his domain stretched right across northern Greece from the Adriatic to the Aegean. Men served him faithfully because it was the only safe and profitable thing to do. He could always raise a Christian army to wreak his vengeance on a Moslem clan, or a Moslem army to do the same to Christians; he could rouse Albanians to slaughter Greeks, or set both those races together to slaughter Turks, and then invoke the Sultan's Turkish troops to put them down. So he maintained a deliberate organized chaos, and kept the only key to the organization.

The final revenge for the insult to his mother was perfectly typical of the way he thought and acted. He waited no less than forty-five years, when everyone but himself and his sister had forgotten the ancient offence, and everyone who had committed it was presumably dead or in his dotage. Then he invited all the male inhabitants of the offending town who were over the age of six to meet him to discuss an offer of military service, and he provided a dinner for them in a large walled courtyard. Six hundred and seventy are said to have attended. The town was Moslem so he promised the sack of it to his Christian soldiery and ordered them on to the courtyard walls, whence they fired with muskets for an hour and a half, until everyone inside was dead. The soldiers rounded up the women of the town and delivered them in hundreds to Ali's sister, who had told Ali (in a letter which was intercepted by a French consul) that she meant in future always to sleep on mattresses stuffed with their hair. The courtyard gates were walled up, the bodies were left inside, and Ali's court poets composed an ode in praise of his deed, which was inscribed on a marble plaque and stuck on the wall for the inspiration of travellers.

Cruelty is infectious: some people disapproved of this particular deed, but other deeds as barbarous were discussed with scandalized admiration all over Greece. So were stories of the debaucheries of Ali's court: the oriental splendour, the gold and silks and jewels, the activities of the concubines and of the scores of pages, the young sons of parents he had murdered, who attached themselves to him like orphaned puppies – and of Ali himself, bored with everything his courtiers had to offer, roaming the streets of Joannina in the night disguised as a merchant, in search of novel adventures. But his court life led to another episode which shocked the country. One of his daughters-in-law, according to the story, complained to him that her husband had refused to give her an emerald ring, but had given it to a young married woman named Euphrosyne whose husband was away from home in Venice. Euphrosyne was a celebrated beauty, and rumour said she had been rash enough to resist the advances of Ali. Again, moved by heaven knows what mixture of sadism, jealousy or revenge, he arranged a dinner. Euphrosyne was bidden, with others of the most elegant and charming ladies of the town and some of the local prostitutes. Then his policemen burst into the house, tied them all up and shut them in a church on the shore of the lake, and told them they had been condemned to death. They were left there all day: it was Turkish or Moslem custom to execute women by tying them in sacks and drowning them, and convention demanded that it should only be done at night. They were not in despair, because they supposed that Ali was waiting for a ransom. But he was not. That night, Euphrosyne and sixteen other girls were taken in boats to the middle of the lake and drowned.

In spite of these habits, Ali continued to thrive. He remained a vassal of the Sultan, but the Sultan was far away. From the capitals of western Europe, even farther away, his rule seemed efficient and prosperous, while the Sultan's was growing more feeble. In the

first decades of the nineteenth century, western governments began to treat him as an independent sovereign. Britain and France
both appointed diplomatic agents to his court. Ali negotiated with
Napoleon in terms of mutual esteem, and always succeeded, of
course, in persuading the French that he hated the British, and the
British that he hated the French.

And such was his fame that adventurous western travellers made
a point of visiting Joannina. Among them were Byron and his
companion John Cam Hobhouse – together with the long-suffering
valet Fletcher, who detested the whole experience. This was on
the grand tour that Byron made when he was 22, the tour which
aroused his romantic love of Greece; and indeed it was at the court
of Ali that he started to write Childe Harold's Pilgrimage, that
traveller's tale in Spenserian verse which later made him 'famous
overnight' and formed the inspiration, for better or worse, of many
men who tried to help Greece when the war began. Ali received
him with hospitality and a show of respect, and characteristically
hit on the very thing to flatter him: he said he could see he was a
'man of birth' because he had 'small ears, curling hair and little
white hands.' Byron knew something of Ali's cruelties, but he was
more than ready to be enthusiastic about the warlike character of
Albanians, who he believed – though here he was in error – were
all brave, rigidly honest and faithful. And he was impressed by the
pomp of the court: 'two hundred steeds ready caparisoned to move
in a moment, couriers entering or passing out with the despatches,
the kettle-drums beating, boys calling the hour from the minaret
of the mosque.' In the letters he wrote, one senses the delicious
fear of a young man befriended by a tyrant who he knows would
be capable of cutting off his head. 'He is guilty of the most horrible
cruelties, very brave, and so good a general that they call him the
Mahometan Buonaparte . . . He has been a mighty warrior, but is
as barbarous as he is successful, roasting rebels, etc., etc. Napoleon
has twice offered to make him King of Epirus, but he prefers the
English interest, and abhors the French, as he himself told me . . .
He told me to consider him as a father whilst I was in Turkey, and

said he looked on me as his son.' And the same sentiments, in due course, appeared in the second Canto of Childe Harold:

> 'In marble-paved pavilion, where a spring
> Of living water from the centre rose,
> Whose bubbling did a genial freshness fling,
> And soft voluptuous couches breathed repose,
> ALI reclined, a man of wars and woes:
> Yet in his lineaments ye cannot trace,
> While Gentleness her milder radiance throws
> Along that aged venerable face,
> The deeds that lurk beneath, and stain him with disgrace.'

Byron's visit was in 1809. Eleven years later, Ali went too far. He became annoyed with a man who was in the Sultan's service, so of course he arranged to have him murdered. The man fled to Constantinople. Ali sent three assassins after him, and they tried to kill him in daylight in a city street. But they bungled the job; and being arrested, they confessed that Ali had sent them and also that he had told them there were plenty of men within the Sultan's government who would protect them. That claim incensed the Sultan. Ali was deposed and ordered to report to Constantinople in forty days. He refused. The Sultan mobilized an army to go to fetch him, and Ali collected every man he could to defend his country.

*

When members of the secret Hetairia heard of this incipient war, they knew that for their own revolution it was now or never. If the Turks beat Ali, the Turkish army would be at large in Greece and free to put down a revolt; and if Ali won, he would certainly expand his dominion, and most or even the whole of Greece would be subject to uncontrolled Albanian despotism, which might be even worse than Turkish rule. The organizers of the Hetairia, the Greeks abroad, did not issue any order to begin, or tell anyone what to do; it was the Greeks in Greece, infected by the society's propaganda and under its oath, who suddenly independently took to arms.

The acting Turkish governor of the Peloponnese gave the final incentive by a typically muddled and feeble act of authority. He knew that trouble was brewing: no plot that was so widespread could possibly be a secret. He might still, perhaps, have cowed the Greeks by a show of force, or appeased them by a show of generosity. But what he did was neither. He made no military preparations, either to quell the Greeks or to protect the Turks, but he ordered all Greeks to surrender their arms, and all bishops and primates to come to his headquarters in the town of Tripolitsa. So every bishop and primate, and every brigand or peasant who had a musket or a sword, was forced to make a quick decision: to obey or to rebel.

It started like an explosion in the spring of 1821, a flame that spread so quickly that no-one could say where the first of the Turks were killed, or who killed them, or why. But the first recorded leadership came from the Church, and the first motives were given the gloss of a holy war. The Archbishop of Patras, whose name was Germanos, set out with misgiving on his journey to Tripolitsa. But he stopped on the way at the ancient monastery of Haghia Lavra, which stands in a wild ravine near the mountain town of Kalavryta. There he met at least four of the primates who had taken the oath and were equally undecided what to do: whether to go to Tripolitsa, or to refuse and face the consequences. While they hesitated, a letter was brought, ostensibly from a friendly Turk in Tripolitsa, warning them that the Turkish governor meant to imprison them or kill them, which was not unlikely. Afterwards, it was widely believed the Archbishop himself had forged the letter to gain time. He let it be read among the local people, and it raised their excitement to a new intensity; and with that encouragement, on 25th March, he raised the standard of the cross and called the people to arms. That day in the year is still a national holiday. But nobody knows whether raising the standard was a physical act or a later metaphorical phrase. Certainly the call to arms was no more than the Church's blessing on something already started which nobody could have stopped.

The Archbishop began to march back to Patras with the primates, and as he went on the devious track through the mountains, an ever-growing rabble of people joined him, armed with the scythes and clubs and slings of a revolutionary army.

Patras was a flourishing city in those days, as it still is, on the south side of the entrance of the Gulf of Corinth, opposite Missalonghi: as a major port, it was one of the few places in Greece that had foreign consuls in it, and some view of the outside world. It also had a good many Turks among its people. Hearing of the throng that was coming down from the mountains, they made for safety in the citadel of the town. The garrison of the citadel started to fire its cannon, and before the Archbishop arrived the town was burning and Christians and Moslems were killing each other in the streets and looting the empty houses. He and the primates were welcomed as deliverers, and hopes rose high of taking the citadel. In solemn ceremony, a crucifix was set up in the main square, and the leaders made a proclamation which simply said: 'Peace to the Christians: Respect to the Consuls: Death to the Turks!' There was really no more to say: for beyond that, nobody had any plans.

It was a brave enough act of defiance, but it could not possibly succeed. None of the leaders knew anything of war, or of how to control a mob in hysterical excitement, or how to turn it into anything like an army. Nor were there any weapons to assault the citadel. For a fortnight, the chaos went on; and then Turkish reinforcements were reported to be coming, and the Archbishop, the primates and most of their followers had to retreat again to the mountains. Nothing had been achieved in Patras except a horrible scene of destruction; and indeed the Turks were never turned out of the citadel and the ruins of the town until the war was over.

Nor did anyone else in the Peloponnese have any plans. All over the country Greeks rose and murdered their Moslem neighbours, perhaps in the name of Christ or perhaps of freedom, or merely to rob them or revenge some petty parochial envy or private grudge. Once they had started, they did not need a reason: they killed because a mad blood-lust had come upon them all, and everyone was killing. It was said there were twenty-five thousand Moslems who lived and farmed in the countryside of the Peloponnese in March of that year, men women and children. In April when Easter was celebrated there were none. A few had escaped to the fortified towns, and they were already hungry. The bodies lay neglected among the flowers that glorify the soil of Greece in springtime, and withered with the flowers when the heat of summer came.

*

It is fair to assume that Archbishop Germanos and other leaders of the Church were soon appalled at the orgy of genocide they had helped to let loose. At any rate, it was a long time before another bishop led an army. But a few other leaders emerged in those early days who continued as heroic figures in their followers' eyes for the whole of the war. In the Peloponnese there were two. One was a hereditary chief called Petrobey, and the other was Theodore Colocotrones, the most successful of all the brigand klephts in the southern part of Greece.

Petrobey's whole name was Petros Mavromicheles, and Bey was a Turkish title; but like many Greeks who had similar honours, he still liked to use it even when he was fighting against the Turks. And perhaps in his case it was not a matter of pride: everyone called him Petrobey as a kind of nickname. He was chief of the wild, peculiar tribe of Mainotes, who lived in the mountains of Maina right down in the south of the Peloponnese. They claimed they were descended straight from the ancient Spartans, and it possibly could have been true: they certainly had a character and customs of their own and lived a Spartan life, and nobody dared to molest them in their mountains. Young Mainotes were brought up to obey the chief, honour their parents, give respect to women and old men, be brave in battle, rob without being caught, keep their promises and never forget an injury; and if this ambitious education was not always more successful than any other, it did succeed in giving the tribe a distinctive moral code. Death was their penalty for seduction; but sometimes a seducer was allowed to leave the Mainote country to make enough money to come back and marry the girl – and if he did not come back at the proper time, the girl was put to death. Blood feuds were handed down for generations, and when a man married, he shared his wife's feuds too. And murder among the Mainotes could be assigned as a right; a debtor could give his creditors a legal right to kill him if he did not pay, or to kill any two of his relations. It was really no wonder that people left them alone.

Petrobey was growing old in 1821, and some people said he was more cheerful and easy-going than a chieftain ought to be; but he had a large number of stalwart sons and nephews united by family pride, so nobody cared to insult the name of Mavromicheles. Everyone seems to have liked him, including the few Englishmen who met him. He was a brigand of course: the Mainotes often came down from their mountains for raiding expeditions. But he was a brigand of high principles, and he had the easy dignity of a patriarch or king. Some people, as the war went on, began to find him a nuisance, but that was because they had failed to learn two lessons his very existence might have taught them. One was that it would not be easy, with people like him around, to turn Greece into a tidy constitutional state on the European pattern. The other was that the moral standards of contemporary Europe were not the only ones. Petrobey was not at all like Ali Pasha. He was a moral man, and that was why he was respected; and it was not his fault that the morals of Maina were not exactly the same as the morals of Canterbury or the Vatican or the chancelleries of Europe. A Scottish highlander would have understood him: he could almost have been a Campbell.

The very moment the revolution started, Petrobey sallied out in person from the mountains, followed by all the able-bodied Mainotes. It would only be guesswork to say what was in his mind: a holy war, a political demonstration, or just a determination not to be left out of whatever excitement was going. He took his men down to the seaport of Kalamata, which was the nearest town to his domain. They were much more effective than the Archbishop's peasant mob at Patras: they raged through the town, killed all the Moslem men and herded away the young women and children whom they could sell or use in servitude. The Church, if it was not leading this massacre, came close behind: on the banks of the river, twenty-four priests assembled with thousands of bandits to sing a Te Deum in victory, and according to one description of the scene, 'patriotic tears poured down the cheeks of rude warriors and ruthless brigands sobbed like children'.

Immediately after, a long elaborate proclamation was issued in the name of Petrobey. It was addressed to the nations of Europe, not to the Greeks. It appealed for help and support in the struggle against the tyrants, and said the Greeks were unanimously resolved on liberty or death, the recovery of their rights and the revival of their unhappy nation. It ended with these words:

> 'With every right does Hellas, our mother, whence ye also, O Nations, have become enlightened, anxiously request your friendly assistance with money, arms and counsel, and we entertain the highest hope that our appeal will be listened to; promising to show ourselves deserving of your interest, and at the proper time to prove our gratitude by deeds.
> Given from the Spartan Head Quarters Kalamata 23 March 1821*
> Signed Pietro Mavromichali, Commander-in-Chief of the Spartan and Messenian Forces.'

It is inconceivable that Petrobey had written this; neither he nor any Mainote, nor any ordinary Greek, would have thought of themselves as a nation, or thought of saying that ancient Hellas had enlightened the rest of the world. Even in translation, its style gives it away: some Greek of foreign education, a Hetairist or perhaps a Phanariot, had already arrived in Kalamata and written the first of many such pieces of florid and romantic prose, and persuaded the old man in the flush of victory to put his name at the bottom. It was seldom that Petrobey did anything so out of character.

*

The Mainotes were not in the habit of going far from home. After their success at Kalamata, they straggled across the southern

* Dates were confused by the use of different calendars. Petrobey's action was a week or so after the Archbishop's, not before it.

Peloponnese to the great fortress of Monemvasia on the eastern coast, to try their skill on that. They could not assault it, so they camped to starve it out; while farther north, the only sizeable gangs of fighting men were being led by Colocotrones the klepht.

Colocotrones had no hereditary rank and no tribe or territory of his own; he said he was born in the mountains under a tree. His forebears had been fighters for at least a hundred years, sometimes as brigands and sometimes in the armed guards the primates maintained as a kind of police force – sometimes, in other words, against the law and sometimes on its side. But in his father's time, the brigands had been too successful and rapacious, and the Turks had made a special effort to put an end to them. His father was killed, and he himself had to flee the country and go into exile in the Ionian Islands. It gave him a standing grudge against the Turks, but to be fair one must add that they were not to blame. It was the Greek peasants who suffered most from the brigands' raids, and they had asked the Turks to protect them from their own compatriots.

The portraits of Colocotrones do not make him look an attractive person. His hair is long and lank, his moustache droops grimly down, and so do the corners of his mouth and eyes: he has a forbidding air of cunning and ferocity. Certainly those were two of his characteristics, and he may have found it useful to look like that. His higher qualities, like most people's in this story, are hard to assess. Some people said he was clear-headed and good-natured, and exalted him as more heroic than any mere man can be; others said he was greedy, selfish and ambitious. But these differing judgements reflected the prejudices of the men who made them, rather than inconsistency in himself. He had two kinds of critics: the men who wanted to do what he did but were not so good at it, and the men from abroad who imported the foreign idea of national patriotism, and expected a leader at least to try to disguise his private ambition with patriotic slogans. In short, he was the kind of leader the peasants and brigands wanted, but not the kind the foreigners thought they ought to want: and it remains a matter of taste to prefer the bare-faced brigand or the wily phanariot.

Prince Demetrius Hypsilantes lands in Greece,
dressed in the uniform of the Regiment

Theodore Colocotrones

Petrobey

Prince Alexander Mavrocordato

Mahmud II, The Sultan of Turkey

When Colocotrones reached the Ionian Islands, they were nominally a republic under the joint protection of Turkey and Russia, for the Republic of Venice, which had owned them for centuries, came to an end in 1797. In 1807 they became a part of Napoleon's empire, and in 1815 they became a republic again, but under British protection. Most of the time, Colocotrones made a living importing cattle from Greece to feed the foreign troops; but the British recruited a regiment of Greeks, and he joined it. He had no special sympathy for the British, but they made him a captain and then a major, so the pay was good. He was one of the early members of the Hetairia, and before the revolution started he left the British service and went secretly back to the Peloponnese and waited. By then, he was fifty.

Thus he became the only native leader in Greece who had served in a European army. His European critics afterwards said he had not learned anything from the experience. But more probably he had the common sense, which they did not, to see that no human power could turn the Greek brigands and peasants into a formal army, or persuade them to drill and manoeuvre and fight in the disciplined ranks that Wellington or Napoleon commanded. When he came home after fifteen years in exile, plenty of men remembered his reputation as a brigand chief and were ready to join him; so he simply became a brigand chief again, with a brigand's technique of strategy and tactics.

He was present at the sacking of Kalamata, and then he set off on his own. He was reported first with thirty followers, and then with three hundred, and a week or two later with six thousand. Probably nobody counted them, and most figures in this war were vastly exaggerated; but certainly he soon had enough to lay siege to a minor town, and through all the vicissitudes of war he was never without a private army of his own. Even when he was imprisoned by his own government, his followers faithfully waited for him to get out again.

His first foray was a failure. His force, whatever its size, was routed by some Turkish cavalry who were numbered at five hundred. Colocotrones had to run with the rest; and in fact he ran so fast that he lost his rifle.

The Greeks' habit of running away when a battle seemed to be going against them was one of many things that scandalized European officers a little later; for the officers, who began to arrive in Greece before the year was out, were schooled in the virtue of fighting to the last round and the last man. But running away was not a custom peculiar to the Greeks; it was the common-sense tactic of guerilla fighters anywhere, and it was really of more practical use than the heroic death that European armies glorified. Colocotrones may have thought the rout of his men was a set-back, but certainly not a major disgrace or disaster: they knew very well they could not fight against cavalry, so it was stupid to try.

That was not the only habit that shocked the foreign officers, who had fought either for or against Napoleon. They disapproved entirely of the Greeks' idea of tactics, and never made any attempt to understand them. The Greeks would not fight in the open like European armies, or march in formation. They always had to take cover, usually behind rocks, and if they could not find rocks they built themselves little walls of stones. From there, they would open fire, and also shout insults and make obscene and derisive gestures at the enemy. Few of them had rifles, most had muskets, and no doubt most of the muskets were very old. A musket at best was a very inaccurate weapon. Even a skilled man using Brown Bess, the musket of Wellington's armies, needed luck to hit a rank of men at much more than seventy paces; and the Greeks – perhaps because their weapons were so old – preferred to fire from the hip and were said to turn their faces away when they pulled the trigger. So what with one thing and another, few men were killed in their battles, and as soon as anyone had that misfortune his enemies were likely to forget the fight in a rush to strip and behead the corpse. It was a method of war that so far had only been tried against rival brigands and small detachments of Turks. It remained to be seen how well it would work against a formal army. But the Greeks had the utmost faith in it.

In the evening of that first abortive fight, Colocotrones was left all alone: every one of his men had vanished. He came to an isolated church and went in, and prayed for victory. By his own account, he had a vision there of the Virgin Mary, who assured him his prayer was granted; and it illuminates this war to think of the brigand kneeling there, and sincerely persuading himself that the Mother of Jesus was blessing the course of slaughter and robbery he was determined to follow.

Soon his men began to emerge from their hiding-places, pleased at their shrewd escape; and with the encouragement of his vision, he marched to war again.

*

By the time when spring was starting to turn to summer, the Greeks seemed almost to have won their independence. The whole of the Peloponnese was free of Turks, excepting the town of Tripolitsa and the fortresses on the coast – Nauplia, Monemvasia, Coron, Modon (Methoni), Navarino, Patras, Rhion and Corinth. These places were cut off from each other and surrounded by eager bandits waiting for them to starve. North of the Gulf of Corinth and in Attica things were much the same, except where they were confused by the presence of Ali Pasha's soldiery, who added a third dimension to the struggle. For the moment, there was not much fighting to do, for the primitive reason that every accessible enemy was dead.

But what was to happen next? Nobody knew. The Greeks had destroyed the Turkish system of government, such as it was; but they had not thought of any system of their own. Each of the bands of brigands roaming the countryside and besieging the towns owed some kind of allegiance to chiefs like Colocotrones or Petrobey. Each of the primates still more or less controlled his village, just as he had before. But the chiefs did not recognize anyone else's authority, and the primates no longer had any superior officials over them, so each of them did as he pleased. By the economics of brigandage, the chiefs were committed to robbery and plunder; without it, they could not feed their men, much less give them any hope of being paid – and men whose chief could not feed them disbanded themselves and went to a chief who could. And the primates, who had always been tax-collectors, now had nobody to remit the taxes to, so they spent them on extravagant whims of their own. It was not that they were essentially wicked men; but none of them, or their forefathers, had ever been set an example of justice or honour in the use of power, and so they began to imitate the pride and ostentation of Turkish pashas.

At this stage, two months after the revolution had begun, the educated Greeks from abroad began to arrive, bringing with them infinite possibilities of confusion. The name of the first of importance was Prince Demetrius Hypsilantes. He landed in June with a small crowd of followers, and with news that astonished the Greeks. His elder brother Alexander, he announced, was the secret head of the Hetairia and was leading an army through the Balkans to attack Constantinople, with the support of Russia. When that was accomplished, he was coming to accept the throne of Greece; and he himself had been appointed to govern the country as regent until his brother arrived. All this was true, or had been. What he did not know was that Alexander had turned out to be a tragically incompetent commander, and had already been disowned by the Russians and utterly defeated by the Turks.

The Hypsilantes were one of the families of Phanariots who had been powerful in Constantinople under the Turks, and the title of Prince that they used was no more royal than Mavrocordato's. Demetrius was not a prepossessing person. He was small, and his appearance was insignificant, even in marvellous uniforms that no Greek had seen before; he was described as having a discordant voice, an awkward manner and weak health; he was only in his twenties, but was nearly bald; and he neither had tact nor any experience of government. And unluckily, his virtues were not really the kind that were needed in Greece at that moment. He was an honourable man, and his honour was doomed to be outraged; he was sincerely a patriot, in a country where patriotism scarcely yet existed; he was a gentleman, as Europeans understood the word, and that was a pure misfortune. The only virtue he certainly had which everyone understood was courage.

The Hetairia had no right whatever to appoint a ruler of Greece without consulting anyone in the country, but nobody challenged the claim. People who had not won any power for themselves were beginnning to see that there had to be somebody with supreme authority. And even the primates and brigand chiefs saw some use in having an outsider as a nominal head of state, if only because each one of them hoped to persuade him to accept his own point of view. This Prince was at least a Greek, although he spoke a kind of Greek they could hardly understand, and was full of ideas they could not understand at all. And what was more, he was believed to be the herald of Russian aid; he had come from Russia, and people argued that the Russians would not have let him out of their country unless they meant to support him. He believed it himself. So they all hurried to meet him, and to stake their claims for high official positions.

One can only be sorry for this bewildered young man, who no doubt had been led to expect a royal reception from happy com-patriots, and some kind of ready-made administration. He found he was like a foreigner in the country he thought was his own; and as for a royal reception, it was hard enough to find anything to eat or anywhere to sleep. He was confronted by innumerable rough and flamboyant men who expected him to confirm their newly-won authority, and warned him against each other's rival claims; and whatever he said, they all went away and issued their own orders in his name. The whole thing was entirely beyond him. With his arrival, the war was neglected and all the self-made leaders began to dispute among themselves. It was anarchy.

CHAPTER TWO

The Navy and the Regiment
September 1821—March 1822

Admiral Miaoulis · Bouboulina
Constantine Kanaris · Frank Abney Hastings
Sir Thomas Maitland
Commodore Gawen Hamilton · Colonel Baleste
Colonel Thomas Gordon

One reason why the Greeks felt safe from counter-attack at home was the faith they had in their navy. To call it a navy, at a time when Nelson's navy still existed, may have been the wrong word for it. It was a sort of home-made navy. It did not have many qualities a proper navy had: no discipline, no training in war, no naval rules or laws, no idea of tactics and no warships. But it did have one excellent asset. Its crew were very good at sailing their ships, while the Turks were very bad at it.

Having said that, one must add that anyone who has sailed in the Aegean Sea must have some sympathy for the Turks as seamen. It is as beautiful as the Ionian Sea, but much windier, and although sailors have crossed it for thousands of years, they have done it by choosing their season and waiting for the weather. In winter there may be storms from any direction. For a few weeks in spring and autumn it is usually expected to be calm, but even then it sometimes does things that are unexpected. My own first ventures among its islands were prudently made in May, but I remember beating up through a sound towards the harbour of Paros against a rising northerly gale, and having to lie to two anchors in a bay for three rather dreary days because the harbour itself was full of spindrift and nobody, not even the Greeks, could approach it. And almost every day for most of the summer, from the middle of June until the end of August, there is a strong northerly wind which is called the Meltemi, pleasant enough in the heat ashore but troublesome at sea. Nowadays, if you want to reach the northern Aegean at that time of year, you probably start your engine before the dawn, when the wind is weakest, and make what northing you can against an uncomfortable sea before the wind rises again in the middle of the morning. But in the 1820's there were no such unfair tactics; and moreover the square-rigged ships the Turks possessed were probably much less weatherly than any boat with a modern rig.

And of course the Aegean has no tide. In northern seas, sailing ships could often make progress, up and down the English Channel for example, by sailing or drifting with the tide and anchoring when it changed. But for the Turks and everyone else in the eastern Mediterranean it was the wind or nothing.

And again, there is friendly shelter now in any of the islands of this fabled sea: not always the perfect shelter you might like for a quiet night, because the sea is apt to roll in to any anchorage on the windward sides of the islands, while on the lee sides the wind tears down from the mountains in alarming gusts. But for the Turks in the early 1820's there was the added discomfort that the people of every island were their enemies.

So it is understandable if the Turkish fleet, lying in Constantinople, waited with trepidation for the Sultan's orders to sail to Greece. They had some imposing ships, line of battle ships of up to eighty guns which were built in France and therefore probably as good as any in the world, and plenty of frigates. But if they had to sail in winter, they had to handle these ships not only by day but by night among the unlit islands in whatever weather came. In spring or autumn, they might be becalmed in hostile seas for days or even weeks. And in summer, they could expect to run down through the islands with the Meltemi, but then to have to beat back against it; and no sailor is happy when he is far down wind. Apart from anything the Greeks might do to them, they had a daunting nautical problem. Nobody but Nelsonian sailing masters and crews would have tackled it with perfect confidence in the warships of that era, and the Turks were far from being that kind of seamen.

*

The Greeks could not have handled a line of battle ship if they had had one. For their purpose, what they had was better; the small brigs and schooners they had always used for trading. These were built to work among the islands: it is a fair guess that all of them, and especially the schooners, were handier and more weatherly than the Turkish men-of-war. And although they were merchant ships, they had always been more or less armed against pirates – which often in the past had meant against each other.

Most of the Greek ships, and their captains and crews, belonged to three islands: Hydra and Spetsai, just off the east coast of the Peloponnese, and Psara, which is much closer to Turkey than it is to the mainland of Greece. On the mainland there was only one considerable fleet: its harbour was the little town of Galaxidhi, on the northern shore of the Gulf of Corinth below the ruins of Delphi.

Hydra especially, in those days, was a prosperous, busy place. Its leading families were Albanian, and their elegant houses still look down on the old piratical port. The Hydriotes are said to have had 115 ships of over a hundred tons. Sailing round their island nowadays, one wonders where and how they kept them safely. The harbour has a new breakwater now, but before that was built nothing like so many ships could have sheltered there, and the rest of the barren mountainous island has nothing but open bays exposed to the Aegean winds. The only remaining signs that Hydra and Spetsai were once such maritime centres are the bollards round the shores of every possible anchorage: most of them are old cannon, stuck in the ground or set in the stones of the quays; and this is the armament of the fleets of 1821, discarded when piracy came to an end about twenty-five years later.

When they were trading, these ships had been organized like ships in England in the middle ages: the captain and all the crew had shares in the profits of each voyage, together with the owners of the ship and cargo. This ancient system had its origin in Grecian seas. The laws that governed it are supposed to have been brought from Rhodes to Bordeaux, and thence to England, by crusaders in the twelfth century; and they were known in England as the Judgements of Oléron, after the island off Bordeaux which was the centre of the wine trade. It was a good old system by leisurely medieval standards, but it had one result that seemed impossibly inefficient in later ages: every man in a crew right down to the cabin boy could claim to have his say in making the plans for a voyage, and captains were bound by law to consult their crews before they sailed and to accept the majority opinion. Such innocent ideas disappeared in England around the time of Drake, but the law had not changed in Greece, and ships were still run like that.

Perhaps it was all very well to man a merchant ship with a kind of committee, but when the same ship went to war it was a disadvantage, to say the least. All through the Greek war, western observers wrote about mutinies in the fleet; and it was true that Greek ships often sailed away and disappeared at very awkward moments. But it was ignorant to judge the crews by western laws and customs and call it mutiny: they were simply using their archaic legal right to say they disliked the voyage and were going home. And to do them justice, one must look at it the other way round: they fought although nobody had any right to compel them, and when they went suddenly home it was seldom because they were scared, but most often because they had not had the money they thought was their due. They were strikers, not mutineers.

In spite of this disability, the Greeks at sea produced some heroic admirals (the fleets elected them), and one at least who had the rarer reputation of being perfectly honest. This was Admiral Andreas Miaoulis, a wealthy Hydriote who never joined the undignified scramble for profits like other leaders, but on the contrary spent his own fortune in the cause of Greece. There was a story about Miaoulis which shows more clearly what people thought of him than any formal description. It was said that he had once been captured by Nelson, but after an interview the great man set him free because he knew a first-class seaman when he saw one. It may not be true: there seems no reason why Nelson should ever have kept a Greek in captivity. But it does not have to be true: the Greeks thought it was, and one would still like to think it was. The Greeks wanted a Nelson of their own, and Miaoulis was the man. Nobody could have expected him to be a tactical genius, and he never pretended to be; but in his different circumstances he had something of Nelson's skill with difficult captains and crews, and he had the merit of being simply likeable and incorruptible.

The Spetsiotes, on the other hand, had a distinction that must be unique in naval history: they had a lady admiral. Her name was Bouboulina, a redoubtable woman, mother of six and twice widowed, whose exploits are still remembered in her island with a mixture of pride and rude masculine humour. They say she could drink any man in the fleet under the table, and that she was so unattractive she had to seduce her lovers at pistol-point. But they also say, and truly, that she was a brave and genuine leader; and perhaps her only defect as an admiral was that she often went ashore and appeared on horseback at battles on land, leaving the Spetsiote fleet to its own devices.

Psara had its admirals too, and the town of Galaxidhi might have done so, but it suffered an irretrievable disaster very early in the war. Three months after the revolution began, the Sultan gave his order, and a Turkish fleet set sail from Constantinople: three line-of-battle ships, five frigates and about twenty brigs. He or his admirals had chosen the best time of year to do it, exactly when they might sail out while the Meltemi was blowing and come home when it had stopped. The fleet was joined by squadrons from Algeria and Egypt, whose Arab crews were much more efficient than the Turks. It rounded the Peloponnese, landed supplies at the fortresses the Turks were still holding, and finally reached Patras.

The Egyptian squadron entered the Gulf of Corinth and found the whole fleet of Galaxidhi in the little harbour below the town, which is the only perfectly sheltered harbour in the whole of the Gulf. The citizens had employed some soldiers to protect them but they ran away, and after a day of bombardment the Egyptians landed, and burned the town and all the ships and boats that were on the beach. Thirty-four brigs and schooners were lying in the harbour ready for sea, and the Egyptians took them all, with thirty men who had not escaped in time.

On the way back to Constantinople, this fleet and its prizes were attacked by Miaoulis, who had already gathered thirty-five ill-organized but enthusiastic crews. One or two brigs on each side were driven ashore, but the Turkish commander, whose name was Kara Ali, reached home again in triumph. There was really no limit to the inhumanity men on each side could display. He kept his prisoners alive until he was entering the harbour of Constantinople, and then hanged all thirty of them from the yard-arms of his flag-ship, so that they should still be struggling as he came alongside. The Sultan promoted him.

Galaxidhi never recovered, but the islands were having their own successes against Turkish merchant ships, and behaving with equal brutality: there were many stories, proudly told, of captured crews who were brought ashore and tortured in Hydra and Spetsai. And they had two victories, almost identical, which were celebrated and magnified until they far outweighed the disaster of Galaxidhi.

From the very beginning, the Greeks were sailing with confidence all over the Aegean and along the coast of Turkey, because they totally scorned the Turks as sailors; and in June a large fleet of the small Greek ships, close to the mouth of the Dardanelles, discovered a Turkish battleship. It fled, and they chased it into a bay where it came to anchor.

But then they were baffled to know what to do with it. Many approached it and shot at it with their piratical guns, but none of them dared to go within range of its broadsides, so their cannon had no effect at all. This was not cowardice but prudence, because most of their ships were privately owned by the captains themselves or their families, and no owner could be sure of compensation if he was rash enough to get his ship sunk or damaged. In traditional style they called a conference. Some people suggested cutting the cable of the Turk, in the hope it would drift ashore. An admiral said he had talked to an Englishman, who told him the Greeks should use fireships; but that benefactor seems not to have told him, or anyone, how to prepare a fireship. So word was sent around the fleet to find out if anyone knew. A Psariote teacher of navigation volunteered; he said he had fought for the Russians at the Battle of Cheshme, when they used fireships with great success against the Turks, and he remembered how it was done – though he must have been an elderly man and his memory sound, for that battle was fought 52 years earlier.

It was all charmingly amateurish, and no wonder. The English routed the Spanish Armada with fireships, which were an ancient weapon then, and all organized navies had used them ever since; but the Greek navy had never fought a war and had to work out the technique as it went along. On this occasion, the committee work went on for three days; and all that time the Turk lay passively at anchor. A captain was persuaded to sacrifice his ship, for the promise of a bountiful payment from the treasuries of the three islands. A crew volunteered to sail it in, for a bonus of a hundred dollars each, and the teacher of navigation soaked its sails and rigging in turpentine. But when they tried it, they set it on fire too soon, and it did no harm to the Turk. At a second attempt with a second ship, the same thing happened; and still the Turk did not dare to put to sea. The third time, they were braver and luckier. A Psariote captain named Papanikolo wedged the third ship under the bow of the Turk and made it fast before he set it alight. He jumped into his boat and rowed away and the Turkish man-of-war went up in flames and its magazine exploded.

Some months later, again off the Turkish coast, they did the same thing with even greater drama. The Greeks had fought a three-day gunnery battle with a major Turkish fleet. Nobody had been hurt and no damage had been done to either side, because both sides fought well out of effective range and because their aim was bad. Dispirited, the Greeks went back to Psara, and the Turkish fleet to anchor off the island of Chios. But then two fireships, ready prepared and unescorted, went back to the attack commanded by Constantine Kanaris, who became a national hero for this and similar exploits. It was the night of the Moslem feast which ends the month of Ramadan. Most of the senior Turkish officers had gathered to celebrate on board the 80-gun flagship of the admiral or capitan-pasha, the same Kara Ali who had commanded the sack of Galaxidhi, and the ship was brightly lit by festive lanterns in the rigging. Kanaris is said to have run the bowsprit of his fireship into a porthole so that it stuck there. He lit the fuse and safely rowed away in the night, and the flagship went up in a dreadful blaze and panic that caused the deaths of hundreds of her crew. In rough justice, one of the yards where Kara Ali had hanged his prisoners fell from the mast, and hit him on the head and killed him.

It was a feat that was brave enough in itself, although the second fireship failed; but as the story of it spread through Greece and out into Western Europe it grew to the size of a decisive victory, until the English poet Walter Savage Landor achieved the final height of exaggeration:

'Twice twenty self-devoted Greeks assailed
The naval host of Asia, at one blow
Scattered it into air – and Greece was free.'

*

These efforts of the Greeks at sea were observed with friendly exasperation by one man who had fought at Trafalgar when he was a boy of 11. He was English, now 27 years old, comfortably rich, handsome in a Nordic fashion, and conspicuously tall among the Greeks: Frank Abney Hastings, an ex-commander of the Royal Navy.

Hastings came to Greece for the same fundamental reason as many other foreign volunteers: he had got into trouble at home. His particular trouble had started in Jamaica, when he sailed the survey ship *Kangaroo* into harbour at Port Royal and came to anchor. The flagship of the West Indies Station was already there, and her captain – according to a report that Hastings wrote – 'thought proper to hail me in a voice that rang through the whole of Port

Royal, saying – "You have overlaid our anchor – you ought to be ashamed of yourself – you damned lubber you – who are you?"' He was so mortally insulted that after a few days' thought he challenged the captain to a duel. That was simply not done in the Navy, and after fifteen years' service he was dismissed.

Out-of-work British naval officers could usually find jobs in foreign navies, and that was what Hastings decided to do: not because he needed the money, but because he had novel ideas of naval tactics and had always hoped he would have a chance to try them. He was in France learning French when he heard of the Greek affair, and early in 1822 he took ship from Marseilles and landed in Hydra, the first and almost the only genuine naval officer who joined the Greeks and fought with them at sea. He was taken for a spy, but when that suspicion wore off he was given permission to go to sea in a Hydriote ship called *Themistocles*.

It was a trying experience for a man brought up in the perfect precision and discipline of British men-of-war. The crew came on board when they felt like it, arguing with the captain; they unfurled the sails, and then found there were no sheets and what there was of the running rigging was wrongly rove; and caught in a squall outside, it seemed to him that everybody shouted orders and nobody executed any of them. And it was a voyage, across to Psara and the Turkish coast, that was full of disagreeable surprises. The captains did not carry out the admiral's orders unless they happened to think they were right, and the crews took the same democratic view of what the captains told them. He could not get used to seeing prisoners beheaded on the decks, or to the way the crews rescued their own compatriots from Turkish ports – for they always extorted all the valuables these refugees had succeeded in bringing with them.

But by what was no more than a matter of habit to him, he won the admiration of the Greeks. The *Themistocles* chased a small Turkish ship into the lee of a cliff, and was becalmed within range of a posse of Turkish soldiers with muskets on the cliff-top. The whole of the crew took cover from the musketry, while the ship was gently drifting ashore. But Hastings perhaps knew better than the rest how inaccurate muskets were, and he stood where he was on deck: so he was the only one who noticed a small eddy of breeze. He went out on the bowsprit alone and backed the headsail, brought the ship's head around and saved her. That revealed another facet of the character of the Greeks. They were full of generous admiration for his bravery, and spread the story of it round the fleet.

He continued to like the Greeks, and they began to like him; he was a friendly young man, even if he could sometimes show the arrogance of a privileged young Englishman. But they just did not want his advice or anyone else's: they liked their own chaotic and casual way of doing things. At that time, the gunnery of the British navy was by far the best in the world, and the Greeks' was probably the worst, with the single exception of the Turks'. Hastings longed to get them bigger guns, and shells instead of cannon balls, and to teach them how to serve a gun and aim it, and how to make red-hot shot in a furnace in the hold. But they were happy enough to blaze away at the enemy and to feel astonished if they ever scored a hit, even though their occasional lucky shots did no visible damage. Nobody wanted to listen. Even Miaoulis, a courteous and reasonable man, rejected a written proposal Hastings sent him for capturing a Turkish frigate; though one must admit the plan seems unrealistic, since it depended on disciplined action and perfect timing. After some months, in a moment of gloomy disillusion, Hastings wrote 'They place you in a position where it is impossible to render any service, and then they boast of their own superiority, and of the uselessness of the Franks (as they call us) in Turkish warfare.'

Yet he remained with them to the bitter end, determined to render them every service he could. It was in this reaction to snubs and disappointments that Frank Hastings differed from almost every other volunteer. Most of the rest were army men, who hoped the Greek war could give them quick promotion. Many promoted themselves before they arrived: corporals called themselves captains, lieutenants posed as colonels, and the few real colonels expected to be commander-in-chief; so when they found there was no army to command, and nobody willing to accept their wise advice, they were doubly disappointed. Hastings himself used the title of captain although he had only been commander. But he never showed any wish to be an admiral or command a fleet. He set himself a lower ambition, and in the end he attained it, and thereby made himself more useful to the Greeks than all the others put together. All he wanted was one small ship, with 64-pounder guns and a crew that he would choose and train himself, and even pay if nobody else was willing. But in one respect this modest plan was twenty years ahead of the British navy itself: for what he wanted was a steamship.

*

The struggle the Greeks had begun was watched by all the governments of Europe with a glum distaste. It was a time when revolt was in the air; Italy and Spain had both experienced it, France was nervously aware of Bonapartist plots, and England of the industrial unrest that had come to a climax, only two years before, with the 'massacre' of Peterloo. Each established government felt itself more or less threatened, and disliked and mistrusted revolt wherever it happened. Each was determined not to encourage the Greeks, but to keep out of the whole affair by careful neutrality – yet each was suspicious that one of the others might cunningly profit by backing the winning side.

The British government seemed the best placed to know what was happening in Greece because it had two observation posts: the Ionian Islands, which were under British rule, and the Royal Navy, which patrolled the seas of Greece, like almost all the seas of the world, with the right it had claimed at Trafalgar.

British rule in the Ionian Islands was one of these exercises of empire that were morally indefensible yet certainly beneficial. Since 1815, the islands had been a nominally single, free and independent state under the protection of the Sovereign of Great Britain. The first Lord High Commissioner was Sir Thomas Maitland, who soon became known as King Tom of Corfu: 'a mortal of strange humours and eccentric habits', one published

48

Byron entertained by Ali Pasha in 1809

Ali Pasha hunting on the lake at Joannina

On the balcony of the monastery where Ali Pasha was killed

description says – and another: 'a man possessing great shrewdness accompanied by excessive roughness of manner.' Between the lines of these and other hints, one may read that he was a bombastic, flamboyant, hard-drinking autocrat, a caricature of an eighteenth-century English squire whose tenants, for the moment, happened to be Greek. Charged with giving the islands a constitution, he decreed an elected Assembly of forty, from which he himself chose six members to form a Senate. He arranged for the Senators to be very highly paid, so that members of the Assembly who hoped for promotion were careful not to offend him; and each senator was allowed to make only one proposal in each session, which was subject to his approval in advance. Just in case anything went wrong, he reserved the right to veto any decision of this dummy parliament.

Each of the seven islands had a British military governor who was also its civil judge. The most conspicuous of them was Colonel Charles Napier, the governor of Cephalonia. He was another man of eccentric appearance who wore steel-rimmed glasses and a magnificent luxuriant set of whiskers; later in life he became a celebrated general in India and he still has his statue in Trafalgar Square (Erected by Public Subscription. The most numerous Subscribers being Private Soldiers.)

The rule of these men was shameless despotism; but it worked, to the good of the islanders, because the intentions of the despots were benevolent. Napier, for one, loved the Greeks and adored his little island, which he covered all over with unneccesary roads and decorated with public buildings of classical design and light-houses modelled on ancient temples. And King Tom himself, in spite of his terrifying rages, was not a wicked man; he was honest and had an overriding sense of natural justice. Under this alien rule, the islanders grew far more prosperous than they had been before. Old-established oppression which dated back to Venetian times was ruthlessly dug out; the rich disliked the loss of their power and perquisites, but the poor found comfort in being judged by foreign officers, who might sometimes be mistaken, but at least could not be bribed.

In 1824, King Tom characteristically died of an apoplexy. His successor, Sir Frederick Adams, was a weaker man who so enraged Colonel Napier by his indecision that Napier wrote and published a book of 600 pages of abuse of his commander-in-chief. Among all the causes of their titanic quarrel the most memorable, after this lapse of time, may be found on page 543: Adams ordered Napier to shave his beautiful whiskers, and Napier sent the hairy remnants in a parcel to Adams' Adjutant-General as proof of his loyalty. (His book is an engaging work, misleadingly titled 'The Colonies'; at the end, it has three totally irrelevant pictures, 'the first attempts at lithography by a talented lady', with no better explanation than the comment: 'It is not surprising to see a very pretty woman draw well – her taste being formed by her looking-glass!')

Most, and probably all of the British officers in the islands were passionately on the side of the Greeks in their revolt. Nevertheless, the British government was neutral; those were the orders from London, and King Tom insisted that neutrality must strictly be enforced. The islanders were extremely annoyed that they were not allowed to go and join the fight, yet were pleased to be peaceful and prosperous while Greece was reduced to anarchy and ruin. And it was certainly useful for Greece to have the civilized amenities of the islands at their backs all through the war. Tens of thousands of refugees escaped to them, and were fed on British rations. And they provided the only reliable route of communication between the Greeks and the rest of the world. Greek mails went in and out by way of Corfu, and rival nations suspected the British of keeping a staff of spies to steam open the envelopes. Probably they did.

The other British observation post was even closer to the centre of events: the Royal Navy was never far below the horizon when things were happening. Frank Hastings, of course, was not part of it: he was a 'loner' working for Greece, without any British status. The senior officer in the eastern Mediterranean from 1822 to 1827 – almost the whole duration of the war – was Commodore Gawen Hamilton of the *Cambrian* frigate. Hamilton is a shadowy figure who appears out of naval obscurity for his tour of duty off Greece and vanishes into it afterwards. But while he was there, he probably knew more of what was going on than anyone else alive. He could cruise anywhere under the British flag, speak to the Turkish admirals on one day and the Greek guerilla captains on the next. He developed a knack of always turning up, calmly sailing into the harbours of Greece, at all the most fearful moments of crisis – a knack that seems uncanny but must have been based on very good intelligence. Like the army officers in the islands, he was evidently a strong supporter of the Greeks, but like them he was bound by duty to act impartially. I have seen a letter he wrote to Adams in Corfu at a time when the fortune of Greece had sunk to the lowest point it ever reached. 'I have not the smallest hope as to any good result of the struggle,' he said; 'I believe that England will mourn over but not save Greece.'

That was the direction of his hope, and duty did not stop him giving the Greeks advice, with all the unshakeable self-assurance of the Royal Navy in the nineteenth century. The advice was not always welcome, but it was always good; the Greeks were in awe of him and of what he represented, and of the martial air and unruffled efficiency of his ship, and they usually, if reluctantly, did what he recommended. In the course of years, he came to know all the leaders; and all of them, at one desperate moment or another, seem to have been thankful to see the *Cambrian* in the offing, and to have hurried on board to be given a sane analysis of whatever crazy situation they were in. He also saved many hundreds of lives, both Greek and Turkish. The British, and their navy in particular, expected in that era to have a finger in every pie in the world, and Hamilton was the finger they had in the pie in Greece. He will keep on turning up in this story.

*

In the autumn and winter of 1821, Prince Demetrius Hypsilantes, in the Peloponnese, was making elaborate proclamations which few people understood, insisting on being treated with regal ceremony, and distributing portfolios of non-existent government departments to his friends. To be just, there was nothing much more, among the surrounding chaos, that the forlorn young man could have done. But there was one folly he might have avoided: he announced that he would march on Constantinople in the following spring.

Among the departments he imagined, the most important was a Ministry of War. He had prepared for it, before he came to Greece, by engaging a French colonel named Baleste to raise and train a national army. If such a task had not been quite impossible, Baleste would have been a good choice for it. He was a capable officer who had served with distinction under Napoleon, and he had lived for a time in Crete; so he was one of the few foreigners who came to Greece and not only knew what he was talking about, but could also talk about it in Greek. In Italy, at Hypsilantes' expense, he signed on a party of other officers, French and Italian, and bought the necessities of an infantry unit: muskets, bayonets, ammunition, trumpets, drums and uniforms of a new design, black with a black hat decorated with a skull and the motto 'Freedom or Death'. So equipped, he landed in Kalamata about two months after Petrobey had captured the place, and began a recruiting drive.

The trouble was, nobody would join. Baleste's intention, of course, was to train his first regiment to drill and fight in disciplined Napoleonic ranks, which he rightly believed would be invincible against the Turks. He named it in advance the Regiment Baleste, and he started to drill as soon as he had enough men to make a platoon. The Greeks of Kalamata watched the performance with admiration, amazement and utter incomprehension. This, they knew, was how the Franks went to war, but it seemed to them to have nothing to do with what they knew of fighting. So far, their own methods had been successful and they were proud of them. To submit to fierce and foreign words of command seemed unworthy of free men; to be seen by their friends marching about the parade ground in mysterious manoeuvres would have been impossibly embarrassing; and it would simply have been un-Greek to have changed their national costume, which they cherished even when it was reduced to filthy rags, for an alien outlandish uniform.

And their natural leaders, men like Colocotrones and Petrobey, mistrusted the whole idea of a national army. Probably all of them, and certainly Colocotrones, knew a well-trained army of the western style would be an efficient means of winning the war, or at least of defending what they had already won. But to what end? They may have been vague about the meaning of the independence they were fighting for, but it certainly did not mean changing the rule of Turks for the rule of phanariots, enforced by troops under European Command.

So the only Greeks who could be persuaded into the Regiment were a few of the refugees from Turkey who had been landed destitute and friendless on the mainland. At the height of its strength, this national army numbered rather less than 350 men, and nearly all the officers were foreigners.

Nobody asked the foreigners to come, but nobody could stop them. At that time, so soon after the end of the Napoleonic wars, Europe was full of disbanded army officers, men unqualified either by training or temperament for any other trade. Many were drifting round the continent as mercenaries in any revolutionary plots they heard of; and many also were in political disgrace or under suspicion in their own countries, and so could never go home. The scent of any war attracted them, and rumours of what was happening in Greece aroused their wildest hopes of glory and promotion. The rumours were truly inspiring. While Baleste was drilling something less than a company of bemused and awkward refugees with muskets, reports in Europe spoke of anything from four to ten thousand European infantry, artillery and cavalry who had already won magnificent victories under French and Italian generals and soon, as Hypsilantes himself had said, would be at the gates of Constantinople.

So the officers gathered. Some managed to attach themselves to rich European Greeks, who were equally deceived and were making their way to Greece, confident of being offered important posts in government and willing to promise commissions in the highest ranks of the army. Others who could scrape up money for the fare took passage on ships in Marseilles and the ports of Italy. Each of them was equipped with a uniform of suitable splendour to his own design, with a sword and a brace of pistols, and with a more or less credible story of his past prowess and distinction.

Small groups of these out-of-work officers in their exotic green and scarlet cloaks and jackets, their elegant breeches and polished boots, medals and braid and epaulettes, and their various monstrous helmets and cockaded hats and caps, were landed in all the primitive little harbours of southern and western Greece in the summer and autumn of 1821. Their first shock was to find they had to carry their own bags ashore. Then they asked where the army headquarters were. None of them spoke modern Greek and none of the inhabitants spoke anything else, so there was plenty of scope at once for mutual misunderstanding. But Greeks had the oriental politeness to tell strangers what they thought they wanted to be told, and so they sent the officers off in the direction where the Greek army might have been if it had been anywhere. And in the course of time, the people of the seaports were asked the same question so often that they really began to believe the foreigners must be right, and that an army must really exist somewhere else in the country. So all over the Peloponnese that year, groups wandered from village to village in their pathetically inappropriate finery, slowly growing more tattered, footsore and dejected, and heading towards the ultimate disillusion when they found the army in which they expected high command was nothing but the Regiment Baleste.

It was really tragic, but one could feel the tragedy more if so many of them had not been such proud and pompous men. It was an age when anyone in authority, and army officers most of all, could display a conceit and self-esteem that would only be ridiculed nowadays. Among themselves, they were always on their dignity, always taking affront, always demanding satisfaction for imaginary insults and fighting duels on trivial points of precedence and etiquette. Their affairs of honour were all the more difficult because they all suspected each other of being impostors, which many of them were; and nothing could be more distressing than for a gentleman to call out another and give him the thrashing he deserved, only to find he was some upstart from the lower classes with whom it was undignified to fight. Not many were killed in these affrays, but plenty were wounded badly enough to have to leave the country. They spent much more time and energy fighting each other than preparing to fight the enemies of Greece.

And to the Greeks they behaved with odious condescension. They expected every Greek to be grateful to them for offering their talents to the cause; they often mentioned the personal sacrifice they had made and the brilliant career they had interrupted, although the fact was that most of them had nothing better to do. In the villages they demanded food and accommodation befitting officers and gentlemen, they complained at what they were given and never considered that the people who fed them were on the edge of starvation. In the early days they got away with it: the villagers did not know who they were and treated them with peasants' humility. But after a while, some Greeks began to ask the obvious question: who asked you to come? And there was no answer.

In Kalamata, the Regiment had one success. A Turkish fleet was sighted, and the inhabitants in a panic prepared to abandon the town. But Baleste paraded his men on the beach, and when the Turks saw them they sailed away again. Perhaps it was a portent of what the Regiment might have done if it had had a chance: the mere sight of what looked like European troops appeared to have frightened the Turks. But that was the only unqualified victory the Regiment ever had, and it may be that the Turkish fleet was rather easily frightened. About the same time, according to a legend in Spetsai, red poppies miraculously grew round the mouth of the harbour where they had never grown before, and the Turkish fleet mistook them for the red caps that guerillas often wore and sailed away in alarm.

*

While the Regiment was drilling at Kalamata, the Greeks under arms were waiting for the fortresses of the Peloponnese to fall through starvation. There were nine still held by the Turks: Nauplia and Monemvasia on the east coast, Coron, Modon and Navarino in the south-west, and Patras, Rhion and Corinth in the north. All those are on the coast: the only one inland was Tripolitsa, which had been the headquarters of the Turkish government. Outside the Peloponnese there were half a dozen others, including the Acropolis of Athens.

The Turks had never prepared these walled towns and citadels to stand a siege: there was not much food or ammunition in any of them, their cannon were rusty and their fortifications already centuries old and more or less in ruins. But the Greeks' blockade was a casual affair by the rigorous standards of Europe. Neither the Greeks nor the Turks expected to fight or keep watch in the dark, or during the afternoon siesta, or when it was raining. There were always Greeks who for pity's sake, or more usually for profit, were willing to sell provisions to the enemy and smuggle them through at night when everyone else was asleep. And some places, especially Coron, Modon and Patras, were well supplied from the sea, either by Turkish warships or merchantmen from Europe. So the sieges were slow.

The first to fall was Monemvasia, five months after the revolution began. Its town and citadel are on a steep rock in the sea, only connected to the mainland by a bridge. The Mainotes of Petrobey had only to camp round the end of the bridge to cut off the place by land, and at sea Bouboulina's ships from Spetsai, a few hours' sailing to the north, had the upper hand. The Turks within, soldiers, tradesmen of the town with their families, and refugees from the countryside, were reduced to eating seaweed, and even to making desperate sorties at night to drag in human bodies. But they knew what would happen if they surrendered to the Mainotes.

Monemvasia brought out the difference between the Greeks who had lived in Greece under the Turks and those who had come from abroad. The Mainotes and other brigands squatting round the town were patiently waiting for slaughter, rape and booty. But Hypsilantes and his few followers had civilized feelings of mercy.

When he heard the fall was imminent he sent a deputation down to Monemvasia to offer an honourable capitulation, and a guarantee that the Turks would be spared and sent in neutral ships to Turkey. Possibly he still believed the brigands would accept his authority and carry out his promise. The Turks believed it, and agreed to surrender. Luckily, since the whole of the rock was in their hands, they could go straight off to the ships, and five hundred were safely aboard before the town gates were opened – when the Mainotes rushed in and plundered the place and murdered everyone who had not got away in time.

This was another great victory to be reported in Europe, both as a feat of arms, which it was not, and as a triumph of Christian principles as Europe understood them. It was indeed a kind of victory for Hypsilantes – but a moral victory over the Mainotes, not a martial victory over the Turks. He succeeded only because of the unique position of the town, and he never succeeded again in protecting Turks against his own bloodthirsty population. Nor is this success quite certain. Some reports say the five hundred Turks were really landed somewhere in Asia Minor; others that they were put ashore on a barren uninhabited island and left there to starve again, and that a French ship that happened to sight them could rescue only a few survivors.

Navarino was the next of the fortresses to succumb. Again Hypsilantes sent an emissary and terms of surrender were agreed: the Turks were promised transport by sea to Africa. Perhaps the emissary meant what he said, but nobody else had the slightest intention of honouring the agreement. Baleste was there, and refused to have any part in what he knew was a trick; and one of the Greeks who signed the agreement proudly told a British colonel afterwards that he had destroyed the only copy of it so that nobody could prove it had existed. The Turks believed, or hoped in their desperation, that the promise would be kept, and they opened the gates. The Greeks swarmed in and killed the whole population, about two thousand people. A priest who saw it all told afterwards how the women were stripped and driven into the sea and shot there, and their babies thrown in to drown or beaten to death on the rocks. The Greeks delighted in cutting off the arms and legs of their victims, and both sides in this war had the habit of decapitating all their enemies and piling the heads in pyramids as trophies – the Turks sent sacks full of ears to the Sultan as proofs of their skill. Months later in Navarino, when fresh volunteers were arriving there by sea, the place still stank of death and the dogs and birds were still eating the rotten dismembered corpses round the walls; and Greeks who hoped to impress the newcomers boasted of the numbers they had personally killed and how they had done it, and offered the services of terrified half-naked girls and boys who had been kept alive as prostitutes and were roaming in the ruins.

Then Tripolitsa. This was a much larger town, and its agony was prolonged because it was known to be rich; it contained the palace of the Pasha who had ruled the Peloponnese, and the homes of the most prosperous merchants. So all the leaders gathered round it with their gangs, Colocotrones, Petrobey, a dozen or so of lesser brigand captains, Bouboulina from the Spetsiote fleet, and Hypsilantes himself. All of them were intent on booty. Hypsilantes would not have used such a word: he justly believed that the treasury of the Turkish pasha, the proceeds of past taxation, should fall by right to his government. But his need was more desperate than anyone's: his funds had run out and the government, if it could be so called, was already bankrupt.

Hypsilantes summoned the Regiment up from Kalamata. But when it arrived, it was a travesty of the splendid force that he and Baleste had imagined. Hypsilantes had paid for its equipment, but he had not been able to pay its wages, and the people of Kalamata had refused to supply its provisions. The officers who had any money left had had enough to eat and more than enough to drink; the others were driven to begging and borrowing. All their beautiful uniforms were tattered. The men, outnumbered by the officers, were hungry and ragged, and many were marching barefooted. The guerillas, especially the leaders, watched them with open scorn.

After they were assembled, Hypsilantes heard there were forty-odd more foreign officers in Kalamata who had come too late to join, and he sent a letter to request them also to come to Tripolitsa. He addressed it to an Italian colonel, the only one of them whose name he knew, and asked him to pass on the message to the others. That innocent request set off a typical outburst among those proud and touchy characters. Outraged Germans and Frenchmen swore they would never serve under an Italian, though that was not what Hypsilantes had said or intended. Italians, bristling and posturing, protested at this insult to their nation, and a general brawl began, which was watched with interest by Greeks who wondered what it was all about. After some hours, somebody took a closer look at the letter and managed to tell them they had all misunderstood it. Then, as usual, the Italians demanded satisfaction, a duel was fought and the French combatant was wounded and had to go back to France. The rest of them set off for Tripolitsa, still scarcely on speaking terms.

And then, outside the beleaguered town, another trying incident made the Europeans look foolish, although it seems to have been no fault of the Regiment's. Hypsilantes had acquired two mortars and one or two other guns, and with no small labour they had been hauled to Tripolitsa and set in position to breach the wall of the town. He had also acquired an Italian named Tassi, uniformed and accoutred, who said he had been Napoleon's chief engineer, and also let it be known that Lord Castlereagh the British Prime Minister and Count Metternich the Austrian Chancellor were both old friends of his. The Regiment might have had its doubts, but the Greeks believed him and Hypsilantes appointed him his Engineer-in-Chief. So it fell to him to supervise the firing of the guns.

When the great moment came, an expectant crowd of Greeks and a few Europeans waited to see the walls fall down. But watching his preparations, the Europeans began to suspect he had never fired a gun before. At last, he applied the match to a mortar. Either he had made a fundamental mistake, or else it was not a good mortar: there was a bang and a cloud of smoke and its barrel exploded, and in the violent recriminations Tassi had to confess: he was a bankrupt saddler from Smyrna.

The captains put off attacking Tripolitsa, because all of them were making private bargains with the wealthy Turks inside, selling them promises of safe conduct to the coast. Lesser Greeks were selling food to them, at prices that men with starving families would pay. Bouboulina herself went in and out of the town by night to persuade the Turkish ladies to give up their jewels. And while there was money to be made in this disreputable trading there was no hurry to start the assault, when the loot would go to the quickest and most ruthless of the soldiery.

And during this time of waiting, Hypsilantes decided to march away with the regiment to Patras. There was a rumour, quite untrue, that the citadel there was also about to fall, and he may have hoped for a personal victory. But most likely, he knew he could not control the mobs round Tripolitsa and simply did not want to see or have any part in the sickening cruelty he knew was inevitably coming. Perhaps also, as a Greek, he did not want his European followers to see it.

But there were about a score of European witnesses when at last the bandits grew impatient at their captains' duplicity and rushed at a gate and broke into the starving town. Among them was Colonel Thomas Gordon, a sober, experienced, rich and independent Scotsman who knew the Middle East, spoke Greek, and had come with an entourage of his own to observe events and see what he could do to help the Greeks. As soon as the war was over, he wrote a history of it; but he 'dared not describe' the torments he had seen at Tripolitsa, feeling perhaps that it was wrong to perpetuate anything so shameful. Even now, it is certainly better not to recount the stories the witnesses told: it is enough to say that within two days, the ten thousand people of Tripolitsa were dead and most of them mutilated and beheaded. Thousands of Greeks retired to their villages, rich by their own standards, to hide away their booty. A vast ephemeral market sprang up where everything of any value was sold or bartered, but the price of slaves fell so low that they were not worth keeping. All the leaders did well out of it, but Colocotrones got the lion's share: he had the authority to claim the money, arms and jewels from the Pasha's palace, and he sent such profits to the banks in the Ionian islands that he was rich enough to maintain his own independent army for years to come. An unbearable stink arose from the corpses, which nobody paused to bury, the wells were poisoned and a plague broke out which ravaged the Peloponnese on and off for the rest of the war.

Hypsilantes, of course, got nothing, and from this time onward the Regiment was reduced to beggary. The foreign officers who saw the aftermath of Tripolitsa were finally disgusted and disillusioned, and most of those who had any money used it to get out of Greece as quickly as they could. But some had no money, and nowhere else to go. They might have been allowed to join the bandits, but that offended their sense of military honour and probably also their residual human conscience; and they could not have survived very long without even understanding the bandits' language. Baleste told Hypsilantes his only hope was to use the Regiment to kill Colocotrones and the other klephts and take back their booty for the government, but Hypsilantes would not hear of it, and Baleste left the country and went to Crete. The remnants of the Regiment, perhaps two hundred of them, wandered from place to place, mostly with Turkish women and boys they had rescued or bought for a few pence. To delay their starvation they began to sell their accoutrements, and afterwards, the prouder brigands could be seen with epaulettes and medals on their sheepskin cloaks. And still, new hopeful volunteers were landing in Greece, with the same resplendent clothes, the same illusions and the same high hopes of command in a glorious army.

*

Some months after the horrors of Tripolitsa, the Turks took revenge with the massacre of the island of Chios.

Chios is on the far side of the Aegean Sea, cut off by only a narrow sound from the coast of Turkey; yet its people were Greek and had scarcely any Turkish settlers among them. They had always been mocked by other Greeks for being slow-witted; a proverb said it was easier to find a green horse than a clever Chiote. But in fact they were simple easy-going people, pious in their own fashion, who had the wisdom to make a peaceful life for themselves under Turkish rule. Their own village primates collected the taxes, which were not much of a burden, a small Turkish garrison manned the citadel in their town and gave nobody any trouble, their girls were well known for being beautiful and obliging, and they had a steady prosperous trade in growing mastic, the basis of chewing gum, which was one of the few indulgences allowed to the ladies of Turkish harems.

They therefore watched the start of the revolution with alarm. Mainland Greeks were almost as foreign to them as Turks, and it was far from certain that they would be better off if they were ruled from Greece, which was far away, instead of Turkey, which was close. They were afraid the taxes would be heavier and collected by greedier hands, and especially that they would lose their mastic trade. So they kept quiet and did nothing.

But that was not good enough for some of the trigger-happy Greeks in their early enthusiasm. One in particular, a man named Lykourgos, decided the Chiotes ought to be liberated. Some reports said he had been a doctor in Turkey, others that he was a grocer who specialized in selling poisons. Whatever he was, he persuaded Hypsilantes to authorize an expedition. The Prince soon changed his mind, and suggested that the venture should be postponed. But Lykourgos had got what he wanted, a patriotic excuse to exploit the Chiotes, and he took no notice of the timid suggestion. By March 1822 he had collected a sizeable force of men who hoped for plunder, and he landed them on the island. And the folly of it was that nobody paused for a moment to think how such an outpost of Greece could possibly be defended.

There was nobody there to plunder except the Chiotes, so they became the victims. Lykourgos deposed the islanders' own authorities, set himself up as a military ruler, and proclaimed that the place was independent. But he was not a military man at all, and did not know how to capture the citadel. His men, with no Turks to fight, ran riot through the town and the neighbouring countryside, and their officers – if any had a right to such a title – set up a protection racket to rob the richer citizens. Some of the Chiotes, who really had no idea what was going on, were persuaded to celebrate their freedom; and Lykourgos did not begin to make plans for defence because he was sure that he and his men could escape by sea if the Turks attacked them.

The counter-attack came sooner than they expected. There was a story that the Sultan's harem had rebelled at the shortage of chewing gum. In the nature of things, it could only have been surmise, but it was a whimsical thought that the dreaded Sultan himself was at the mercy of wives and concubines, clamouring among the fall of empires that whatever happened the chewing gum must be saved. At all events, the defection of Chios was an affront he could quickly avenge, and he did. Three weeks after Lykourgos landed, the Turkish fleet arrived and put ashore an army, and hordes of Moslems, incited by their rulers and priests, began to cross the narrow straits intent on holy war. Lykourgos and his followers fled in Psariote ships, and left the defenceless Chiotes to pay the penalty.

On the Sultan's orders, the Archbishop and seventy-five of the leading citizens were executed, and possibly that was as far as the Sultan himself would have gone: he had no interest in killing off his tax-payers or his mastic growers. But the army was out of hand, and the fanatical volunteers who had crossed the straits were under nobody's orders. They took their own revenge for what the Greeks had done in the Peloponnese. No-one knows how many of the harmless islanders were murdered or herded away. It was at least ten thousand, and for a long time afterwards the slave markets of the empire, from Algiers to the Caspian Sea, were glutted with the merchandise of Chios.

CHAPTER THREE

The Philhellenes Arrive
September 1821—July 1822

Lord Byron · Percy Bysshe Shelley
Prince Alexander Mavrocordato

Nowadays, sailing or wandering around in Greece, it is hard to believe in the frenzy of cruelty that overcame the Greeks in 1821. They seem the kindest of people. In summer on the tourist routes they may be mercenary, but tourism anywhere in the world disrupts human relationship, and I do not think the Greeks are often dishonest with their tourists, as many nations are. And of course their ways of governing their country are still erratic and sometimes deplorable. I am told they have two sayings almost as true today as they would have been 150 years ago: 'Every Greek thinks he ought to be a captain', and 'Wherever there are six Greeks there are seven political parties.'

But off the tourist track, and politics apart, they have an instinct now to trust a stranger and make him welcome. I am very sorry I started to visit their country when I was old enough to have forgotten the Greek I was supposed to learn at school, except the alphabet, and when I felt too old to begin again. But classical Greek would not have been much use to me, and I have been lucky with interpreters. Moreover, there is nobody more loquacious in signs and gestures than the Greeks. They want to know all about you, and you can find without understanding a word that you have told them where you live, and how and why you have finished up in their harbour, and how old you are and how many children you have, and how many horse power your engine is. It is an endearing kind of inquisitiveness. They make you think they like you, although you cannot see any possible reason why they should.

Some of them are very rich and some are very poor, but poverty makes no difference to their kindness. You are left with innumerable memories of it, each trivial in itself but indelible in sum. You try to buy fish from a fisherman you have never seen before and will never see again: he will give them to you, and when you say four are enough he gives you seven because seven is a lucky number. If they are having a party, you may be whisked into it, and whatever you intended to do has to wait for another day: I have a hazy recollection of being stuffed with wine and cake by a huge crowd of people in a country tavern who turned out, so far as I ever understood it, to be the annual outing of the Athens Plumbers' Union. And I remember the very first time I ever anchored in an empty bay in Greece. It was that blessed time of day when the sails are stowed and the chain has rattled out and you switch off the engine and total peace descends; the first glass of ouzo is in your hand, a drink deceptively strong and ludicrously cheap, the warm air is scented by rosemary and thyme and the hills are mirrored as if the world had stopped. An old man came rowing out with creaking oars from the shore that had seemed deserted. He looked like one of Colocotrones' brigands, and we waited for him anxiously, expecting some kind of request or complaint we would not understand. But he had come to give us some pomegranates. Of course he accepted a cigarette and a drink, and a cynic might say he had hoped for this sort of bargain. But I do not think so. I think he came only because he was Greek and wanted to show his goodwill – and of course to ask who we were and where we had come from.

Sometimes, one must admit, their geniality is complicated by a belief that any northern woman welcomes being instantly seduced. But that seems to be a common opinion in the Mediterranean, and if his rebuff is explicit a Greek will accept it cheerfully; it was worth trying, he seems to say, and was meant as a compliment.

And sometimes they explode with Olympian rages which look and sound as though they would end in murder, but usually end in a crowd of conciliators with drinks and embraces all round. Most of these thunderous outbursts seem to be caused by offences against the quality they call philotimo, which means something between self-esteem and personal honour. Their sense of philotimo is powerful, and among themselves they try to avoid offending it; a Greek is normally careful not to make another Greek 'lose face', because he knows himself how much it hurts. I am glad I have never been the target of an angry Greek, but I have seen foreigners outrage a Greek's philotimo, either by mistake or by bad manners, and the result has always surprised them. You can travel all over Greece relying on the people's courtesy, but you cannot bully a Greek, however humble, into doing what you want him to do. I have not come across this concept in histories of the war, but it explains a lot. The foreign officers in their pride must constantly have offended the Greeks' philotimo, and seldom if ever have understood what they had done.

Philotimo is a personal affair, but it has a racial parallel which even more illuminates what happened in this war. I do not know a Greek word for it, only a word of Greek derivation: it has been defined as ethnic truth. A Greek, at least until the recent past, lived his life on two separate planes of truth, the ordinary factual everyday truth and a kind of ideal truth. The first described things as they unfortunately were, and the other as they ought to be to accord with his ideal of Greekness, and he could sincerely believe them both. Things could happen on the factual plane, and everybody could know they happened, but on the other a Greek could deny they had ever happened at all. This was the quality that enabled the Greeks, for example, to glorify their brigands. On one level they might know from experience that they were dirty, lousy, greedy and callous thieves; on the other they could see them as knightly heroes and guardians of a noble tradition. To a Greek, both could be equally true. Their own government, on one level, was a gang of self-seeking rogues; on the other, it was a model of wise democracy, simply because it was Greek. Or their own battles: they could laugh about them as farcical skirmishes, or boast about them as

66

glorious victories against enormous odds – and be sure in the latter case that no other Greeks except their mortal enemies would offend their philotimo by contradicting them.

Every race has some of this gift of self-deception: it is the only basis for national patriotism. In the Greeks it is, or was, much stronger than most because it was not national, but fundamentally religious. A Greek by definition was a member of the Greek Church. For most of the Christian era, that church had been quite separate from western churches. Its adherents believed it was the only true church; the Empire of Byzantium where it had been supreme was the Kingdom of God on earth, and Greece was its heritor. Consequently, it was a matter of Christian faith that everything Greek, on the level of ethnic truth, must be near perfection, and critics were blasphemers.

The bizarre excesses of this dual truth lasted all through the nineteenth century. In the end, some Europeans came to understand it and make allowances for it; but during the war, so far as I can discover, not one of them understood it at all. They simply wrote off the Greeks as liars. Nowadays, the Greeks have the redeeming virtue of laughing at themselves, but the optional truth is not far below the surface; the best of their friends must admit that they still have what Byron called an incapacity for veracity. Every Greek has a pretty high opinion of Greeks, and of the quality one can only call Greekness.

So have I. No open-minded traveller could help being fond of them; the more so perhaps for their frailties, which they do not disguise by hypocrisy. And being grateful to them for their kindness, I have puzzled a long time over the reason why their ancestors 150 years ago suddenly behaved so atrociously. The usual explanation then was that they hated the Turks and took revenge for centuries of oppression. But I think there was more in it than that. The oppression had not been so very bad, and hatred is a poor excuse for cruelty. I believe the cause was rather the opposite: that in those days they were very much like the Turks. For 350 years they had been exclusively under Turkish influence, and only their church had kept them a separate people. Despite their Christianity, they had become more eastern than western in their manners and customs, and in their moral judgements too. I doubt if they have ever quite recovered from this influence. People who know them better than I do, and like them as much, will point out that they still have a streak of vengefulness and cruelty, which shows in the way they treat their political prisoners. Certainly, in the history of their war, one always finds that the only people who really understood each other were the ordinary Greeks and the ordinary Turks. Both sides were angry when the other massacred, cheated and decapitated their own, but they were never surprised – no more surprised than people in modern wars when their enemies drop bombs on them. Given the chance, it was what they would do themselves.

The Europeans were surprised and shocked by the massacres because they had never seen an eastern war. So were the westernized Greeks like Hypsilantes. The kind of war they knew, the Napoleonic wars and other western wars for a long time past, had been almost gentlemanly affairs, controlled by convention; armies and navies slaughtered each other ferociously, but they seldom slaughtered anyone else. Eastern wars, on the other hand, were not controlled like that and never had been. They were more like modern wars in their horrible thoroughness. Nowadays, people burn women and babies with incendiaries or blow them up in their homes with high explosives; then, in eastern wars, they cut their throats. The Europeans judged the Greeks of the time by inappropriate standards; but now, I need hardly add, we have lost any right to judge them at all. They were fighting an eastern war, because it was the only kind of war they had ever heard of.

*

Very few Europeans who were not in Greece knew what was happening there. Reports of the massacre of Chios were sent home by ambassadors in Constantinople, and they caused a thrill of horror. Ever since the Turks besieged Vienna in 1683 they had been vaguely dreaded as an eastern menace, and massacre was the kind of terrifying act that people expected of them.

But from Greece, the only reports with any official air were sent out by the followers of Hypsilantes. Like most reports of partisans in wars, they were far from the factual truth, and moreover they were gilded to fit the ethnic truth. So, while everyone in Europe condemned the Turkish massacres, not many knew the Greeks had done the same and had done it first. All governments regarded the Greeks as legitimate subjects of the Sultan, but public opinion regarded them as Christians gallantly fighting against the Moslem hordes.

And it was not only Christianity that distinguished the Greeks from the Turks in European eyes, it was also the early history of Greece. Education then was mainly classical, and the language, philosophy and arts of ancient Greece were a basic part of it. And misunderstanding was increased to fantasy by the people who came to be known as the Philhellenes. They were classical scholars, idealists, poets, romantics and radical politicians all over Europe, and they proclaimed a new kind of ethnic truth which the Greeks had not thought of at all. This was that the modern Greeks were direct descendants of the ancient Greeks and still, in some latent form, possessed their wisdom and heroic qualities.

In the next few years, men not only died for this belief but subscribed quite large sums of money for it. But in any factual sense, it was not true at all. The modern Greeks were not more closely related to the ancient Greeks than the modern British were to the ancient Britons. The blood of both had been thoroughly mixed and diluted by thousands of years of migrants and invaders. The ancestors of modern Greeks were not only Greek but Roman, Albanian, Goth, Venetian and Slav, not to mention Turkish. The only Greeks who might have had an almost unbroken descent were the few small clans like the Mainotes who were so fierce, and lived so far up in the mountains, that invaders had left them alone.

As for the ancient genius of Greece, it was indeed a foundation of European culture, but in Greece it was almost forgotten. The Greeks did not want to remember it. They looked back with pride to the Christian empire of Byzantium, but never to the pagan age before it; the relics and monuments they valued were ikons, the tombs of saints and the beautiful dilapidated little Byzantine churches in their villages, not the marble columns and broken statues scattered in the hills. Very few of them could have read the classical authors if they had tried, unless they had been translated into the modern language of Greece, which they called Romaic, and all that most of them knew of the ancient times were some scraps of the warlike legends. When Lord Elgin's workmen in the first decade of the century were wrenching the sculpture off the Parthenon, it was not the Greeks who protested, it was other Europeans, most notably Byron.

The Philhellenes had hit on a kind of self-deception the Greeks did not yet possess. The belief did not last very long in Europe; it was withered by harsh blasts of fact. But as it died in Europe, it was born in Greece. The Greeks were told it so often they began to be proud of it, and in due course it became a part of their ethnic truth. I think it is fair to say they believe it still.

But it was certainly unfair to inflict this belief on the Greeks in 1822. It was the passionate, poetic creed of the Philhellenes that the genius of classical Greece was still in existence and would flower again as soon as the Turks were gone. They proclaimed that this was what the poor Greeks were fighting for, and so gave them a reputation they could not possibly live up to. They created yet another aim for this peasant revolution. It was not the anarchic freedom the peasants themselves had in mind, nor the lordly ambitions of the captains of the klephts, nor the holy war the Church had hesitantly blessed, nor the national patriotism of the 'foreign' Greeks. It was what they called Regeneration, the revival of the ancient glory of Greece: or, as they would have preferred to say, of Hellas.

*

Men like Hypsilantes and his colleagues were well aware of the European belief. They never stated it as a fact, and they certainly knew their own countrymen too well to take it literally. But they made every possible use of it. They needed money from Europe and America, and the ancient glory of Greece, to put it crudely, was their best selling point. It began with the proclamation old Petrobey had signed, and all Hypsilantes's proclamations and dispatches were slanted in the same direction. Calling the Greeks to arms, he reminded them of ancient battles, Marathon and Thermopylae, and of ancient heroes: 'The blood of our tyrants is dear to the shades of the Theban Epaminondas, and of the Athenian Thasybulus who conquered and destroyed the thirty tyrants – to those of Harmodius and Aristogeiton who broke the yoke of Pisistratus – to that of Timoleon who restored liberty to Corinth and to Syracuse – and above all to those of Miltiades, Themistocles, Leonidas –'

Such a muddled sentiment, such language and such a list of names would have meant less than nothing to the soldiers or brigands they were ostensibly addressed to. But they were like a bugle call to professors of classical studies in western universities, not many of whom had ever been to Greece. These men made the assumption Hypsilantes only implied, and added art, philosophy and statesmanship to the martial heroism the Greeks were supposed to have inherited. 'The Greeks of the present day are descendants of those whose wisdom and science have become the common property of the world.' That was a German professor of theology; this a German professor of Greek literature: 'Could any man suppress his desire to see reborn in Greece the days of liberation of Marathon and Salamis, and if possible the blessed age when Plato listened to Socrates and when the songs of Homer and the choruses of Sophocles resounded through the court of Pericles and the temple of Phidias?'*

From the professors it spread to the poets. In France and Germany there was a sudden outpouring of books of verse on the romantic theme of Turkish barbarity and Greek civilization. And in English, there was already Byron. Byron himself, by the time the war began, was tired of the poetry that had made him famous, and indeed of being a poet at all. But there it was: Childe Harold, the Giaour, the Corsair, the Siege of Corinth, the Curse of Minerva, parts of Don Juan and many lesser poems, all returned in one way or another to the theme that had inspired him when he made his youthful journey

* Quoted by William St. Clair in 'That Greece Might Still Be Free'.

to Greece in 1809: the romance of its past glory and its present enslavement to the Turks.

Some biographers make too much of Byron's poetic influence on the Philhellenic idea and on the war in Greece. He was not the originator of the romantic attitude to ancient Greece; many others had said the same sort of things before him, but had not said them in quite such a popular way. What he did, for better or worse, in the ten years before the war, was to make the romance of Greece a best-seller. A great many people read his poetry, not only in Britain and America but almost all over Europe; and when the time came there were certainly some who turned up in Greece saying he had been their inspiration, and knowing not only the famous stanzas from Childe Harold, but more obscure passages from his other works:

> 'Clime of the unforgotten brave!
> Whose land from plain to mountain-cave
> Was Freedom's home or Glory's grave!
> Shrine of the mighty! Can it be
> That this is all remains of thee?
> Approach, thou craven crouching slave:
>   Say, is not this Thermopylae?
> These waters blue that round you lave, –
>   Oh servile offspring of the free –
> Pronounce what sea, what shore is this?
> The gulf, the rock of Salamis!
> These scenes, their story not unknown,
> Arise, and make again your own.'

But the influence of Byron's poems was fortuitous. He seems not to have dreamed, when he wrote them, that they would be read a few years later in the context of a genuine bloody revolution. It is one thing to incite a people in verse to throw off their yoke, and quite another to think of the horror and grief it causes if they really try to do it. Byron's distaste for his own early poems may have been partly artistic. But also, he may well have had a sense of guilt when he heard of the atrocities in Greece and remembered the rhetorical incitements to revolt he had composed so carelessly when he was young. Certainly he was embarrassed when anyone mentioned them.

Byron had the merit of being realistic about the modern Greeks. He never quite committed himself to the ultimate illusion of the Philhellenes. But Shelley did. When they were together in Pisa, after the war had started, he took up the theme where Byron had left it. His poem Hellas was an even more direct encouragement to revolutionaries. And since, like most of the Philhellenes, he had never been to Greece, he could make the usual false assumption in the preface of the poem: 'We are all Greeks. Our laws, our literature, our religion, our arts have their roots in Greece. But for Greece, we might still have been savages and idolators . . . The modern Greek is the descendant of those glorious beings whom the imagination almost refuses to figure to itself as belonging to our kind, and he inherits much of their sensibility, their rapidity of conception, and their courage.'

And the poem ended with the Philhellenic dream: 'The world's great age begins anew, The golden years return –'. And again:

> 'Another Athens shall arise,
> And to remoter time
> Bequeath, like sunset to the skies,
> The splendour of its prime;
> And leave, if naught so bright may live,
> All earth can take or heaven can give.'

This was perhaps the height of Philhellenic naïvety, and it was written at the height of the massacres in the Peloponnese.

The same idea was taken up by all kinds of people who opposed their own governments; for while governments prudently disapproved the revolution, the popular feeling for Greece was a useful weapon with which to attack them. Artists also followed the Philhellenes with paintings as romantic as the poems: the most distinguished of them was Delacroix. And journalists joined in it too, especially in England where the press was free and opposition journals flourished. Newspapers took their information from the meagre reports that came out of Greece, but they took their style

73

from the Philhellenes. Reports of battles began as boastful stories told by brigand chiefs. Hypsilantes's colleagues turned them into propaganda. They grew as they were re-told by enthusiasts abroad, and when they got into print they had to be compared to famous ancient battles. So any skirmish in which a few aimless shots were fired and insults hurled at the enemy became in European papers a second Marathon or Thermopylae, and any chief whose name was known was a second Leonidas or Epaminondas. One journalist got his period wrong and called Bouboulina a second Joan of Arc, a comparison that would have delighted the ample matron of Spetsai. But for most it seems to have been a chance to display their erudition, perhaps a little more erudition than they really had – a temptation every professional writer finds hard to resist.

In England, *The Times* was comparatively sober and printed optimistic reports with reservations, but anti-establishment journals accepted any new story as fact and competed to think of new classical embellishments. Leigh Hunt, the friend of Shelley who edited the Sunday paper the *Examiner*, reported battles that had never happened at all, even as skirmishes. As early as May, he destroyed a Turkish army of 30,000 in the Peloponnese. In July, he captured Athens without the loss of a single man. In August, quoting an 'official report of the Admiralty of Hydra and Spezzia', he said a Turkish admiral's ship of 120 guns had been blown up, which was true excepting the number of the guns, but added that three more Turkish ships of the line had been sunk, seven frigates stranded and sixteen other ships captured. Very occasionally, one must add, he recorded a disaster which was not recognizable in any other report: in December, he said the Greeks had sent two fireships against a Turkish fleet, when the wind changed and blew them back again and 23 of their own ships were destroyed. He ran out of classical comparisons and had to go one better: 'To behave as the Greeks have done at Malvasia is to dispute the glory even with those older names.' Malvasia was the Italian name of Monemvasia, and the glorious behaviour was in fact the scene of rape and knifing when it fell. And in October he wrote a call to arms: 'Now is the time for young men of fortune and education who wish to distinguish themselves . . . Will they encounter dangers to behold Athens and Mount Parnassus and do nothing to rescue them from degradation ? Will they be enraptured with the Elgin Marbles, and with the very names of Phidias and Praxiteles . . . and not do what they can ? Surely not, or they can never again take up their Aeschylus or Sophocles with comfort.'

So the fantasy grew, but the fact remained: the Greeks had slaughtered a great many Turks for reasons of their own, but so far they had not fought a single battle against a substantial army.

Looking back, one cannot avoid a heretical suspicion about the ancients. The nineteenth-century Greeks were certainly good at boasting about their own achievements, especially their bravery. It is still an endearing characteristic of Mediterranean people. Could this be one facet of character that had really survived? At the battle of Marathon in 490 BC, according to the Greek historians, 192 Athenians were killed and 6400 of the Persian enemy. At Thermopylae, Leonidas defended the pass with 300 Spartans against the entire army of Xerxes. At Salamis, the Greeks lost 40 ships but the Persians lost 200 and an army corps. It all sounds unmistakably like the reports of the insignificant skirmishes of 1821. But of course there was no suspicion in the minds of the Philhellenes.

And looking back, the activities of the Philhellenes seem irresponsible. Europeans in general came to believe that the Greeks themselves were consciously fighting for Regeneration of the Golden Age, and were doing it with legendary heroism. And under that fictional inspiration societies and committees sprang up to send them aid, at first in Germany and Switzerland. The wish to help them was generous and sincere, but one may doubt whether it was wise. A few hatfuls of money collected at meetings, a few weapons, a few volunteers and plenty of popular sympathy – these things could perhaps prolong the fight a little, but they could not decide its outcome. Only the full-sized armies and navies of governments could have done that. It was still the Greeks who had to do the fighting, and if they lost in the end, amateur help would only have

made their suffering longer and their devastation worse. At best it
was a very dangerous gamble.

*

Shelley's *Hellas* was dedicated to Prince Alexander Mavrocordato,
the man who later welcomed Byron at Missalonghi. In the summer
of 1821 he had been waiting in the wings, so to speak, at Pisa, and
passing some of the time in teaching Mary Shelley to read Greek.
On April 1st she wrote in her diary 'Alexander Mavrocordato
calls with news about Greece. He is as gay as a caged eagle just free.'
And with more familiarity three weeks later: 'Alex calls in the
evening with good news from Greece.' And in August, when the
Peloponnese was conquered and the massacres in the towns had just
begun, this fat little eagle landed in Greece with a fresh entourage
of overseas Greeks and some boxes of muskets, bayonets, powder
and shot – a second phanariot prince to add to the infinitely complicated rivalries between the leaders who were already there.

Mavrocordato was the oddest and most enigmatic of all the
Greeks the war made prominent. Mrs Shelley was the only person
who recorded gaiety as one of his qualities, and perhaps he lost
it when he arrived in Greece. Some people thought he had a kindly
expression, but most said he was cunning, devious and deceitful,
a man who would never do a straightforward deed or give a
straightforward answer. Yet he survived every vicissitude; he
always bounced up like one of those round old-fashioned dolls
that cannot be knocked over (he looked like one) and he became
president and three times prime minister of Greece.

One reason for his survival was that in the turbulent politics
of Greece he had the Greek guerillas' knack of always knowing
when to run away: whenever things got too hot in government,
he made strategic retreats to Hydra or Missalonghi, or anywhere
else that was reasonably calm. And another reason may simply
have been that he was cleverer than any of the rest of them. He was
cosmopolitan and well educated: he spoke fluent Italian, Turkish
and Romaic, read classical Greek and could understand English

and French. Of course he was ambitious, as any politician has to be, but he was sincere in wanting the freedom of his country. And although he sometimes looked like a coward, he sometimes found a genuine streak of courage. Even when everything seemed lost, he did not run away from Greece.

His most obvious oddity was his appearance, and perhaps in part it was deliberate. Everyone else with any claim to authority, Greek or foreign, dressed either in garish versions of European uniforms or else in the elaborate embroidered costume of wealthy Greeks, with a battery of elegant knives and pistols in their belts. Mavrocordato, with his portly little figure, could never have competed with the ferocious martial finery of the others, but he made himself more conspicuous than any of them. Even through the heat of the Greek summer and through the physical trials of a guerilla war, he always seems to have worn his sober morning dress, his high collar and stock, his gold-rimmed glasses and flat cap, an outfit that in modern eyes at least makes him look like a caricature of a Ruritanian civil servant. Yet in spite of the strictly unmilitary clothes, he had one dangerous illusion: he fancied himself as a general in command of armies, and that was the cause of disasters which were ignominious for him and fatal for a good many of his followers.

It would be pointless and boring to try to follow all the convolutions of rivalry in Greece in the winter of 1821. All the different kinds of leaders were grouping and re-grouping, forming alliances and breaking them up with threats of assassination: the klephts, the primates, the bishops, the islanders and the Greeks from abroad. And the two phanariot princes instantly became rivals of each other.

Mavrocordato used the title of prince in his dealings with Europeans, but he had no pretensions, like Hypsilantes, to royal status in Greece. What he foresaw for the country was a constitutional republic which would later become a monarchy under one of the many available genuine princes of Europe, with himself as the power behind the throne: it is said he already had it in mind to invite Prince Eugène, the adopted son of Napoleon, to become the king of Greece. But for the present, he only saw that Greece as a whole was ungovernable, and that Hypsilantes was running out of money and losing what little authority he had had. So he quickly removed himself from the turmoil of the Peloponnese by the first of his subtle retreats. He went to Missalonghi, where there were no rivals and no Turks, and began to try to organize some kind of government there for the western part of the mainland.

Soon afterwards, Hypsilantes made a final bid for power by summoning a National Assembly to meet in the Peloponnese. The place he chose for it was Argos, because Tripolitsa was riddled with plague and there was no other capital. Most districts of Greece that were free sent representatives: some sent a few, and some sent large delegations to make their voices heard. Mavrocordato came back from Missalonghi. On his way, he had the idea of commanding an attack to capture the citadel of Patras, hoping perhaps to arrive in an aura of military glory. But this was the first of his disasters. He did not know what he was doing, and the Turkish garrison made such a sudden sortie that he lost his own luggage; and so he reached Argos with nothing but the morning dress he was wearing, and the reputation of having made a fool of himself.

All the same, it was he who dominated the new Assembly, for what it was worth. That was not much. Its very existence, and all its claims to be a government, were violently opposed by the klephts and primates, who had a rival institution they called the Senate of the Peloponnese. With their armed bands, they made Argos so unsafe for the delegates that the Assembly had to retreat to the village of Piada, about twenty miles away to the east in the hills near the ruins of Epidauros. There, in January 1822, this power-less government proclaimed the political existence and independence of Greece. Mavrocordato was elected President, and Hypsilantes Chief of the Legislature, and a written constitution was published: the Constitution of Epidauros.

Many people in hindsight have said this document was only written to impress Europeans, especially European governments. Certainly the name they gave it was likely to impress the Philhellenes, who would know Epidauros as the site of the temple of Asclepius the God of Medicine – but would not need to know the Assembly only met there because it had been chased there by its much more powerful rivals. But it seems impossible that the Constitution was written during the meeting, which was short and disorganized. It is much more likely that Mavrocordato had drafted it, with expert foreign help, in the long hopeful months before he came to Greece, and that he published it now because he simply could not bear to give up hope. With things as they were, he must have known that any constitution, and this one in particular, was irrelevant. It was a blameless liberal aspiration. Among other things, it proclaimed the freedom of the press, although Greece had never had a newspaper; the abolition of slavery, although no Greek had owned a slave before the massacres began; and religious tolerance, although almost everyone in the country was a member of one church, and although they were still killing every Moslem they could lay hands on. Nobody in Greece took the slightest notice of this constitution, and it is said the only lasting decision of the Assembly was the design of the blue and white flag which is still the national ensign.

*

Since Mavrocordato was now the nominal President, it fell to him, not Hypsilantes, to receive a new generation of volunteers who began to arrive uninvited about the turn of the year. He may have noticed that they were a different kind of people. There were still some officers among them, more or less mercenary, like those who had formed the sad Regiment Baleste. But now there were also young men who had no military training but were bright-eyed with the inspiration of the Philhellenes. And while most of the Regiment had come from France and Italy, most of these new young men were Germans.

It was in Germany that the professors of classics had been most active in founding committees to help the Greeks. At least a dozen had done it independently in different university towns, and had

collected subscriptions and issued calls for volunteers. They may
have been more successful than they expected; for the cause of
Greece caught on as a youthful protest movement. The past glories
the war was supposed to revive were vivid then, from school or
university, to any young man with an education, and it was a
thought that truly inspired them to fight in the land of the heroes.
To some it also appeared a crusade in defence of Christianity
against the Moslems. Volunteering was also a protest against oppression and tyranny, and a protest against what now might be called
the Establishment, the governments which persisted in regarding
the Sultan as the proper ruler of Greece: the government of Prussia,
indeed, made volunteering illegal, and so made it all the more
attractive. And above all, perhaps, the idea of travelling to such a
distant romantic country was a promise of high adventure at a
time when adventure in Europe seemed to be dead.

So hundreds, probably thousands, of young men all over Germany,
and in Poland, Denmark and Switzerland, gave up their jobs, broke
their apprenticeships or interrupted their studies and set off to
find the committees, mostly on foot. But the committees had
been more idealistic than practical; they had not thought out the
logistics of sending men to Greece, and they were baffled by the
numbers who applied. The volunteers wandered from town to
town, calling on one committee after another. They learned that
the governments of Italy and Austria had closed their ports against
them for fear of offending the Turks. The only possible way was
through France and down to Marseilles. Some gave up in despair,
but after making the gesture of leaving home on such a heroic
mission, it was humiliating to admit defeat and go back again. A
dwindling number marched down the valley of the Rhône and
began to meet others who were heading in the same direction. And
in Marseilles itself they met officers coming back from the débâcle
of the Regiment. These veterans, disgusted with Greece and the
Greeks, tried to tell them the truth as they saw it. One Prussian
officer, an eye-witness of Tripolitsa, stopped in Marseilles to write
a warning to the youth of Europe, and it contained three sentences

which summed up everything the others were trying to say, the antithesis of the Philhellenic creed: 'The ancient Greeks no longer exist. Blind ignorance has succeeded Solon, Socrates and Demosthenes. Barbarism has replaced the wise laws of Athens.'

But still, nobody listened. The young men had their dream, and they could not bear to be woken. They continued to come like lemmings, and about once a month the German or Swiss committees chartered a ship to take everyone who was waiting in Marseilles. Each Captain was told to land his passengers at any port in Greece that was not in Turkish hands. If he fell in with Turkish ships off the coast, he was to say the passengers had forced him to come there against his will.

But the committees had not asked the Greeks if they wanted volunteers, or what the volunteers could do or where they should go when they landed.

CHAPTER FOUR

The Battle of Peta
January—July 1822

General Normann · Marco Botzaris
Brengheri

Three weeks after the National Assembly met at Epidaurus something ominous happened on the other side of Greece. Ali Pasha of Joannina was defeated.

For most of a year, the old tyrant's defiance of the Sultan had seemed to prosper. His armies defended all the mountain passes by which the Turks might have come from the east, which seemed the obvious threat. But Joannina was not so well protected from the west, where there are only fifty miles of gentler hills and valleys between the town and the coast of the Ionian Sea. The Turks did not even try the mountains. During the summer of 1821 they advanced very slowly round the south of his domain, close to the northern shore of the Gulf of Corinth. And towards the autumn, their army reached the western coast and joined the naval expedition that captured the fleet of Galaxidhi. So Ali was surrounded.

But the campaign was not mainly a matter of battles. It was fought by bribery, intrigue, secret meetings between the opposing captains and promises of future power and favours. Both sides were using a large proportion of Albanian mercenary fighters, for whom it was only common sense to finish up on the side that won. Ali's men were not united by patriotism or any of the other ideas men fight for. Their loyalty depended entirely on being paid and on their belief in his power; and the moment they lost that belief his power was certain to vanish. The Turks spent most of their energy in undermining it.

In the end, it was his own three sons who brought his downfall. Each of them was a pasha in his own right, governing one of the old man's outlying dominions. Each of them, coming face to face with a Turkish army, had to weigh up a choice: to inherit a share of his father's domain in permanent opposition to the Sultan, or else to make peace while he could. Each of them started to parley with the Turks and was promised pardon and another pashalik somewhere else in the empire. And each of them accepted, abandoned his troops and put himself and his harem under the Turks' protection. As soon as that became known, the rest of Ali's followers began a stampede to change sides before it was too late.

The Turks closed in on Joannina itself. Ali ordered his town to be burned and shut himself up in his citadel with the remnants of his own harem and a small and nervous garrison. He has been described as living there in a bomb-proof cellar, deserted by almost all his sycophants, wrapped in a bundle of dirty embroidered garments. In January 1822 the Turks broke into the citadel by treachery and surprise, and he retreated again to the last and strongest tower, where he kept his treasures and his powder magazine.

From there, he began to bargain with the Turkish commander. Nobody knows what arguments he used, but certainly the Turkish commander wanted the treasure, and probably Ali threatened to blow it all sky-high. Once again, he won what he wanted. The Turk promised to spare his life, and said he believed the Sultan's pardon was on its way from Constantinople. The Turk in fact was under mandatory orders to send Ali's head to the Sultan, while Ali in all his long life had never kept such a promise or spared an enemy. Yet still, at the age of 82, he seems to have believed he could trick and argue his way out of anything, even the Sultan's implacable displeasure. And he was allowed to retreat once more, this time to a small monastery on the island in his lake, taking with him his favourite wife.

The monastery is still there, empty, decrepit and beautiful above

the rushes on the lakeside. There is a tottering little church. Its
interior walls and dome are covered all over with early sixteenth-
century frescoes; two caves open off it in the overhanging rocks, and
beside the altar there is an escape hatch with a tunnel to the lake, a
relic of the sudden alarms of Ali's domain. There is also a tiny gatehouse, with an archway below and a wooden balcony above, approached by an outside stairway. Two small rooms open off the
balcony, and it was in them that Ali was confined. There are no
monks now, and some enterprising person has made an Ali Pasha
museum in the gatehouse, with reproductions of pictures of him
and his times. The whole place is shaded by two immense plane
trees, with trunks now thirty feet in girth. I sat under them in the
heat of a summer day in 1974 and had a picnic, and supposed they
must be aged enough to have shaded Ali too.

Perhaps in that calm and timeless place, among the emblems of
humility and poverty, the old man had a glimpse of a kind of life
he had never led, and a hope of being left to die in peace. But it
was not for long. On the 5th of February, another of the invading
pashas came to see him. They talked alone in the room above the
archway. When the visitor rose to leave, the two of them, being of
equal rank, moved together towards the door and out to the balcony
with the indestructible etiquette of the Turkish world. Ali, fat and
ungainly, bowed low; and in the second when he was off his guard,
the visitor drew a dagger and stabbed him to the heart, and then
walked down the steps and said to his attendants: 'Ali is dead.'

But according to the story the local people told afterwards, he
was not quite dead. He crawled back to the inner room. It seems
the Sultan's soldiers were afraid to enter the room and attack the
famous old fighter face to face. They went into the archway
underneath and fired their muskets up through the wooden floor,
and so succeeded in killing him at last. Thirty years later, an English
traveller reported he had seen the bullet holes in the floor, and they
are still there now. To me, they look too small for musket shot.
Perhaps the Turks used pistols.

They cut off his head, and before the sordid relic was packed up and sent to Constantinople it was shown to his few remaining Albanian troops. These men put up a token fight, but the Turkish Pasha intervened to say he would pay the arrears of their wages; whereupon they cheered and eagerly shouted 'The dog Ali is dead. Long live the Sultan.' The head was duly exhibited at the gates of the Sultan's palace, and soon afterwards four others were added to the show: those of his three sons who had rashly accepted the Turkish promises, and that of his grandson. The house of Ali was extinct; and not only the Turkish army but most of Ali's too was at the Sultan's disposal to attack the Greeks.

*

When this news reached the Peloponnese, Hypsilantes was at Corinth, trying to supervise the surrender of the vast fortress of Acrocorinth, which stands high on a hilltop behind the town and had dominated for thousands of years the isthmus connecting the Peloponnese to the mainland. He failed as tragically as he had at Navarino and Tripolitsa. He promised safe conduct to the starving garrison and ships to take them home. But when they marched down with their families to the town on the shore far below, exactly the same awful scenes were enacted again: the Greeks fell on the defenceless Turks and slaughtered them all except the girls and boys they could sell.

Apart from the wanton cruelty of these massacres, their stupidity was remarkable. If the Greek mobs had shown any sense of forbearance and had sent home one surrounded garrison, all of the others would have surrendered at once, and not a single Turk would have been left in Greece. As it was, garrisons held on in isolated fortresses all through the war, a constant threat behind the backs of the Greeks and a series of nuclei for every counter-attack.

As for the Turkish property and treasury of Acrocorinth, Hypsilantes and the government again got nothing at all. He insisted that men of his own should be the first to enter the fortress, to put government seals on everything of value. But Colocotrones was also there – whatever his faults or merits, he was always present when there was booty – and he and his men swarmed into the place, tore off the seals and took everything worth taking; what they could not carry out by the gates they threw over the walls to confederates waiting outside. And the fortress was left empty. It was the most important strategic point in the country and was impregnable except through starvation. There was every reason to think a Turkish army sooner or later would come across the isthmus, and the Greeks would have to try to hold the fortress. But the government could not afford to stock it with food or ammunition, and Colocotrones had no intention of spending his winnings on anything so far-sighted.

Mavrocordato turned up in Corinth soon after it fell, and all the foreigners made their way there if they could: the remains of the Regiment followed Hypsilantes, and the newcomers trudged across from ports on the western coast. There was soon a motley collection of some hundreds of them in and around the town. Those who survived to write about their adventures gave strangely diverse accounts of the next few months. Some remembered it as a carefree easy-going time when spring was in the air and wine was cheap, and cheerful parties were held in taverns and makeshift cafes. Those were the minority who still had some money left. The rest remembered the ration the government gave them, which was half a loaf of bread and nothing else, and the raids they made on the country-side to steal corn from the mills and cattle from the pastures. A Frenchman who went there said the officers were paid the equivalent of five French centimes a day. He did not say what that would buy in Corinth, but it was certainly very little indeed, and he went away again to try his luck in Hydra. Most foreigners who had come with such high ambition became the beggars of Corinth, much poorer than the Greeks who had all had some share of the booty. The only people even worse off were the soldiers of the Regiment, the refugees from Turkey and more recently from Chios: they were so ragged they were almost naked, and for the most part were weak from starvation. Still, some of the foreigners retained a grudging affection for the ordinary Greeks and a few admired Mavrocordato. But everyone despised poor Hypsilantes.

The one purchase most of them seem to have afforded was a Turkish woman or several. They were being sold at thirty to forty piastres, according to age and beauty. Again, it is impossible to say what a piastre was really worth, but the point was that a woman cost next to nothing. It is fair to assume that the Europeans who bought them succumbed to the wish that lurks within most men, the wish to own a harem. But at that time and place it seemed a perfectly moral project because it often saved the women's lives; and of course the men made the most of this aspect of it when they wrote about it afterwards. An Italian named Brengeri told a story that was typical. On a road before he came to Corinth he found a dead Turk, and a little farther on he found his wife and baby, still alive but very hungry. He and his friends gave her a few small coins, in the hope that she would be able to feed herself and the baby a little longer. Before they had gone another hundred yards they heard two shots: some Greeks had seen what they had done and killed her and the baby and taken the coins.

So he knew better when he witnessed the massacre of Corinth. He saw some Greeks killing a Turkish family, a man, two children and two slaves. Before they killed the mother they tore off her veil to see what she looked like, and at that moment Brengeri rushed up and begged or demanded they should spare her. Fifty piastres, they said. He left some friends in charge of the situation, ran to a Greek shopkeeper he knew and borrowed the money. The Greeks tried to take her clothes which they said were not part of the bargain, but Brengeri found himself, whatever he intended, the undisputed owner of a human being. For five days the poor woman lamented her husband and children and would not eat; but in time she became a comfort to him, and he no doubt to her. And in general, the women seem to have been pitiably grateful and affectionate; for the foreigners did not share the Greeks' genocidal frenzy and probably treated their women with a remnant of western chivalry. But everyone knew it was only a short reprieve.

It was in women, oddly enough, that the government made its only recorded profit. By some unaccountable chance, the only part of the booty of Tripolitsa that fell to the government was the Pasha's harem, forty ladies in all. It is said they owed their lives to Bouboulina, who had sold or even given them a promise of safe conduct and was the only leader at Tripolitsa who kept the promise. The Pasha himself was away when the town was sacked, commanding the attack on Joannina; and while Mavrocordato was in Corinth a British ship came in to ask the price of the forty ladies' ransom. Presumably it came from the Ionian Islands, but nobody recorded and possibly nobody knew whether the message came from the Pasha himself or from an enterprising tradesman who wanted to make a profit. Mavrocordato or his spokesman asked a large sum of money and the ship went away and soon came back with the cash. It was paid to his Minister of War and the forty were herded on board. Among them was the Pasha's principal wife, who was said to be the Sultan's sister, and she went unwillingly. She had not expected to see her husband again, and during her months of captivity she had fallen in love with one of the very handsome sons of Petrobey. Now the poor girl expected her husband would find out, and she would be tied in a sack and dropped in the sea. But when she left Corinth she vanished from history, and her fate is not recorded.

*

One of the new arrivals was a German general called Normann. He was yet another man who had come to Greece to be commander-in-chief, but he had a little more reason than most for this expectation, and among so many eccentrics and rogues he seems a genuinely tragic figure.

There was no doubt about Normann's qualifications. He had been a highly distinguished Major-General. But in the shifting politics of Napoleon's era, he had found himself on the wrong side, not merely once, which happened to many men, but three times. He served first in the Austrian army. When his native state, which was Wurttemburg, joined the French, he was recalled and had to fight against his Austrian colleagues. When Napoleon's star was waning, he led a battle against another German force which had already abandoned the French. Finally, he took his own troops over to Napoleon's enemies; but the King of Wurttemburg remained stubbornly loyal, and Normann was disgraced and cashiered and forced into exile. It was the kind of muddle that many honest men got into.

By mid-winter of 1821, the German and Swiss committees had sent off hundreds of men in the direction of Greece, all destined, they believed, to accept commissions in the national army. So they had the reasonable idea of sending a general senior enough to command them all, and they offered the command to Normann. After some hesitation, he was talked into accepting. No doubt he sincerely believed the cause of the Greeks was good and that they did possess an army, and it seems he also hoped to redeem his disgrace.

He landed in Navarino in February 1822, and like everyone else he stepped ashore into chaos. There were some hundred volunteers in the town with nowhere to go, drinking and gambling, still picking infantile quarrels with one another and fighting their pompous and sometimes lethal duels. Normann soon learned that the Greeks had never heard of him and did not want him, and that the army he had come to command did not exist. He sent out junior officers to find the government and announce his arrival, and waited for a welcoming summons. But nothing happened. At length, he set off to make his own way to Corinth.

When he got there he found Mavrocordato still talking of raising 30,000 men. But this was only a dream, no longer a hope. Everyone knew that Colocotrones and the rest would never allow such a thing to happen; and if by some miracle their opposition were removed, the Greek guerillas in any case would never join an army. The reality was there for Normann or anyone else to see. The thousands of guerillas or brigands were in control. The remaining officers of the Regiment, mostly Italian refugees who could not go home, were still drilling their tattered barefoot troop which was scorned by everyone. An Italian had taken over command and the

Regiment now bore his name instead of Baleste's: the Regiment Tarella. The crowd of superfluous Europeans was doing nothing. There was only one way out, and Normann saw it. The Europeans would have to form a military unit of their own. They would have to give up their inflated ideas of promotion and serve in much lower ranks than they claimed to have held at home.

This despairing idea evolved. Some officers refused the indignity of it and went home, but more accepted it because they had no money or no home to go to. Mavrocordato offered good rates of pay, one third in cash and the rest in government promissory notes, and the first month's third was actually paid, probably from the money the government got for the Pasha's harem. Colonels were to be subalterns, captains to be sergeants, lieutenants to be corporals and everyone else to be privates. A commission of three was appointed, one German, one Frenchman and one Italian, to sort out everybody's claims and allot the ranks. It dug out several impostors, whose swords were ceremonially broken. The most engaging perhaps was a Dane who had become a favourite of Hypsilantes: Baron Friedel von Friedelsburg, who was always talking about his castle and his important friends. When other Danes turned up and proved he was not a baron at all and there was no such place as Friedelsburg, he burst into tears and left Corinth in a huff. But in fact, he had a better claim to fame: he was a very competent artist. He spent most of the rest of the war wandering round on his own and drew most of the portraits in this book.

At last, after bitter arguments, it was all arranged and the new force was given a name, the Battalion of Philhellenes. It had all the organization of a Napoleonic army, quartermasters, paymasters, standard bearers, a medical corps and a drum major. One company was mainly Italian and French and was commanded by a flamboyant Italian colonel called Dania; the other was mainly German, but the man in command was a Swiss who had defeated at least one German in a duel back in Marseilles. His name – or so he said – was Chevalier.

A ceremonial parade was arranged by the shore in Corinth.

Mavrocordato requested everyone to swear to serve for six months: anyone unwilling was told to fall out of the ranks, and eight men did so. Then he presented its standard to the Battalion, as Napoleon presented standards at the Champ de Mai. For a moment, the Philhellenes felt the pride they remembered from their armies at home, the pomp, precision, flamboyance and unity of purpose, the ringing words of command and the drums and trumpets that could swell the chests and bring tears to the eyes of military men. Yet in retrospect the glory they glimpsed seems sad, for the strength of this international force was no more than a hundred men.

On the same evening, it marched to its first campaign. But there had been another shock. Mavrocordato with equal pride had announced that he was commander-in-chief: General Normann was to be his chief of staff. And of Mavrocordato one wise contemporary wrote: 'He neither knew what he ought to do nor what he ought to leave undone, so that his military operations were generally determined by accident.'

Mavrocordato's army marched along the southern shore of the Gulf of Corinth and crossed to Missalonghi. The plan was to intercept the Turks who at any moment would march south from Joannina.

The Battalion of Philhellenes was only a small part of it. For once, most of the factions in the Peloponnese were united in a single enterprise. There was the Regiment Tarella, and a band of brigands commanded by a son of Colocotrones named Geneas, and another under one of the numerous sons or nephews of Petrobey, Kyriekules Mavromicheles; and there were also some volunteers from the Ionian Islands and a group from the fierce Albanian tribe of Suliotes. All in all, the frock-coated little commander-in-chief led nearly two thousand men. The army grew as it went along, both in numbers and disbedience, for the only groups which accepted his orders were the Battalion and the Regiment. He had no cavalry, and for artillery he had two small guns.

Among the motley band, the Suliotes must specially be mentioned. They were the only ones who distinguished themselves in subsequent battles, and their leader, whose name was Marco Botzaris, became a celebrated hero. They were an ancient tribe, separate like the Mainotes from their neighbours, and they lived in remote defensible mountains near Joannina. They were proud and aristocratic in their fashion and they were not ordinary klephts or brigands; rather than raid the peasants in their district, they maintained them in a sort of serfdom. Sometimes they had been allies of Ali Pasha and sometimes his enemies, and life in those desperate borderlands of Albania had made them arch-masters of guerilla war. They had developed its logic into a rigid soldiers' code. Their speciality was defending passes and gorges, and they always fought as individuals, each man in a battle making his own decisions. They reckoned a dead or wounded Suliote was useless, and therefore a man who got himself killed or hurt had failed to do his duty. A good man knew how to use his musket from the lee of rocks, and how to use his sword if he had a chance; and he also knew exactly when he should run and keep himself alive to fight again. This sensible philosophy had kept the tribe intact for centuries; but in the last years of Ali's reign he had outwitted them and driven them out of their mountains and down to the coast, where they put to sea and joined the assorted refugees who lived under British protection in the Ionian Islands. Some were still in exile there, some under Marco Botzaris had joined the Greeks, and some were still skirmishing in the recesses of their mountains.

When the Philhellenes left Corinth, they had to say goodbye to their Turkish women. Brengeri the Italian had grown fond of his 50-piastre girl and she begged to come with him and die with him in battle, but he gave her to a salacious middle-aged shipmaster who said he would take her to Italy and have her baptized. Most men simply left their women in Corinth, although they knew the Greeks would kill them. But the drum-major of the Battalion astonished everyone by insisting on marrying a girl he had bought for two piastres. He had her baptized and married her in a single ceremony, and dressed her in a man's clothes so that he could take her on the march. There is something extremely tragic in the thought of the love or pity he must have felt, and the remnants of conventional morality he must have brought with him. The first time she went out alone to gather herbs for his supper, some Greeks shot her dead.

The people of Missalonghi were not at all pleased to have an army quartered in their town, and they persuaded Mavrocordato to march farther on to find and fight the Turks. The two armies met before the town of Arta, sixty miles north of Missalonghi, early in July. The Turks were in the town, which is on the banks of the River Arachthos and had a powerful citadel and a single medieval bridge. Both are still standing, the citadel with a modern hotel inside it, and the bridge with a miraculously delicate central arch of stone. The Greeks settled down to confront them in and around the mountain village of Peta, a few miles short of the bridge. There they were joined by an aged local brigand named Gogos, who had a thousand men at his command.

The village of Peta has grown bigger now, but the square in the middle of it is much the same as it was that summer when the Philhellenes sauntered round it in the evenings, grumbling about a French officer who had found a stock of brandy but refused to give any to his companions unless they could pay. Storks nest on the top of the belfry above the square, and below it, beyond a parapet, the foothills and lower spurs of the mountains, covered with olives, pines and cypresses, half-hide the wide valley of the Arachthos. On the far side of it, when the air is clear, you can see the bridge and citadel of Arta.

I have sat there on a dusty morning at a café table under the trees, watching a group of old men, including a priest, at one of their inexplicable games of dice. Again it was early July: the valley wavered in the haze of heat. Some small boys, directed by a schoolmaster, were hanging strings of Greek flags from tree to tree, the same flag that was decreed at Epidauros. I wondered if they were taught what happened in their village, and I wondered also why anyone, even Mavrocordato, could have thought of defending the place with sword and musket. Nobody now could claim to be an expert in the tactics of those weapons, but Peta seems to have nothing to commend it as a scene of battle. It has neither the kind of defile where guerilla tactics might have been successful, nor the open country where the Europeans might have manœuvred in Wellingtonian formation. It is not even on the way to anywhere. The road from Arta to Missalonghi leads past it on the river flats, far out of range, and the Turks in Arta could perfectly well have marched towards Missalonghi if they wished and left Mavrocordato's army sitting where it was. A dashing commander might have sallied out from here and trapped the Turks by capturing the bridge, or even blowing it up; a prudent one would have fallen back to one of the defensible passes on the road to the south. But Mavrocordato did neither one thing nor the other. Here, on the foothills in front of Peta, he ordered his troops to set up a line of defence, believing the Turks would attack it and be routed.

The preparations for battle were peculiar. Mavrocordato set up his headquarters fifteen miles in the rear: one cannot help comparing him to the Duke of Plaza-Toro, who 'led his regiment from behind – he found it less exciting.' General Normann was left in a situation somewhat worse than Ney's at Waterloo; he could not get immediate orders from his commander-in-chief, and had not been given enough authority to issue them himself. Both Dania the Italian company commander and Tarella of the Regiment would only take orders directly from Mavrocordato, and nobody else would take them from anyone. Geneas Colocotrones, when battle was imminent, suddenly decided to return to his father in the Peloponnese. Petrobey's son was making an expedition of his own to the coast. Between Gogos and Marco Botzaris there was a blood feud, because Gogos had murdered Botzaris's father, or caused him to be murdered. Gogos also detested Europeans, and especially detested Mavrocordato for his European ideas and his morning dress. He was one of the many brigand chiefs who did not really care in the least who was ruler of Greece, so long as he was left to rule his own small part of it. All the Europeans observed that men and mule-loads of provisions came out of Arta every night to the camp of Gogos, and they expected every morning to find he had deserted. Finally, Marco Botzaris grew impatient and took his band of Suliotes out alone to force a way past the Turks and join the part of his tribe that was isolated in the mountains near Joannina.

General Normann knew from the outset that Peta was a bad position. The army had halted there only because it could not go any farther. He felt so strongly about it that he wrote a letter to Mavrocordato to say so. The Regiment and Battalion, he said, were both being thinned by sickness and hunger. The former had about 300 men but the latter only 90, of whom about 20 were sick; he might have added, but did not, that their incessant quarrels and duels had accounted for several. But Mavrocordato, with the confidence of total ignorance, replied that the position was strong and could be held against an army of at least eight thousand, and that Gogos would 'maintain his post with honour.' Normann forlornly showed this answer to the assorted European commanders, and his lifetime's training obliged him to stay where he was.

Everyone knew the Turks had planned to attack on 16 July, and that morning the dust of their army was seen as it crossed the bridge and deployed towards the hills of Peta.

The Turks, unlike the Greeks, had some notions of battle tactics, but they were archaic. They had standard bearers, who would rush forward and plant their standards; then the troops marched up to them and stopped to fire, and the standard bearers ran forward again. And this was done with complete disregard for casualties – the foremost of whom, of course, were the standard bearers.

They came in this fashion across the river valley. The Regiment, trained by Baleste and Tarella, held its fire until the Turks were in range, and shot them down. The Philhellenes were elated. 'We laughed at their mode of fighting,' Brengeri wrote. 'We continued our fire very coolly, seeing the hundreds of dead before us, while we had not lost a man . . . We shouted victory, and fancied we should dine in Arta.'

And suddenly more shouts were heard behind them. They thought it was Greeks coming up to reinforce them. But it was Gogos and his brigands running away. A great gap was left in the middle of the line. The Turks poured through it, and all the rest of the Greek guerillas, seeing the day was going against them, fled for the hills. The Regiment and Battalion, imbued with European traditions, stood their ground a few minutes longer, and then it was too late. They were surrounded, vastly outnumbered, shot down and slaughtered. None would have escaped if the Turks in their eastern manner had not stopped for the usual competition to strip the dead, especially the Europeans whom they expected to be rich. As it was, 67 of the 90-odd Philhellenes were killed that day, and of the rest who struggled out of the holocaust with the remnants of the Regiment, almost all were wounded. Tarella, Dania and a few others were captured alive, taken to Arta with the heads of their comrades, and there, with two exceptions, were hanged on trees. The two were a young and beautiful Greek lieutenant and a German doctor who became the personal physician of the Pasha.

Among those who straggled back to Missalonghi was one who would certainly rather have died where he stood: General Normann. He had come to Greece in the hope of redeeming his past disgrace. Now further disgrace was added to it: he blamed himself for foreseeing what would happen at Peta and failing to prevent it. Ten days after the battle he paraded the Battalion for a service in remembrance of the dead. There were 25 of them left. Then the Battalion was formally disbanded: from its first parade to its last, it had existed seven weeks. The remains of the Regiment were sent away to the Peloponnese, where they dissolved into destitution and oblivion. Normann himself lingered in Missalonghi three months more. He was penniless, sick and utterly miserable. It was said that Mavrocordato refused to pay for a boat to take him to the Ionian Islands, where he might have recovered. But perhaps he did not want to go. When winter was coming on, for no medical reason that anyone knew, he died.

*

Those minutes of utter disaster at Peta were the only active result
of all the devoted work of the Philhellenic committees. The Greeks,
half-fearing and half-despising the European way of making war,
had always wanted to believe it was useless, and now they were
sure of it. For the time being, Mavrocordato was discredited: he
resigned as President and stayed in Missalonghi.

One cannot deny the Greeks were right. No doubt any good
European army could have beaten the Turks in battle, and quickly
captured the remaining citadels. It might have used a few guerillas
as auxiliaries: Wellington himself had done so in the Peninsular
War. But no European power was willing, or probably able, to
send an army to Greece and maintain it there; and what was more,
no Greeks except the Phanariot princes wanted a foreign army in
their country. They were fighting to get rid of foreign armies.

And the alternative, to mix small European units with large
guerilla bands, was certainly useless. They simply did not and would
not understand each other. Pride and tradition made the Europeans
stand and fight at Peta. Left to themselves, the Greeks would have
had more sense. They would have run for the hills before a disaster,
not afterwards, and then have let the Turks come on, and harassed
them when they could. Guerillas in their own mountains always
have a final impregnable defence: to be and remain ungovernable.
And at that, nobody was more expert than the klephts.

Yet the lesson took time to reach Europe. The committees
heard of the defeat, but did not understand that the whole idea of
sending volunteers was at fault. So they did not stop; on the contrary, they worked even harder. They set themselves to raise a
bigger army with all its equipment and to send it bit by bit, and
they gave it yet another name: the German Legion. The first
contingent of 120 men was recruited and left Marseilles in December
1822, nearly six months after the battle, and its fate was exactly
the same as all the rest. The men landed – this time in Hydra and
then in the town of Nauplia – and found that nobody had ever heard

of them or wanted them, that nobody would pay them or feed them, or even tell them how to go home again. They were left bewildered, slowly selling or being robbed of all they possessed, to sicken and die of plague, starvation and exposure.

It was the French who put a stop to it in the end. They had quietly been collecting reports from men who found a way back, and soon after the German Legion sailed they came to the conclusion that young men were only being sent to disillusion and useless death. They followed the example of Austria and Italy, and closed the port of Marseilles to volunteers. There was no other practicable route to Greece, and so this first phase of philhellenic endeavour withered away and died. In Germany and Switzerland where it had flourished, devout believers began to waver and admit that the premiss must have been wrong: that the modern Greeks were not the same as the ancient Greeks and really did not want to be thought the same. It had all been a tragedy of mistaken enthusiasm.

CHAPTER FIVE

The Brigands Win
July—October 1822

Odysseus Androutsos

In this same autumn after the Battle of Peta, the belief of the Greeks in their own ways of making war was increased by some spectacular successes. In three separate parts of Greece they met at last the full strength of Turkish armies, and everywhere, by their own peculiar methods, they won. The first was at Missalonghi, the second at Athens, and the third and most decisive in the Peloponnese.

When the Battle of Peta was lost, Missalonghi waited to be besieged. There was nothing to stop the Turkish army coming, and the sea behind was controlled by Turkish ships that were based in Patras. Most of the inhabitants crowded on to the muddy dunes that separate the marshes from the sea, and waited there for small boats to escape to the Peloponnese. But Mavrocordato, who had seemed so cowardly in the battle, showed one of his unaccountable changes of character. He stayed where he was, and that was a brave thing to do.

At that time, no doubt Missalonghi was an even more gloomy place than it is today. Its marshes were perhaps no wetter, but its streets were muddier and smellier, and its people poorer and weakened by centuries of malaria. And its siege was a bizarre example of the military art which could hardly have happened anywhere but in Greece.

To begin with, the Turkish army took three months to advance the sixty miles from Peta. The time was not spent in fighting, excepting minor skirmishes, it was spent in negotiating with local leaders, a kind of formalized game of mutual double-crossing. At least five of Mavrocordato's captains thought the moment had come to change sides and take their forces with them – though all of them changed back at later stages, and some made several journeys from one allegiance to the other. The remains of the Suliotes had to surrender, but they refused to join the Turks; and rather than slaughter them or leave them in his rear, the Turkish pasha sent them to join the rest of the tribe in exile in the Ionian Islands, where the British took charge of them. But Marco Botzaris the Suliote leader contrived to come to Missalonghi.

When at last the Turks arrived outside the town, Mavrocordato inside it commanded two hundred men, including a dozen assorted Europeans, and Marco Botzaris commanded twenty-two. There were also a good many townspeople still in the place, but they had no military standing. The besiegers, if any figures can be believed, had fourteen thousand men. The Greeks had plenty of time to attend to their defence, but they did nothing about it until the last minute. There was already a ditch round the landward side of the town which was eight feet wide, and a mud wall five feet high, and the other side was protected by the marshes; but the wall in some places had fallen into the ditch. Mavrocordato authorized everyone to break into the houses the Missalonghiotes had abandoned and take anything that could be used to reinforce the wall. It was an agreeable occupation with endless scope for pillage, especially of the cellars of the rich. Among his own baggage, he had 300 bayonets, the last remains of the armament he had brought to Greece. When he distributed his muskets the Greeks had refused the bayonets, which were not a weapon they knew; but now Marco Botzaris had the idea of cleaning them up and fixing them on poles and setting them behind the wall to look like a row of vigilant defenders. There were also two broken old drums, but nobody who claimed to be a drummer. Men marched round thumping them as loudly as they could, hoping to give an impression of armies continually drilling. The Greeks had unbounded faith in the Turks' stupidity.

They had a fairly good stock of powder. Some had been brought by a young Italian called Nicholas Sciutto, the prodigal son of a Genoese merchant. The year before, Sciutto had been appointed maker of letter bombs by Ali Pasha. The novelty of these weapons appealed enormously to the old man's sense of fun. The first of Sciutto's letters that Ali dispatched blew up a priest he detested, and he gave Sciutto a standing order for more, an elegant house in Joannina and all the money he asked for. In the course of a month, Ali demolished four neighbouring rulers by sending them letters, but the idea had come too late in his career, and with the Pasha's downfall Sciutto lost his job. His next project was to get his father to give him a cargo of powder and lead for making shot, which he meant to sell to the government of Greece. He made the mistake of handing over the powder to Mavrocordato without insisting on cash, so of course he was never paid for it; and rather than part with the lead he buried it in Missalonghi. This curious man survived the whole of the siege and its shortages without digging up his lead, and indeed without doing anything but gamble unsuccessfully. Afterwards, he set himself up as a pirate, but so far as his history goes he was not very good at that.

Early in November, the siege began in earnest. So did the rains, and Missalonghi dissolved into winter mud.

Whether it was the bayonets, the drums or the mud, or perhaps a matter of policy, the Turks did not make an immediate attack, which would certainly have succeeded and indeed would not have been resisted. They began to build barracks round the town, instead of tents, as if they were preparing to stay for years. From time to time there were exchanges of musketry when Turks came near the wall, and sometimes also a duel of artillery. The Greeks broke up old anchors and pots as ammunition and managed with luck to send a blast of scrap-iron in the direction of the Turks. The Turks fired back with shells. Most of them missed the town entirely, whizzed over the rooftops and fell in the marshes behind, and the few that landed within the wall splashed into the mud and sank without exploding. One fell down a chimney into the fire below, where several people were gathered to warm themselves, but even that one failed to go off.

The Turks were notoriously bad shots either at sea or on land: when Byron saw them he said they would be dangerous enemies if they did not take aim. But the artillery at Missalonghi had a special reason for being bad – or so the defenders believed. The Turks had captured a picturesque professional pirate called Bassano. He was Italian, and was said to have captured many British ships under cover of the Napoleonic Wars. Afterwards he had attached himself to Ali Pasha and then, in a vague kind of way, to the Greeks, though he only used the pretext of war to enrich himself. Off the port of Prevesa, not far from Arta, he had taken a British ship which was full of wine; and during the party that followed he rashly attacked two Turkish warships and was beaten. His men were executed, but he was taken to the Turkish Pasha for a decision of the details of his fate; and such was his skill and reputation that he talked himself out of a lingering death and into the post of commander of the Turkish artillery. But his heart was still with the Greeks; and at Missalonghi the siege artillery was in the charge of a man who would have changed sides if he could. This, according to the defenders, explained why the Turkish guns at the shortest range could not even hit a target the size of a town, and why their shells had fuses that went out. And it is hard to think of a better reason; unless perhaps Bassano, in spite of his talk, was even worse as a gunner than the Turks.

Soon the Turks asked for a parley, and Marco Botzaris went out alone to meet them. A carpet was laid in an olive grove, and he sat down with two pashas while the garrison watched from the wall. The Turkish army, he found, was really two, one mainly of Turkish soldiers and the other of Albanians, and the pashas were not on good terms with each other. One greeted him by his first name and hoped they would be friends; the other seemed impatient to start the attack. He told them the town was defended by 800 Europeans and 2000 Greeks with 24 pieces of artillery. The friendly Pasha offered him command of any city he chose, and proposed to pay the Europeans fifteen thousand Turkish piastres each and to send ships to take them home to Europe. Marco thanked him and said he was sure he could persuade the garrison to accept such generous terms; but, he added, it was a delicate matter and would take some time.

The heroic reputation of Marco Botzaris was based on battles he fought, but perhaps he deserved it more for his single-handed battle of wits with the pashas, who were no mean exponents of that game. He went on meeting them for several weeks, playing on their mutual disagreement and coming back each time with better terms. Each time he went out, he certainly ran a risk that they would call his bluff and instantly cut off his head. And each time he came back, he ran an equal risk that someone in Missalonghi would decide he was double-crossing and would stab him in the night. Clearly he enjoyed it all; but nobody has left a close enough description of him to explain what personal charm he had that kept him alive.

While he procrastinated, the rains washed away Turkish barracks, filled the ditch and turned the flat land to a lake of filthy mud. The besieging army began to sicken from Missalonghi's abominable winter climate, and the garrison cheerfully waited for reinforcements. The Turks' Albanian troops formed a habit of strolling up to the wall unarmed to gossip with the sentries and grumble about the conditions in their camp; and a local fisherman who supplied the pashas with fish came back to the town every night with reports of what they were doing and what they intended to do.

Towards the end of November, reinforcements began to arrive. Six brigs from Hydra turned up, and the Turks' blockading ships retreated to Patras. A few days later, Petrobey himself and two or three other chiefs came across from the Peloponnese with a thousand men. The Hydriote sailors landed cannon and shot: even a 36-pounder was brought by some ingenious means across the miles of marshes. A week before Christmas, everyone knew in the town that the Turks had lost faith in Marco's promises and had planned a surprise attack by night on Christmas Eve, when they thought the Greeks would be in church.

It was nearly a surprise. The Greeks as ever were reluctant to keep a watch in the dark or in the rain, and still firmly believed that Turks never fought at night. It had become a nightly routine for Mavrocordato himself to go round the walls with one or two wakeful Europeans to thump and shake the sleeping sentries who turned over and went to sleep again. On Christmas Eve the whole garrison was put on the alert. But by four o'clock in the morning everyone had decided it was a false alarm and had settled down to rest. They were woken rudely by shouts and the Turkish artillery. A mass of Albanians had approached unseen by any sentry and were throwing logs into the ditch and swarming over the wall with sabres and pistols.

Of course the accounts of the battle are confused and partly incredible. Brengeri the Italian was in the thick of it and reported that the only defenders killed were two sentries who had not woken up in time, while the enemy left six hundred dead behind them – a proportion that outdid the ancient reports of Marathon. But the attack was repulsed and the garrison was triumphant.

In the next few days a noticeable silence fell on the Turkish camp. After a fortnight some Suliotes ventured out to see what had happened. It was empty: the enemy had gone. They probed in the muddy ground and dug up a quantity of cannon and cannon balls which the Turks had buried for future use, like dogs who bury bones.

*

That episode certainly proved that a Turkish army, however large, was not irresistible. Yet after reading Greek or Philhellenic accounts of such affairs one is always left with doubt. The Turkish commanders may not have been very skilful, but could they possibly have been as stupid as the Greeks believed they were? It seems unlikely, and so there must be another explanation of the things they did. The Greeks expected an army to advance with ruin and massacre, and

Colonel Baleste,
first commander
of the Regiment

Overleaf inset Greek Guerilla
on the march
Overleaf A Turkish army
advancing through a pass

Officers of the Regiment

Marco Botzaris

Odysseus

The Bridge of Arta

if it did not they took the credit for stopping it. But the Turkish armies had been sent not merely to crush the Greeks' rebellion but also to re-establish the Sultan's government. Marco Botzaris said the friendly Pasha told him he wanted to be 'father of the good and judge of the bad.' It sounds as though he meant it. He had every reason to try to talk a town into submission rather than force it. He had succeeded already with the five captains the rest of the Greeks called traitors. But he could not go on talking all the winter. The rain, the mud, the diseases of Missalonghi, the hundreds of miles of unsettled country behind him and Marco's time-wasting eloquence – these were what beat him, and made him give up what may have been a real attempt at conciliation.

Most wars are simplified by clear divisions of loyalty. Almost everyone knows which side he is on, and why. But this one was complicated by such webs of rivalry and misunderstanding that enemies may seem on reflection to be right and traitors wise, and heroes sometimes foolish.

*

While these events were happening in the west, one such heroic traitor had risen to prominence and power in the east. His name was Odysseus Androutsos, and opinions of him were even more widely diverse than of most of the leaders. One Englishman who knew him wrote that he was a man 'of most wonderful mind – a glorious being . . . brave, clever and noble.' Another wrote: 'He has a very strong mind, a good heart, and is brave as his sword.' And a third: 'He was false as the most deceitful Greek, and vindictive as the most bloodthirsty Albanian. To these vices he added excessive avarice, universal distrust, and ferocious cruelty.'* Among the Greeks, Mavrocordato and others were in favour of murdering him, but the brigands put him on a hero's pedestal and told stories of his physical strength and skill. He was said to be able to jump over seven horses standing side by side, and it was part of his heroic reputation that

* These three, who all come into the story later, were Edward Trelawny, Colonel Leicester Stanhope and George Finlay.

he had run away from an unsuccessful battle faster and farther than anyone else – his troops had been beaten by the Turks and he ran for eight leagues through the mountains before he stopped.

In fact Odysseus, like Colocotrones, must have been a born leader and fighter; but what he was fighting for was not what the government thought he ought to be fighting for. In other ways he differed from Colocotrones. Colocotrones looked grim and sour, but Odysseus was young and handsome and looked like a hero; and to judge by his portraits, he was vain enough to know he looked the part. And Colocotrones in the Peloponnese had been forced to have dealings with Hypsilantes and Mavrocordato and their western ideas; but Odysseus, away in the east, was cut off from them and never understood them or wanted to understand them.

He was born in the island of Ithaca, which was where he was given his Homeric name. But in his teens he had been one of the page-boys who decorated Ali Pasha's court, and that was where he was given his education. He had won the old tyrant's special favour and grown up to become a captain in his forces; so when Ali was dead and Odysseus found his own skill in leading men, he naturally began to see himself as another Ali. Probably he had never heard of national patriotism. What he wanted, and thought he deserved, was to rule his own district with a minimum of inter-ference from anyone, either Greeks or Turks. And that district, broadly speaking, was the whole of the eastern part of the mainland of Greece from Athens to Corinth and as far north as Lamia. On the western borders of this domain, in the cliffs of Parnassus, he had a true brigand's stronghold, a large fortified cave accessible only by ladders, where he kept his family, his booty and his stores of arms.

At the time of the Battle of Peta, this part of Greece was mostly free of Turks, excepting the island of Euboea and the Acropolis of Athens, where their garrison was still holding out. But it was even more chaotic than the Peloponnese. Here, a Greek eye-witness wrote, 'almost every political or military chief was engaged in a plot to supplant or massacre some rival.' It was in this chaos that Odysseus rose to the top, because he was better at such plots than anyone else. Mavrocordato himself made a plot to get rid of him, but he did it so badly that it had the opposite effect. He sent two men to Athens, one to become the provincial governor and the other to supersede Odysseus in command of the local troops. Their mission was supposed to be secret, but Odysseus knew all about it, and also suspected they had come to murder him, which was not in the least unlikely. So he received them with deference and cere- mony, entertained them at dinner, showed them to the sleeping quarters he had provided and murdered them in the night. And thus having shown what he thought of the government, he resigned his nominal rank as a general in the army and acted entirely for himself.

Another event confirmed his dominance: the fall of the Acropolis. In this most famous of all the citadels of Greece, 1150 Turks had lived forlorn and forgotten for over a year among the august and celebrated ruins. Nobody molested them, except a small party of Philhellenes who tried and failed one night to force an entrance. But they could not get out. They looked down from the rocks across a town and countryside where any man would have cut their throats with pleasure.

What defeated them was not an attack or an organized siege: it was thirst. The winter of 1821 was unusually dry. In the heat of the summer, the cisterns on the rock dried up, and presumably also the springs in caves which can still be reached by underground stairways. The only water supply that remained was from the springs on the lower slopes outside the walls, and the Greeks kept an eye on those. By June, the Turks had nothing to drink. They had to ask for terms of capitulation and an agreement was signed: the Turks were to give up their arms and half of the money they still possessed, and the Greeks were to send them home in neutral ships.

It was the same promise the Greeks had made and broken at Monemvasia, Navarino and Corinth. This time, to prevent another massacre, the Bishop of Athens made all the civil and military leaders swear by the holy mysteries of the Church that the promise would be kept. And he was not the only man who felt unsure of it. Athens was only a small town then, but there were foreign consuls there because its harbour of Piraeus was the most important in eastern Greece, as Patras was in the west. As soon as negotiations began, the consuls of France and Austria sent urgent letters for warships of any nation to come to Piraeus.

When the gates of the Acropolis were opened, on 21st June 1822, it was no warlike garrison that came limping down the paths and begging water. Of the 1150 Turks, only 180 were men who were 'capable of bearing arms'. The rest were refugees from the town, the old, the sick, the maimed, the women and their children. No ships had yet come to take them, and they were herded into buildings which stood at that time within the Stoa of Hadrian. For a few days, they were left in peace, but then the violence of the Athens mob began. The Turks were driven out and chased through the streets: four hundred, mostly the weakest, were killed. The rest were saved by the foreign consuls and shut in the consulates. After more days of terror, two French warships arrived at Piraeus and sent parties of armed marines ashore; and the survivors were escorted down the long road to the harbour through crowds of soldiers and citizens screaming threats.

The news that the Greeks had taken the Acropolis gave a profound emotional satisfaction to the Philhellenes in Europe: no other place in Greece had the same symbolic importance. And of course it appeared again as a noble feat of arms. But the Greeks, who had not fought for it, did not know what to do with it when they had it. Odysseus was somewhere up in the north, and the government far in the south. A whole series of minor captains took possession of it and made fearsome proclamations. Each of them lasted a week or two and then was turned out by somebody else: it was like the game that children used to play – 'I'm the king of the castle.' 'Come down you dirty rascal.' Athens fell into chaos and anarchy worse than ever before. At one stage, the shopkeepers of the town decided to garrison the citadel themselves, and when that attempt dissolved into wordy arguments, they invited Hypsilantes to come and command it. He tried to come, for he understood the symbolic prestige it would give him, but on the road from Corinth the soldiery stopped him and told him they would not have him. At last, they sent for Odysseus. He hurried to Athens, and in September he marched up to the Acropolis with a small band of followers.

Odysseus was only another brigand, but he was a much more effective brigand than most. Installed in the Acropolis, he had an authority nobody dared to challenge. He formed a provincial assembly which appointed him commander-in-chief of eastern Greece. He collected taxes and used the money to pay his men and stock the citadel against another siege, and he had the exceptional wisdom to build a new wall which enclosed a reliable well.

So Odysseus won the power he had always wanted; and he set about making sure that nobody could take it from him. The government was hardly worth his attention, it was impotent. The only people who could have threatened him were the Turks; and therefore he made an armistice with them, offering his submission to the Sultan in return for a promise that he should be left in power where he was. It is unlikely that either side intended to keep this agreement longer than it suited them, but for the moment it suited them both. The last wandering Turkish armies withdrew to the north. The brigands went home to their fields, and began again to plough and sow with some hope of reaping a crop. To them it appeared that Odysseus had won the freedom they had fought for, and the war was over.

*

But in the meantime another huge Turkish army had marched un-opposed through the western part of Odysseus' country and crossed the isthmus of Corinth to repossess the Peloponnese; and it was there that the third of the great encounters happened. This army was said to have over twenty thousand men. Eight thousand were cavalry, and its baggage, provisions, forage and armament was carried by a vast train of mules and camels: for a century, according to one historian, since the Turks recaptured the Peloponnese from Venice in 1715, 'Greece had not seen so brilliant a display of military pomp.' The Greek guerillas vanished before it. Corinth and the citadel of Acrocorinth were abandoned without a fight, and the whole mass of it penetrated slowly through the mountains south of Corinth, devastating the country as it went, and emerged on the plain of Argos which is the heart of the Peloponnese. The people of Argos were woken in the night by musketry and rumours that the Turks were at the gates, and they started a panic flight to the south. The members of the government, which was meeting there, threw dignity to the winds and rushed on board ships at the head of the Gulf of Argos, leaving behind them their archives and state papers and what little funds the government possessed.

This episode brought into prominence the town and fortresses of Nauplia, which were still held by a Turkish garrison. Nauplia, at the head of the Gulf of Argos, had the misfortune to have three fortresses. The town itself and the harbour lie at the foot of a very ancient acropolis. Seven hundred feet above it, on top of a crag, is the great Venetian fort of Palamedes, whose outlying bastions seem to flow like lava down the cliffs; and below, on a rock in the harbour, is a smaller fort called Bourdzi. This was a misfortune because the town lies in the middle of the triangle of strongpoints, and for several years, whenever they were held by opposing sides or by rival bands of Greeks, the shot they aimed at each other fell largely in the town.

When the Turkish army began its march, the Turkish fleet set sail from Constantinople escorting a merchant convoy. The army and navy were to meet at Nauplia and relieve it, and the convoy carried the army's winter supplies. The garrison of Nauplia was at its last gasp. It had exchanged hostages with the Greeks and had been negotiating a surrender for several weeks; indeed, the Greeks could already have possessed it, but they had prolonged the negotiations because they were making good money, as they had at Tripolitsa, by selling food and bogus safe-conducts to Turkish families. And in July, 1822, a week after the disastrous battle at Peta, an advance force of 500 Turkish cavalry entered Nauplia, seized the Greek hostages and brought the negotiations to a sudden end.

At this moment the Greeks were on the verge of losing all they had won or hoped to win. Everything depended on the Turkish fleet: if it entered the gulf with its convoy, the army would be invincible. The weather was fine, there was nothing whatever to stop it. But July ended and the weeks of August passed, and the gulf remained calm and blue and empty.

The fleet in fact was hovering off the mouth of the gulf, its commanders in a state of futile indecision. And again, given that they were incompetent sailors, one must spare some sympathy for them. The Gulf of Argos is 25 miles long, and in summer the prevailing wind blows out of it. It is a long beat to windward between the mountains on either side, and in the last mile or two, even on the finest day, fierce squalls may blow from the hills where Palamedes stands and take a ship aback when the harbour is almost in sight. Right in the mouth of the Gulf is the island of Spetsai, where Bouboulina was admiral, and 25 miles up wind is the island of Hydra.

It would be pleasant to record that the fleets of these islands fought the enemy and saved their country, but they did not. They put to sea when they sighted the Turks, but their main worry was to protect their own islands; and they sailed to and fro, without any plan or formation, waiting to see what the Turks intended to do, and taking care to stay out of range of the Turkish guns. Yet the very sight of their mass of small brigs and schooners completed the confusion in the Turkish admirals' minds. The Turks by then were terrified of fireships. Any Greek ship they saw could have been ready stuffed with combustibles and soaked with turpentine, and they could not bear to find themselves to leeward. They did not know what ships were in the gulf, and they did not dare to begin to beat to the head of it.

While they waited trying to make a decision, the wind at least once blew fair for Nauplia, straight into the Gulf, not out of it. That night, the entire fleet could easily and safely have been in Nauplia by morning. Yet this situation, to the feeble minds of the admirals, seemed even worse: to sail in with the wind behind them, and a host of possible fireships also behind them – they could not contemplate it. And after two attempts with a space of some weeks between them, they sailed away and went back to Turkey, and so condemned their army to extinction and their country to defeat.

Only two people came out of this naval affair with credit. One was Bouboulina and the other was Frank Hastings. Bouboulina was not the woman to mess about off Spetsai hoping the Turks would go away: she was up at the head of the gulf in her flagship bombarding Nauplia from the sea and perfectly ready to tackle the Turks if they came. As for Hastings, he still had no ship of his own. The next best thing was the island fort of Bourdzi, and he volunteered to take command of that.

This little fort is well known to tourists now. It stands in the middle of the harbour of Nauplia, looking as though it were specially built to enhance the scenery. Recently it has been a hotel and a restaurant, and it has the unusual reputation of having previously been a rest-home for retired executioners. The Greeks that summer had a few men in it, but they did not know how to fire its guns. Nor were they anxious to try, because it is only three hundred yards from the town and would or should have been a sitting target for the Turks if it showed any sign of activity. A French colonel named Jourdain said he could provide some incendiary shells which could be fired from the fort and set the town on fire. The Greeks told him to go ahead and do it, but he politely excused himself. So Hastings went, with two young artillery officers, an Englishman and a Dane, who had attached themselves to him.

For several days, Hastings and the Turks kept up a noisy cannonade. By all the rules, the fort should soon have been demolished and Hastings buried in a heap of rubble. The stories of the Turks' bad markmanship are sometimes not easy to believe, but Bourdzi is a proof of them. Standing on the shore, one would think that no gunner in the world could miss it. But it is an indubitable fact that the Turks could not hit it, except with a very rare shot which luck or chance propelled in the right direction. Nor was Hastings very successful. His shots hit the town, of course, but the colonel's incendiary shells produced nothing but an enormous amount of smoke without any heat, and set nothing at all on fire: when Hastings remonstrated with him, he said rather lamely that that was what they were meant to do. From a very occasional hit and the concussion of its own guns, the walls of the fort began to crack. But before it fell down, some shattering news came from Argos: the Turkish army was preparing to retreat. The Turkish gunners lost heart and stopped their shooting, and the Greeks, in hope again that the town and its booty would soon be theirs, told Hastings also to stop; and he went away to look for something more useful to do.

The huge and cumbersome army in Argos began its retreat because the navy had failed it: without supplies from the fleet, it could not stay where it was. But its high commander had made no plans for retreat: he had not manned or fortified the passes in the mountains on the way to Corinth. And quite suddenly, the fortunes of the war reversed. The Turks had seemed invincible, the Greek guerillas powerless. Now the army, hungry and perhaps demoralized, had to pass again through country where a dozen guerillas, given the will, could threaten any number of organized troops.

With the first hint that the Turks were leaving Argos, a wave of excitement, hope and enthusiasm swept through the Peloponnese. Men set out from every village with what arms they had and joined any chief they knew. Untold numbers of them took to the mountains, blocked the passes and hid behind rocks along the route. What they hoped to do was to cut off and plunder the trains of baggage-mules and camels. But by sheer numbers, they did much more than that. It is about forty miles from Argos to Corinth, and every yard of the road the Turks were under fire from snipers they could not see, and assaulted by shouted threats of death and occasional sudden murderous forays in narrow places. Their nerves broke. The great army disintegrated into scores of small groups each desperately searching for a safe way through the mountains, the cavalry charging ahead and leaving the infantry and the baggage train to look after themselves. Some reached Corinth, and some Patras. But the great majority vanished on the way and were never heard of again, except in macabre stories travellers told of the heaps of bones they saw. It was not a battle, it was simply the sum of thousands of single fights, of musket shots from rocks on the hills above, and of men with knives who suddenly leaped in the dark.

Colocotrones was given most of the credit for this astonishing victory, because at that moment he had the title of commander-in-chief of the Peloponnese. But in fact he did nothing to organize it, and did not even take much active part in it. The whole thing was too big for any central command. Men came from all directions to join the fight and coalesced into groups; but none of the local captains knew where the others were, or had any means of exchanging messages or making a unified plan. It was not Colocotrones who won it; certainly not the government, which did absolutely nothing; not even Prince Demetrius Hypsilantes, who in the moment of crisis forgot his follies and proved himself a soldier. It was the peasants who won it, the shepherd-brigands, each man for himself with his musket in his hand and his battery of knives in his belt. And even if booty was more in their thoughts than freedom, these men were the strength of Greece.

*

When their army and navy were gone, the Turks in the town and citadel of Nauplia gave up hope. Soldiers sent from the fortress of Palamedes into the town to fetch rations climbed down the 700 feet of steps, but they were too weak to climb up again. So the fortress was abandoned, and the Greeks one night found it empty. They fired off all its guns to announce their victory. Capitulation was agreed; the Greeks, as they so often had before, promised to send the Turks home, and swarms of them surrounded the gates of the town, itching for plunder. Everything was set for another massacre, a repetition of Navarino and Corinth.

But this was one of the moments when Commodore Hamilton hove into sight. He sailed up the gulf, anchored his frigate in front of the town and requested a meeting with Colocotrones and the other captains. And he told them 'in strong language' that if they murdered their prisoners again the name of Greece would be despised in Europe and her cause would be ruined. He insisted they should charter ships to take the Turks to Turkey, and reluctantly they did so. But it was more than imperious interference: he took five hundred of the verminous emaciated Turks in his own ship. So many passengers in a frigate would have been hellish at the best of times, and these brought typhus with them. Sixty-seven of them died of the plague on board, and so did several of his British crew. But he landed the rest at Smyrna.

*

As soon as the Turkish armies were beaten, the leaders of the country threw victory away in an orgy of greed and jealousy: as ever, when there were no Turks to fight, the rival Greeks began to fight each other. A National Assembly was summoned in February 1823. For want of a capital, it met near Astros in the Peloponnese, in an orange grove which had a convenient stream down the middle to divide the warring factions. Petrobey, of all people, was elected president of the executive. Colocotrones, who was not elected to anything, insisted on being vice-president and claimed control of the Peloponnese; whereupon the rest of the executive, for fear of their own vice-president, fled to the island of Salamis. Mavrocordato was chosen as president of the Senate. He declined the perilous honour, and the Senate threatened him with prosecution unless he accepted. So he did – but immediately resigned and made another of his quick strategic retreats, this time to the island of Hydra; for the first shots of civil war were being fired. In spite of his abrupt disappearance, the Senate continued to call him president.

So by the summer of that year, Greece was divided into four quite separate parts. The Peloponnese was controlled by Colocotrones and a large number of lesser war-lords who more or less did what he told them. The west of the mainland, with a kind of capital at Missalonghi, mostly regarded Mavrocordato as its leader, although he was a refugee in Hydra. In the east, Odysseus ruled undisputed from the Acropolis of Athens, half in league with the Turks; and in the islands, the people did what they wished without consulting anyone. Admiral Miaoulis had come back from a cruise in despair. His sailors had refused his orders and fought each other, Hydra against Spetsai, and both against Psara. Then they refused to go to sea again because there was nobody to pay them, and the Turkish navy, for all its inadequacy, was left to blockade the mainland wherever it would. The educated Greeks from abroad had failed so far in everything they had tried to do. The Philhellenes had vanished with their daydreams. Law had ceased to mean anything, and robbery and murder were unquestioned. The Greeks, in short, had got rid of the Turkish rule, but had not yet begun to discover how to govern themselves.

Just as the session in the orange grove was breaking up, a young man called Edward Blaquiere turned up in Tripolitsa. In spite of his name, he was Irish. At this inauspicious moment, a few men in London had started to take a practical interest in what seemed to them to be the cause of freedom.

PART TWO

Lord Byron

1823–1824

CHAPTER SIX

The Crown and Anchor
February—September 1823

Edward Blaquiere · Jeremy Bentham
Edward Trelawny · Count Pietro Gamba

Edward Blaquiere has been described as a radical international busybody, but that is rather less than fair to him. He was a young ex-naval officer who had served in the Mediterranean (he called himself Captain), and he spent his time travelling in Mediterranean countries, involving himself in their revolutionary causes and writing books about them – a man of tremendous energy and intense enthusiasm which he never allowed to be blunted by awkward facts. He was in Spain when he first met a Greek: John Louriottes, a friend of Mavrocordato, who had been sent there in the forlorn hope of raising a loan of money for the government. Blaquiere saw a new cause to support and persuaded Louriottes to come with him to London, where he introduced him to everyone he knew who had shown any sign of an interest in Greece. And Blaquiere's zeal, combined with the presence of a real live Greek, was the immediate cause of the founding of the London Greek Committee, which began to hold meetings at the Crown and Anchor Tavern in the Strand and became known as often as not as the Crown and Anchor Committee, especially by people who disapproved of it.

The British took up the cause of Greece just at the time when the efforts of Switzerland and Germany were foundering. The London Committee was run by a different kind of people: not by classical professors but by radical politicians and a few financiers.

And its motives were different. Its members might have called themselves Philhellenes, but they had no idea of reviving ancient glories. A strong majority of them were disciples of the liberal theorist Jeremy Bentham. Thirty years before, Bentham had published his *Principles of Morals and Legislation*, which offered a complete constitution and code of law, all designed by logic, in the phrase he made famous, for the greatest happiness of the greatest number. Ever since, he and his followers had longed to find a country which would put the theory into practice. And it seemed to them that Greece, a virgin state uncluttered by any existing legal system, was the opportunity of a lifetime. So yet another foreign aim was grafted on to the peasant revolution.

Jeremy Bentham was 75 at the time, but still hard at work extending and propounding his theories of morality and government. He was a great man, and if his principles of legislation had ever been thoroughly adopted, the world would no doubt be a better place than it is. Yet he was always on the verge of seeming ridiculous. His followers treated him and spoke about him with rather too much reverence. Guided by him, they were perfectly certain they knew what was best for the rest of the human race; and that is always an annoying belief even when it is true. People who would have called themselves men of the world were always ready to laugh at Benthamites and call them visionary cranks.

Perhaps that was why the Committee's first efforts were not much of a success. They launched a national appeal for funds for the Greeks and organized banquets and exhibitions. But in several months, they raised only £7000. The Quakers, in their own quiet way, had already collected more than that and used it in helping refugees from Greece.

When even these meagre funds began to come in, the committee had to decide how to spend them. The most ardent Benthamites would have used them to found schools and newspapers in Greece and to translate suitable books, because a well-informed public opinion was the basis of the ideal of Benthamite government. But other members pointed out that the war was still to be won, and Louriottes, if he had any say in the matter, would certainly have wanted either the cash or the armaments it could buy. There was also an ecclesiastical group, in favour of sending Bibles and preachers to Greece to combat what they saw as the superstitions of the Greek Church.

But behind all this was another much more grandiose scheme, discussed in secret at first among the financier members. England at that time had an enormous surplus of capital. Huge sums were already invested in foreign government bonds and loans to poorer nations. And what was in their minds was to raise a loan on the London Stock Exchange which would finance the war for the Greeks and set the country on its feet, and would also make a good profit for themselves and their friends. They were thinking not of a few thousand pounds but a million or two.

At the committee's inaugural meeting, on 28th February, 1823, one firm decision was taken: to send Edward Blaquiere to Greece (it was his own suggestion) to report on what was happening. Four days later he was ready to set off, again taking Louriottes with him. In Marseilles they were turned back by the French authorities, and in Rome by the minister of the King of Naples, and they finally had to take ship down the Adriatic to Corfu. It took them two months to reach the Peloponnese. Blaquiere had never been to Greece before, but three months later he was back in London with a long report and had also 'nearly completed' a book on the origins and progress of the war. He read the report to the committee, and then it was published in a quarterly called The Pamphleteer, together with 'The Leading Principles of a Constitutional Code for any State' by Jeremy Bentham, an article on the Cruelty of Employing Children in the Odious, Dangerous and often Fatal Task of Sweeping Chimneys, and an account of a newly invented Device which enabled one-armed men to eat boiled eggs and also to sponge their hats. 'In my attempt,' he wrote, 'to vindicate the rights of Greece from the effects of envy, malevolence and falsehood . . . I shall be guided by the strictest regard to impartiality and truth.'

Perhaps he saw no contradiction in this sentence; in his enthusiasm, he saw only the things he wanted to see. The government of Greece, he reported, had met – in the orange grove – in dignity and moderation, drawn up civil and criminal codes, introduced trial by jury, established schools and carefully examined the public accounts and national resources. Excesses attributed to the Greek soldiery were most wantonly exaggerated; the Greeks were eminently moral and religious people, more abstemious and industrious than any others in Europe; but to the Turks, the virtues of pity and benevolence were totally unknown. He advised the committee not to send troops to Greece, and in that at least he was right. But he did not observe, or at least he did not mention, that the Greeks were already fighting an intermittent but murderous civil war.

And right at the end of his report he came to the point the financiers wanted to hear. The land was so fertile that Greece would become one of the wealthiest countries in Europe. Nineteen twentieths of this land had been held by Turkish owners, and was now reserved by the Government as a guarantee for any foreign loan it might contract. This of course was as blatantly far from the facts as all the rest. Only a small proportion of the land of Greece is fertile, and the Turkish lands were now parcelled out in small-holdings among the klephts and their thousands of followers. That was what they had fought to win, and certainly they would fight again if anyone tried to take it away from them. The government had not reserved an inch.

Thus Blaquiere added another dose of pure misinformation to all that earlier Philhellenes had said. Anyone who knew the Greeks would have recognized what he wrote. Some interpreter had dished up to him a perfect expression of the ethnic truth, as opposed to the factual truth, and he had swallowed it whole. The committee swallowed it too, and on this basis its future moves were planned.

*

Blaquiere had not meant to travel through Italy. It was only the unexpected rebuff at Marseilles that made him take the road to

Rome. On that road, he had to pass through Genoa, where the most famous of all protagonists of Greece was living. 'My Lord', he wrote in his hotel on the morning of 7 April 1823, 'Having reached this place last night on my way to Greece, I could not pass through Genoa without taking the liberty of communicating with your Lordship and offering you my best services in a country which your powerful pen has rendered doubly dear to the friends of freedom and humanity . . .'

It seems to have been his own idea, although the hope of getting Byron to join the committee had been discussed in London. Byron had the reputation of being difficult to approach and of churlishly avoiding English travellers, and Blaquiere must have been immensely flattered at his reception. The famous man was in his most cordial mood, and listened intently to all that Blaquiere said about Greece and the committee and its plans. He promised to help in any way he could, and said he was willing to go to Greece himself. It was far more than Blaquiere could have hoped, but it did not owe much to his power of persuasion. The fact was that he had arrived at a crucial moment in Byron's turbulent life, and suddenly given a glimpse of reality to one of his idle dreams.

The fate of all who analyse the character of Byron is to be neither wholly right nor wholly wrong: so Harold Nicolson wrote in 1924, and no doubt he meant to include his own analysis. And Byron himself, at just about the time of Blaquiere's visit, gave the clue to the difficulty. 'Now, if I know myself,' he said to Lady Blessington, 'I should say, that I have no character at all . . . I am so changeable, being everything by turns and nothing long.' But everyone who has tried to unravel Byron's motives in going to Greece is more or less agreed – both those who knew him and the much larger number who only knew what he wrote and what he was reported to have said. The motives were mixed and complicated, and in the beginning at least they were mainly selfish: they related to his own extraordinary needs, and not to the needs of Greece.

In the nine months since Shelley was drowned, the circle of friends that had centred on him and Byron at Pisa had broken up in querulous disagreement. Edward Trelawny, the robust and untruthful adventurer, had gone away to Rome, and most of the people on the periphery of the circle had disappeared. The only English who were left were Mary Shelley and Leigh Hunt with his wife and six hooligan children, who depended on Byron for money; they were fascinated by him but secretly disliked him, and he found them a perpetual irritation. Teresa Guiccioli had been his mistress for four years, much longer than any other woman: she was still devoted to him and he was still fond of her, but her stormy emotional demands had become rather trying. 'He is kept in excellent order,' Mary Shelley wrote cattily, 'quarrelled with and henpecked to his heart's delight.' And while Teresa was with him he also had to house her tottering arthritic old father and their train of followers. His only uncritical friends in Genoa were his banker Charles Barry, perhaps more a servant than a friend, and Teresa's young brother Pietro Gamba, charming, modest and faithful, but hopelessly ineffective and far from clever.

Byron was also intensely dissatisfied with himself. At the age of 35 he was growing old. His physical beauty had gone. The curly hair that had enchanted so many women was wispy, thin and greying, his teeth were loose and rotten; if he ever went back to England, he had recently said, it would be to see a dentist. During his year of debauchery in Venice he had grown fat and sallow, and that had so disgusted him that he had taken to living largely on biscuits and soda water, with an occasional lapse that gave him acute indigestion and had to be followed by doses of magnesia. On this unhealthy diet he had made himself unnaturally thin, so that his clothes, of a dandyish style some years out of date, were much too big for him. There was nothing left of the romantic, passionate and notorious lover. He had lost the power to play that role again, and had lost the will for it too. And it was only rarely now that he showed the irresistible wit and gaiety his friends in England remembered, or laughed in the way they remembered best of all.

What was worse perhaps was his feeling that fame was slipping away from him. He was still at work on Don Juan, but he believed the public was tiring of his poetry: the journal he had started with Leigh Hunt had been a disaster, and he had quarrelled with his publisher John Murray, who had told him Don Juan was 'outrageously shocking'. He himself was tiring of it too: 'a man ought to do something more for mankind than write verses.' Yet it was poetry that had made him famous, and the fame that had overwhelmed him when he was 24 had become essential to him. He might be annoyed when English travellers recognized him and stared at him in awe, or stood outside his house and peered at his windows, but he might have been much more annoyed if they had failed to do it. He could not have borne to become a faded nonentity.

So these were his needs: to get away from the sordid petty life he was leading at Genoa, and to find a new source of fame. For the first, he had often talked aimlessly of plans: to go to the United States, or to buy a principality in Chile or Peru or Mexico, or even to settle in Venezuela. Sometimes, but never for long, he thought of returning to England. He envied the eccentric Lady Hester Stanhope who lived in Syria, and said he would have gone there if she had not forestalled him. And often, since long before his present discontent, he had thought about Greece, where he had spent those two years of uncomplicated contentment before the fame and before the scandal of his marriage. Like many other men, he had dreams of buying an island and living on it inaccessible: he had considered, not unambitiously, the islands of Naxos, Ithaca, Antiparos or Zante, though he never went nearly so far as to find out who owned them or whether they could be bought.

In the beginning, these thoughts of Greece had nothing to do with the war; they were simply a yearning for the happiness he remembered, and for escape from the present. His nostalgia was for Greece, not for the Greeks. On his youthful journey, he had been more impressed on the whole by the Turks and Albanians than by the Greeks themselves. Remembering them as 'hereditary bondsmen', he did not believe when they started their war that they had any chance of winning. When it had lasted two years, he began to hope they might, and it was only then that he began to think of helping them. He mentioned it in a letter to John Cam Hobhouse, who had shared the Grecian journey with him. But he had no connection with Greece, and no friends or correspondents in the country.

The new source of fame was a more intractable problem. Three years before, when he was in Venice, he had written to his old friend Thomas Moore: 'If I live ten years longer, you will see that it is not over with me. I don't mean in literature, for that is nothing; and – it may seem odd enough to say it – I do not think it was my vocation. But you will see that I shall do something – the times and Fortune permitting – that "like the cosmogony of the world will puzzle the philosophers of all ages." But I doubt whether my constitution will hold out.'

Neither to Moore nor to anyone else did he hint what his new vocation might be, and it seems unlikely that he had thought of anything. Perhaps there was a glimpse of it in the abortive Italian revolutionary plans of 1820. He had enjoyed the plotting then, the secret meetings and the stores of arms that were hidden in his house. He had been able to imagine himself in a heroic role, fighting for the freedom he had written so much about. Yet freedom, to a wealthy English aristocrat, could only have had a limited practical meaning. It could mean the overthrowing of a specific tyranny, but certainly not the overthrowing of privilege or the hereditary right to govern. He might perhaps have defined it as the right to think for one's self. But Moore was cynical about it: Byron, he thought, 'would ultimately have shrunk from the result of his own equalizing doctrines; and, though zealous enough in lowering those *above* his own level, rather recoil from the task of raising up those who were *below* it.' As for the fighting, Byron was certainly deceiving himself, like other men who imagine glory in war but do not imagine its sordid cruelty. In practice, whenever he encountered any violence, his reaction was to prevent it or mitigate it. But the Italian revolution came to nothing, and left his illusion intact.

One thing was certain: whatever new vocation he found, he would have to start at the top, for he was too proud, too consciously aristocratic and already too famous to take a second place in anything. But he was also indecisive and lethargic. All that winter in Genoa, he drifted and did nothing.

And then Blaquiere turned up: and quite suddenly, everything fell into place. He heard of the committee: Hobhouse himself and other men he knew were founder members of it: they wanted him to join. Could he not do much more? Under their auspices, he could go to Greece again: it would be a new adventure like the old one. It was a worthy use for his wealth: he would offer his fortune to Greece – not through the committee, but directly and in person, a philanthropist in the cause of freedom. He would lead them in battle: the poet of Greece's freedom would fight for it. His reputation would make his position unique. Both his needs would be answered: it was an escape from Genoa, and it would renew his fame.

Next, as always happened when Byron was carried away by a new idea, he felt a reaction against it, a kind of shame at the indignity of being enthusiastic. First there was a muddle of letters wrongly addressed, and for six weeks he heard nothing from Hobhouse or the committee. He felt he was being 'grossly illtreated', and petulantly decided to withdraw his offer of help. And there were endless, complicated and tedious arrangements, letters of credit to be organized, furniture and carriages and livestock to be sold or stored, a ship to be chartered, servants to be paid off, all kinds of minor decisions to be made and nobody on the spot to help except Barry, who had his own work to do, and Pietro Gamba, who usually managed to make a muddle worse. There was the problem of Teresa Guiccioli: he did not want to hurt her, and he dreaded the scene she would certainly make when she knew he was going away. He hated to disrupt his own routine or to dig up his roots in any place he had settled.

At last, however, in May, he heard that the committee had passed a resolution of thanks for his offer of help and had elected him a member. There was no proposal that he should go to Greece: they merely requested him 'to favour us with any suggestions or communications likely to advance the cause', and they seem to have thought of him only as a useful name in fund-raising. But he wrote at once a long letter to the secretary: 'Sir, I have pleasure in acknowledging your letter, and the honour which the Committee have done me. I shall endeavour to deserve their confidence by every means in my power. My first wish is to go up into the Levant in person, where I might be enabled to advance, if not the cause, at least the means of obtaining information which the Committee might be desirous of acting upon; and my former residence in the country, my familiarity with the Italian language (which is there universally spoken, or at least to the same extent as French in the more polished parts of the Continent), and my *not* total ignorance of the Romaic, would afford me some advantages of experience. To this project the only objection is of a domestic nature, and I shall try to get over it . . .'

The tone was unusually humble, and he went on to offer his suggestions. The materials needed, he said, appeared to be 'first, a park of field artillery – light, and fit for mountain-service; secondly, gunpowder; thirdly, hospital or medical stores.' He meant to contribute some of the latter two, but was pausing because if he should go himself, he could take them with him. If a brigade were to be formed, he would presume to suggest – but merely as an opinion – that the Committee should send a small body of officers of experience, rather than enrol raw British soldiers, and they should be aware that they were not going to 'rough it on a beefsteak and bottle of port.' Finally, the resources for British emigrants in the Greek islands were rarely to be paralleled. None of these suggestions was original, not even the thought that Greece might become some kind of British colony. But at that stage he knew no more than anyone else of events in Greece, so it was unfair to expect originality.

A fortnight later he sent a letter to Edward Trelawny. Trelawny was the only one of the Pisan circle who could or would have claimed to be a practical organizer: Byron, he wrote afterwards, always 'exhausted himself in planning, projecting, beginning, wishing, intending, postponing, regretting, and doing nothing.' But Byron knew his own weakness as well as anyone, and he wrote to him now: 'I can do nothing without you, and am exceedingly anxious to see you. Pray, come, for I am at last determined to go to Greece: – it is the only place I was ever contented in. I am serious; and did not write before, as I might have given you a journey for nothing. They all say I can be of use to Greece; I do not know how – nor do they; but at all events, let us go.'

He did not know how, but he had thought of a good many possibilities. He wrote to Douglas Kinnaird, his financial adviser in England, for a credit of £5000. 'There may be prisoners to ransom,' he said, 'some cash to advance, arms to purchase, or if I was to take an angry turn some sulky morning and raise a Troop of my own (though this is unlikely), any or all of them would require a command of credit.' The last of these he mentioned with irony, but he did not really think it was unlikely. He certainly hoped for military glory, and half-secretly saw himself leading Greek armies in battle. He knew nothing whatever of the military arts: at the time of the Peninsular War and Waterloo, when most young men of his class were eager for glory, he had stood aloof from it all and hoped that Napoleon would win. Yet it was not an entirely bizarre conceit. Even in Wellington's army – at least in the lower ranks – an officer was expected to be a gentleman rather than know the technique of the job, which was simple enough to be learned as he went along; and if any foreigner could have led a Greek army at that stage of the war, Byron might have done it as well as any.

He had not wholly confessed to anyone this somewhat school-boyish dream, but he gave it away by the accoutrements he ordered. There were magnificent green and gold and scarlet uniforms for himself, others of slightly less grandeur for his immediate staff, at least ten swords for different occasions, and a battery of firearms. And there were three gigantic helmets of his own design: for Pietro Gamba, who was eager to come with him, one that resembled a Prussian shako, of brass, green cloth and black leather, bearing on the front a semblance of Athene, and for himself and Trelawny plumed and brazen creations of the most menacing Homeric aspect, his own embossed with his coat of arms and his motto *Crede Byron*. He was delighted with the effect, and had his portrait drawn in full array. But when Trelawny arrived, he refused point-blank to put his helmet on. Byron was downcast, feeling no doubt that he had gone too far and made a fool of himself. The helmets and uniforms were packed away in boxes, and were not mentioned again until the time came to land in Greece.*

With Trelawny's arrival, the preparations abruptly accelerated. In the midst of them all, Byron felt trapped by the events he had set in train. 'It is not pleasant,' he said to Lady Blessington, his confidante of the moment, 'that my eyes should never open to the folly of the undertakings passion prompts me to engage in, until I am so far embarked that retreat (at least with honour) is impossible . . . My position excites such ludicrous images and thoughts in my own mind, that the whole subject which, seen through the veil of passion, looked fit for a sublime epic, and I one of its heroes, examined now through reason's glass appears fit only for a travestie.' And he promised that if he survived the campaign he would write two poems on it, 'one an epic, and the other a burlesque, in which none shall be spared, and myself least of all.'

But he did not expect to survive. He was always haunted by morbid superstition, and a fortune teller in his youth had warned him of his thirty-sixth year. He told several people he had a strong presentiment he would die in Greece. To Lady Blessington, in another of their intimate conversations, he said he hoped to die in

---

* There are conflicting stories about the uniforms. Trelawny said he gave him a military jacket during the voyage because he had nothing fit to wear; others that the uniform he landed in at Missalonghi was borrowed from a colonel in the Ionian Islands. It almost seems that after the helmet episode he avoided telling anyone he had the uniforms, but they appeared in an inventory the valet Fletcher made of his effects – 6 military jackets, 4 full dress uniform coats, 7 pairs of trousers, 2 helmets, 4 dress hats with gilt and silver ornaments and feathers, 10 swords and a sword stick, 8 pairs gold and silver epaulettes, and other accoutrements & weapons in proportion.

battle, because that would be a good ending and he had a horror of death-bed scenes: 'but as I have not been famous for my luck in life, most probably I shall not have more in the manner of my death, and that I may draw my last sigh, not on the field of glory, but on the bed of disease.'

Three months after Blaquiere's visit, everything was ready. The mansion Byron had lived in was empty and deserted. The baggage, the horses, the dogs, the servants, the private physician, Trelawny and Pietro Gamba were aboard the brig *Hercules* which had been chartered for the voyage, together with some nine thousand pounds in cash and letters of credit, and medical stores for a thousand men for two years. Teresa Guiccioli, hysterical with grief, had been carried screaming to her coach and driven away with her father. It was no scene of glory when the shrivelled, dyspeptic, doom-ridden little man came limping across the Genoa quay and climbed on board, a sombre victim of an impulse he regretted. At the very last minute he confessed to Barry that he would cancel the expedition even then, 'but that Hobhouse and the others would laugh at me.' Perhaps that is a common spring of what the world calls heroism.

CHAPTER SEVEN

Doubt and Discord
September—December 1823

William Parry
Colonel The Hon. Leicester Stanhope

Byron regarded his own expedition as part of the London Committee's enterprise. But he had no encouragement from the committee and no news of what it was doing – nothing but vague thanks and flattery. He wrote forlornly to the secretary: 'It would have given me pleasure to have had some more *defined* instructions before I left.'

The fact was that the committee was much too preoccupied to care what Byron did or what suggestions he made. It shamelessly used his name to raise more funds and get other rich or influential men to join it. But while the *Hercules* was very slowly sailing round the south of Italy, the committee members were busy with their own conflicting plans.

They took rather more notice of the opinions of Colonel Gordon, who had been present at the sacking of Tripolitsa and then had gone home to Aberdeen, partly perhaps in disgust at what he had seen, but mainly because he had been seriously ill with the plague that struck the ravaged town. Gordon, like Hastings, was one of the very few Philhellenes who were perfectly level-headed and sensible, who understood the tortuous politics of the Greeks and spoke their language, and still were anxious to help them. He advised the committee to spend its funds on the tools and equipment of an arsenal for making munitions and repairing weapons, and on a field force of artillery – and to send out experts who could operate them both. He had already begun to organize this on his own account: he had bought some howitzers and other guns, and engaged an artificer named William Parry from Woolwich Arsenal. He offered to pay a third of the cost if the committee would pay the rest, and the committee responded by asking him to go to Greece in command.

With Gordon in charge, this plan might have had some limited success. But in the course of weeks of discussion in the Crown and Anchor it slowly fell to pieces. Gordon knew too much about Greece: enough to disbelieve the report that Blaquiere wrote, and enough to see the hopeless impracticality of the Benthamite section of the committee, who insisted the money ought to be spent on printing presses and paper, and on school books, maps and mathematical instruments. In the upshot, Gordon gave his guns to the committee and withdrew, saying he was willing to go to Greece as soon as he saw any chance of being useful. The committee decided there was not enough money for all three projects, the arsenal, and the artillery unit and the printing presses. It discarded the artillery. And in Gordon's place as its emissary it chose the strangest of all Philhellenes, Colonel the Honourable Leicester Stanhope – who was indeed a serving lieutenant colonel in the British army and the son of an earl, but was also the most passionate, single-minded, pedantic and humourless Benthamite.

Thus in the autumn of 1823, three separate British expeditions converged on Greece. First, there was Parry the Woolwich Arsenal man, embarked direct from London in a ship named *Anne* with eight fellow-artificers – a clerk, cartridge-maker, turner, wheelwright, carpenter, foundryman, tinman and blacksmith – and a cargo including their tools and equipment, Gordon's guns and the printing presses, the school books and maps, the mathematical instruments, 322 Greek bibles and a set of musical instruments for a military band. Second, there was Stanhope, travelling overland, completely confident of founding a Benthamite state single-handed. And third, there was Byron who, more reasonably, did not know what he was going to do. Byron was the only man among them who had ever seen Greece before.

He was also the only one who questioned whether the Greeks would be glad to see him; the committee took it for granted, like all the earlier Philhellenes, that the Greeks would be humbly grateful for whatever help and advice they were offered. But Byron consulted the only Greeks he could find, those who for one reason or another were exiled in Italy. It was the best he could do, but naturally they could do nothing more or less than thank him for his generous interest. One went so far as to hint that he might be made King of Greece. Byron took that for what it was worth, but it was not an impossible thought and it seems to have stuck in his mind. Later, other Greeks had the same idea, and Trelawny quoted him as saying that if the offer was made he might not refuse it – he could always abdicate.

Blaquiere also wrote to him from Greece. At first he urged him to come as quickly as possible: the government expected him without delay – 'The effect produced by my mentioning the fact of *your* intention to join (the cause) has been quite electric.' Byron was used to sycophancy, and may have reflected that though he was famous, the number of Greeks to be electrified by an English poet was likely to be small. In a later letter, Blaquiere warned him that conditions were harsh; at Tripolitsa, even Mavrocordato had no bed but slept on the floor wrapped only in a greatcoat. And in a third he said the present moment was most inopportune and advised him to postpone his visit indefinitely. But these warnings reached Genoa after Byron had left, and it is not at all clear why Blaquiere changed his mind. Perhaps he had begun to suspect there were two kinds of truth in Greece.

What else had Blaquiere 'mentioned' to the Greeks? Nobody knows; but after his visit a rumour reached every man in the country that a vast sum of money was coming from England, and everyone assumed that Byron was bringing the first instalment.

*

Byron's expedition was the first to arrive within sight of Greece. Most people had advised him to go to the Ionian Islands, since they were safely under British rule; there, they said, he could gather up-to-date news from the mainland. Trelawny dissented. He wanted Byron to buy a fast armed yacht, so that they could sail around in Greece under the British flag, and see for themselves what was happening. That might have been a much better idea, but Byron had already chartered the slow old *Hercules*. Accordingly, early in August, they put in to the island of Cephalonia, which lies off the entrance of the Gulf of Corinth.

The rumour of money had penetrated even there, to the Suliotes who had been exiled at the time of the Battle of Peta. On the morning after the *Hercules* anchored, everyone was roused by a horde of these fearsome tribesmen who leaped on board with happy expectant shouts. The dogs barked, Lega Zambelli the steward rushed to save the money chest, and the captain prepared to defend his ship with a marline-spike. But Byron came up on deck and was enchanted to see them. In their wild Albanian robes, they were the very kind of men he remembered from his visit to Ali Pasha, the very kind he had hoped he might lead in battle. Although he had thought he remembered a little Romaic, he could not decipher a word of what they were shouting about. Nevertheless, he enrolled forty of them as a bodyguard and paid them a month in advance. He soon regretted it. Trelawny wrote that they clung to his heels day and night like a pack of jackals until he stood at bay like a hunted lion. And he himself wrote, in his journal, that they were not quite united among themselves in anything but exorbitant demands for more money. Soon he was happy to buy them off with another month's pay and the price of their passage to the mainland.

That was a small taste of what was coming. As the news of his arrival spread, almost all the self-styled leaders of Greece either wrote to him or sent emissaries. Most of them had the grace or cunning to request him to come at once to their own headquarters. Colocotrones invited him to a national assembly of his own creation. Mavrocordato, still a refugee in Hydra, said that was the only place where Byron could do any good: so did the primate of the island. The acting governor of Missalonghi said Greece would be ruined unless Byron came to him. Odysseus invited him to go to Athens. But Petrobey, a more straightforward man than the rest of them, said what all of them meant to say: he asked for a thousand pounds. And the worst of it was that each of them claimed he was the genuine leader and the others were charlatans and rogues.

The only exception was Marco Botzaris the Suliote hero of the siege of Missalonghi. He was still fighting the Turks, and he did not write to Byron. On the contrary, Byron wrote to him, before the disillusion of the Suliote bodyguard. Two Greeks in Italy, one a bishop, had recommended Marco as 'one of the bravest and most honest of our captains.' Byron's letter is lost, but not Marco's answer. 'Your Excellency is exactly the person we need,' he wrote. 'Let nothing prevent you from coming to this part of Greece . . . I shall have something to do tonight against a corps of six or seven thousand Albanians, encamped close to this place. The day after tomorrow I shall set out with a few chosen companions to meet Your Excellency. I thank you for the good opinion you have of my fellow-citizens, which God grant you will not find ill-founded.' But he never came. That night, he led an attack on the enemy camp and was shot. Greek heroes who lived too long were always dragged down by jealous rivals, and that might have happened to Marco Botzaris. But by his death he remained heroic in their eyes, and he is remembered still.

It would be easy to say the leaders' only motive when they wrote to Byron was private greed. All the Europeans said so at the time. George Finlay the historian, who arrived in Cephalonia soon after Byron, wrote that 'to nobody did the Greeks ever unmask their selfishness and self-deceit so candidly.' But in fairness one ought to look at their greed more closely. What they all wanted was power, and money was the means of power. Greed for power is not usually reckoned a sin; if it is, no politician can hope to go to heaven. These men may have thought as sincerely as anyone that they were fitted to make a good use of power. Certainly Mavrocordato and Colocotrones, at the two extremes, both passionately believed the kind of rule they advocated was the best for Greece; and neither of them, nor the others, could rule without money – first and foremost to pay enough soldiers to overcome their rivals.

Nobody in England had foreseen what happened. The mere rumour of English gold intensified the rivalries in Greece and made them more deep and bitter; all the leaders believed that whoever could put his hands on the gold would come out on top. As a corollary all of them, even the klephts, were suddenly eager to be polite and obsequious to the new set of foreigners. They did not send their fawning letters to Byron because he was a famous poet, or because he was a lord, or even because they cared in the least what he advised them. It was solely because they thought he had the cash. All the rivalry suddenly focused on him.

The truth of this only came to him slowly, and never perhaps completely. But from the beginning, it was a problem he could not solve. The London Committee had not yet sent any money at all and – though he did not know it – it had no money to send: it had spent it all on Parry's exotic cargo. Nor had it sent him any useful advice. Blaquiere had promised to meet him in the Ionian Islands but had gone back to England instead. A letter from London told him he was appointed the Committee's chief agent in Greece, but not what his duties were. 'Your presence there will increase our funds and our influence at home and abroad,' it added: the Crown and Anchor still thought of him only as a fund-raising name. The only money he had was his own nine thousand pounds. He was gallantly willing to spend it all on the cause, but he had expected some kind of recognized government to make good use of it. If he had any illusions about the Greeks he quickly lost them – but without losing his sympathy. 'I did not come here to join a faction, but a nation,' he wrote in his intermittent journal, 'and to deal with honest men, not speculators or peculators (charges bandied about daily by the Greeks about each other) . . . When the limbs of the Greeks are a little less stiff from the shackles of four centuries, they will not march so much "as if they had gyves on their legs". At present the Chains are broken indeed; but the links are still clanking, and the Saturnalia is still too recent to have converted the Slave into a sober Citizen.'

He did not know where to go in Greece or how to begin to help, or whom if anyone he could trust, and nobody could tell him. He soon discovered that almost everyone else who had tried to help had given it up in disgust. But he could not give up. Retreat, at least with honour, was still impossible; Hobhouse and the others would laugh. So he rented a house in Cephalonia and settled down to wait and see what happened; and he waited for nearly four months.

Trelawny wrote in one of his shallow and malicious comments: 'I well knew that, once on shore, Byron would fall back on his old routine of dawdling habits – plotting, planning, shilly-shallying and doing nothing.' Up to a point, it was true. Byron was happy in Cephalonia, and lapsed gently into the kind of life he had led in Pisa and Genoa – but without the domestic irritations. He went out riding and shooting at targets with pistols, and made a week's sightseeing expedition to Ithaca with the train of friends and servants of every degree who always accompanied him. He wrote every day, but not poetry, only long letters which were sane and well reasoned but limited by his lack of information. And he talked. For the first time since he left England he was surrounded by new English acquaintances, the officers of the garrison and the travellers who constantly passed through the islands; and when he found they had all forgotten or never heard of the scandal that drove him into exile he began to enjoy their company and their open admiration. He would have been very content to stay there and never to take the next inevitable step. For one of the contrasts in this infinitely complex man was between his pride and his diffidence: the pride that always made him insist on being the centre of any circle, and the diffidence that made him doubt his own ability in novel situations. He had persuaded himself he was not afraid of death, but he dreaded being unable to master the events and people he would find in Greece. Pride made him unable to retreat, and diffidence made him unwilling to advance.

Trelawny had no such doubts about himself. He was simply impatient. In September he insisted on leaving Byron and going to the Peloponnese, and began to play a more conspicuous part in the war than he merited.

This strange companion had said the Suliotes were like jackals, but he was a jackal himself in his friendship with Byron and Shelley. He had attached himself to them at Pisa for no obvious reason except reflected glory, and they accepted him perhaps because he had the practical ability they lacked. For the rest of his long life, he alternately boasted about his intimate friendship and slandered Byron in a way that revealed his jealousy. He was also one of the great liars of history, though one has to admit that his lies were often more interesting and amusing than the barren truth. The most ambitious was the autobiography of his youth, *Adventures of a Younger Son*, in which he claimed to have deserted a naval ship as a midshipman in the east and led a heroic and colourful life as a pirate. It was written after the episode in Greece, and some of its characters and events looked suspiciously like those of Greece and Pisa transposed to an eastern setting. The character he gave himself, both in the book and in life, resembled Byron's Corsair. Long after he died, people were still debating whether his tale was true, and it was only in recent years that research in Admiralty archives proved that he had never deserted at all, but had meekly returned in the naval ship to England. It is still a good story as fiction, and only a very weird man would have insisted, as he always did, that it was fact. Byron once said that if they could only teach him to tell the truth and wash his hands, they might make a gentleman of him yet. They never did; but Byron was fond of him and missed him whenever he went away.

Luckily, most of the racy story Trelawny told about his adventures in Greece can either be proved or disproved from other sources. When he left Cephalonia, Byron gave him two commissions. One was simply to find out what was happening, and the other to find the government, if he could, and pass on a request from London: the Committee was ready to negotiate the loan on the Stock Exchange, and it needed two delegates with power to act for the Government. Trelawny did both these jobs. His report of intrigue and deceit was much the same as everybody else's, and the delegates he found were personal nominees of Mavrocordato, whom he detested; but they sufficed. One was the same Louriottes who had travelled with Blaquiere, and the other a man called Orlandos. And having done that, Trelawny went on to Athens and met Odysseus. He was enraptured by that wild romantic hero. 'I have desided,' he wrote to Mary Shelley, with his usual eccentric spelling, 'on accompanying Ulysses* to Negropont to pass the winter there – there being excellent sport between Turk and woodcock shooting – I am to be a kind of Aidecamp – my equipments are all ready – two horses – two Zuliotes as servants – I am habited just like Ulysses – in red and gold vest with sheep-skin Capote – gun pistols sabre &c. red cap and a few dollars or dubloons.' So Trelawny had found what he wanted in Greece.

*

Among the letters that poured into Cephalonia were two at least from Frank Hastings, who for want of a ship had spent the summer in charge of artillery in Crete. They were a sailor's letters, prejudiced in favour of the sea, but they gave a far more intelligent analysis of Greece's needs than Byron received from anybody else. He argued, in a form of question and answer, that Greece could not win the war except through superiority at sea, because the first necessity was to prevent the Turks from relieving their fortresses and supplying their armies. 'We now come to the question,' he went on, 'How can the Greeks obtain a decisive superiority? I reply, By a steam-vessel armed as I shall describe. But how is Greece to obtain such a vessel?' And this question he answered by offering to pay £1000 towards the cost provided he had the command, and proposing that the London Committee might make a contribution. In case that was not enough, he made the rather naïve suggestion

* The English often used the Roman form of the name, which must have puzzled the Greeks.

of a loan which would be repaid by the prizes the ship would take.

And he described the ship he wanted in some detail. She would be built of iron, 150 to 200 tons, and carry two long 32-pounders fore and aft to fire red-hot shot and two 68-pounder carronades amidships for use with explosive shells. The tactics he proposed were to steam in circles firing each gun as it came to bear, and to fire them all point blank or at only two degrees of elevation, depending on his shot to ricochet off the water. Even with only one such ship, he believed he could enter the Dardanelles and destroy the Turkish fleet where it lay. 'The surprise caused by seeing a vessel moving in a calm, offering only a breadth of about eighteen feet, and opening a fire with heavy guns at a considerable distance, may also be taken into account. I am persuaded, from what I have seen, that in many cases the Turks would run their ships ashore and abandon them.'

It was a revolutionary scheme, and Byron was out of his depth in such technical matters. If he answered the letters, his answers have disappeared. He sent on the proposal to the committee, saying with an air of condescension that men of experience agreed it was 'on the whole faithful, intelligent and scientific.' And of course the committee did nothing.

There are many moments in the story of Byron's journey to Greece when one is tempted to write 'if only', and this is one. Both Byron and Hastings were men of exceptional vision, the one poetic and the other practical. Both were rich and aristocratic, and willing to devote their lives and fortunes to Greece. If only Byron had recognized Hastings' quality and made him his ally instead of the allies he chose, they might have achieved between them all they wanted.

Hastings' letters may have had one influence on Byron – whether beneficial or not it is hard to say. Louriottes and Orlandos, the deputies the government had chosen to go to London, called at Cephalonia on the way, and they brought yet another request for money: £6000 to 'activate' the fleet. They may not have explained in detail that the fleet was on strike and refused to go to sea without a month's pay in advance; but Byron perhaps remembered Hastings' argument, and he agreed, at least to the extent of offering £4000.

Mavrocordato again had been a little cleverer than any of the rivals. He proposed that the fleet should first sail up the west coast to Missalonghi, which again was blockaded by sea and in danger of attack by a Turkish army on shore. And when it sailed, at the end of November, he sailed with it. Missalonghi was as close to Cephalonia as he could go, and so he put himself in a better position than anyone else to get Byron to come to him.

At almost the same time, Colonel Stanhope arrived from London in Cephalonia, like a rather small tornado. Unlike Byron, he had no intention whatever of wasting time in a neutral island: if Greece had no government, he seemed to believe, that only showed that they needed him to tell them how to make one – and if they had no law, it was a positive advantage: the slate was clean for the law of Jeremy Bentham, for the greatest happiness of the greatest number.

Indeed no Englishman could have been more unlike Byron. Most writers who have tried to describe Colonel Stanhope have been at pains to say he was not a buffoon; which suggests they have all been tempted to say he was. He had most of the qualities it is difficult not to laugh at. He was a do-gooder who had no sense of humour at all and was always perfectly certain he knew best. He had a fixed idea – the doctrines of Bentham – which was a religion to him, or something more: one did not question or discuss it. And he was one of those men who are never aware of the impression they make on others and never pause to imagine it might be adverse.

Yet there is no denying he got things done. He rushed ahead on his chosen course and was never diverted by obstacles, dangers or difficulties, simply because he never saw they were there. And he made the unlikeliest people do what he wanted, because they seldom had time to draw breath for any futile attempt to argue. Not even his first encounter with Byron altered his train of thought. Byron asked if he had brought any new books from England, and Stanhope offered him Bentham's 'Springs of Action'. Byron took one look at it: 'Springs of Action? What does the old fool know of springs of action? My — has more spring in it.' The dash was put in by Hobhouse, who heard of the exclamation; so one will never know precisely what word he used.

The rest of the conversation is not recorded verbatim. But no doubt Stanhope told Byron what he intended for Greece – he told everybody. He had decided the Swiss and United States systems of government would be the most appropriate models since they were democratic, republican and unmilitaristic. Monarchy was out of the question. The legal and monetary systems of Geneva would be best: they were the nearest so far to the Benthamite ideal. So would the Swiss type of army – reservists called up for one month a year, with the structure, of course, of military academies and staff. Museums and record offices were important. The Greeks should be taught to breed silk-worms – and proper hospitals must be established at once. He agreed with Byron that a people so long enslaved could not be all virtuous, but the grand object of the London Committee was to give freedom and knowledge to Greece, which were the springs of order, morality and power. That was why the first care must be to found newspapers and schools and a reliable postal service. A shortage of teachers could soon be overcome: the schools would be organized on the Lancastrian principle, by which older pupils passed on their knowledge to their juniors. And books, elementary books on education, war, agriculture – these must be put into Greek. The present government? He would have a word with the military leaders: he was sure they would obey the government if it was seen to be virtuous.

So saying, Stanhope took ship for Missalonghi to get to work. Byron wrote to the committee that they were acting in perfect harmony: Stanhope had come with 'some high-flown notions of the sixth form at Harrow or Eton, etc.,' but he had put him to rights. Stanhope said he found Byron was rather lacking in drive.

It was only too true. But Byron's reasons for waiting in Cephalonia were wearing thin. A series of letters came from Stanhope and from Mavrocordato. So did a series of ships: they were sent to bring Byron to Missalonghi, but none of them were allowed by the British to enter the harbour. 'You will be received here as a saviour,' Mavrocordato wrote, 'Be assured, My Lord, that it depends only on yourself to secure the destiny of Greece.' And again: 'Yes, My Lord, the present moment will decide the fate of Greece. If ever I have done my duty, I shall redouble my activity and my zeal when I find you beside me.' And yet again: 'Your presence will do the greatest good; our forces will be electrified; the enthusiasm of all will be kindled to follow the impulsion which you will give them . . . I shall repeat myself no longer; My Lord, I only wait for the moment when we can join forces.'

So he went on, for page after page of flattery, and never once mentioned what was really on his mind, the cause of his desperate haste. Stanhope was rather more specific: 'The Prince is in a state of great anxiety, the admiral looks gloomy, and the sailors grumble aloud . . . Your loan is much wanted; and if the money arrive not speedily, I expect the remaining five ships (the others are off) will soon make sail for Spetsai.'

And that was it: the sailors of Hydra had demanded a second month's pay in advance, and since nobody had it they had gone home; in fact they timed it to arrive back in Hydra on the very day the first month's pay expired. Only five brigs from Spetsai were left, and their crews had also told their admiral they were going. If they did, Missalonghi would be left unguarded again, and Mavrocordato would be in jeopardy. It was still not Byron himself he wanted so desperately, it was the cash.

One cannot tell whether Byron entirely saw through the deception, but at any rate he recognized that he could not delay any longer. He hired two local boats so that he could make the crossing under the neutral Ionian flag – a large one for Gamba and most of the servants, money and luggage, and a small fast one for himself, Dr Bruno the medical attendant, Fletcher the valet and Loukas the young Greek page. Once he had made up his mind to uproot himself again, one of his moods of boyish adventure came over him. As they were rowed to their boat, he laughed cheerfully at Bruno and Fletcher who were getting wet with spray: he often laughed at them. Night fell while they were making the crossing, and they all sang patriotic songs, first one boat then the other. When the smaller boat drew ahead, they made signals by firing pistols and carbines, and shouted that they would meet at Missalonghi tomorrow.

CHAPTER EIGHT

Missalonghi
January—April 1824

Loukas Chalandritsanos · Dr Bruno

A few years after my first visit to Missalonghi, I sailed in there again. It still seemed to me as sad a place as ever, though there were some fresh signs of civic enterprise – new buildings were going up, some more of the rutted streets were being paved, and somebody was evidently working on the drains. The crowds of soldiers I had seen the first time had disappeared – perhaps because Greece, though I did not know it, was on the edge of another war with Turkey. The big harbour was still entirely empty, except for a dredger which seems to fight an endless battle with the mud. But there was a shack on one of the quays that I had not noticed before, and it had the one word *psari* daubed on the front of it, which means fish. So we went in, and had a good dinner of fish from the marshes, and another small example of the courtesy of the Greeks.

I asked the way, in all the languages I could muster, to the site of Byron's house, but nobody could understand what I wanted. It is always rather especially difficult to ask about Byron in Greece because the letter beta in modern Greek is pronounced as a V, so that some people call him Byron or Beeron and others Veeron. The people in the café were greatly put out at being unable to help me. More and more were drawn into the discussion, and I was ashamed to have given them so much trouble by my own stupid ignorance. At last they took me to the telephone in the kitchen. They had rung up a woman who spoke French. I told her and she told them, and there were happy shouts of Veeron, more telephone calls and more wine, and at length a young man who spoke English came pedalling down the dusty road on a bicycle. I got on the back and he pedalled me right through the town to show me the place where the house had been, bumping on a half-flat tyre across the pot-holes. My crew sat laughing at this vision of an author doing his research.

Missalonghi, I found, is still well aware of its part in the War of Independence, and of its one distinguished foreign visitor. There is a war museum in the town hall, and just inside the walls of the town – which were repaired and heightened after the first of its sieges – there is a Park of the Heroes; here, among some splendid palms and eucalyptus trees, are the graves of men who were killed in the town's defence, including some of the Philhellenes, with a large statue of Byron himself and a monument to Frank Hastings.

The house where Byron lived disappeared long ago, probably in the second siege which was two years after his death. What they say is the site of it is now a vacant lot among newer houses. It is laid out as a little park, with dusty flower beds, a few palms and some curious spiral-shaped concrete benches; at one side is another memorial, with an exceptionally good portrait of the poet in relief. It stands about a hundred yards from a part of the marsh which is dry in summer now, an expanse of sun-baked mud. Here, where the foreshore is littered with bits of old bicycles and empty oil drums and plastic bottles, Mavrocordato and the gentry of the town assembled to welcome Byron on that mid-winter morning in 1824, and without doubt it was littered then with the garbage of that era. I was surprised, on the back of the bicycle, to find it on the west side of the town, not the south, which is nearest to the harbour and the sea. But the old entrance to the marshes and the town was farther west than the present canal. It has silted up, and the ruins of a fort called Vasiladi which guarded it in 1824 stand now on a mud-bank all alone and miles from anywhere.

On my first visit, I had known about Byron, but on the second I also knew about the war. Wandering round the town that second time, I felt I understood what happened to Byron much better than I had from his biographies. Perhaps I am being presumptuous; but the last chapters of even the most scholarly biographies draw their facts from his letters and the stories of six men who were in Missalonghi and published their own accounts of it all. Neither he nor any of these six knew much about the events of the preceding years in Greece, and some of them knew nothing; and so they all more or less misunderstood the reasons why things happened as they did. Now, I cannot help seeing the well-known story as one of a series of episodes in the war, and that is how I must tell it. Seen thus, it has a poignant air of doom.

*

When we left Missalonghi after that second visit we sailed west; we were leaving Greece, and going up the Adriatic to Venice. The low-lying coast stretches 25 miles to the westward and ends at a rocky hill called Scrofa, an ancient island stranded now like a whale in the silt. Off shore is the island of Oxia, very tall and craggy, and between the two is the channel that leads to the north. It was here that the last great naval action was fought in galleys rowed by slaves, the Battle of Lepanto in 1571, when the Christian states of Europe defeated the Turks, and 250 Turkish galleys were sunk or captured and 15,000 galley slaves set free.

It was also here, not at Missalonghi, that Byron saw the dawn of New Year's Eve in 1823. Probably his Ionian skipper preferred to make his landfall at a place he could recognize, rather than the featureless and almost invisible shore near the town. During the night they had run close under the stern of a larger ship which proved to their astonishment to be a Turkish brig-of-war, and in the dawn light they saw it again and thought it was chasing them. They also saw their other boat, the one which carried Pietro Gamba and their luggage, being escorted by a Turkish ship towards Patras. Byron's skipper abandoned the course towards Missalonghi, ran into the Oxia channel and anchored in a small bay on the landward side of it. I also went into that bay and anchored for lunch and a swim when I passed it. It is a charming little inlet, still deserted and beautiful, but certainly not a good place to hide from a Turk.

Byron was disposed to enjoy the adventure. His only worry was to make sure that Loukas should not be captured – the boy was not an Ionian but a mainland Greek and had been attached for a time to Colocotrones, so he could not expect much mercy. Byron put him ashore in the bay to make his way overland to Missalonghi with a message for Stanhope and Mavrocordato. The skipper, feeling unsafe, raised anchor again and fled farther north, away from Missalonghi. There are some good hiding places up that coast, but perhaps he was too far from home to know them; and they sailed all day to the nearest town, which was then called Dragomestre and is now called Astakos.

There was consternation in Missalonghi. The fleet of Hydra had gone on strike and sailed for home, the Turkish ships had come out from the Gulf of Corinth, and the Spetsiotes, seeing them, had either weighed anchor and prudently put to sea or abandoned their ships and gone ashore. The town was blockaded again, Byron had disappeared, and so had the money. But when Loukas arrived, Mavrocordato managed to round up three ships for a rescue expedition. Loukas not ungallantly went with them, and three days later they found Byron's boat at Dragomestre and began to escort it back.

The passengers in this boat were a landlubberly lot, except perhaps Tita the gondolier, and the crew seem not to have been much better. Fletcher the valet had caught a cold and had to lie down on the only mattress on board, Dr Bruno was prone to wring his hands and weep at any threat of disaster, and Loukas could not swim. Byron himself liked boats, but had never learned much about them. And as they returned through the Oxia channel, the boat missed stays and ran aground in a squall. Two thirds of the crew climbed out on the bowsprit and jumped ashore, Byron told Loukas he would save him, and Dr Bruno stripped to his flannel waistcoat and running about like a rat (it was Byron's description) shouted 'Save him indeed! By God, save *me* rather – I'll be the first if I can.' Thereupon, after striking twice, the boat blew off again. The crew was removed from the rocks by one of the escort

ships, and that evening, without any more alarms, Byron reached
the entrance to Missalonghi.

Pietro Gamba's boat was already there. It had been taken into
Patras with the rest of the servants and the compromising cargo
of money, horses, guns and baggage, including Byron's helmets,
pistols and swords – everything except his correspondence, which
Gamba weighted with shot when capture seemed imminent and
dropped overboard, to the loss of historians. The captain of the
Turkish warship recognized Gamba's captain, who had saved his
life some years before in a shipwreck, and after three days the boat
was released. They all put it down to the captain's gallant deed and
the intervention of saints, but Byron's prescience in sailing under
the Ionian flag had something to do with it. It was a shocking
misuse of a neutral flag and there would have been endless reper-
cussions if the Turks had looked in the hold of the boat; but the
ruse succeeded better than it deserved.

Nobody had been in mortal danger, either from the rocks or
from the Turks, but it had been a most exhilarating start; and
Byron was elated on the morning of 5 January, when he put on
one of his scarlet uniforms and was rowed across the shallows to
the town. 'Hope and content were pictured in his countenance,'
Gamba wrote in his journal. 'I could scarcely refrain from tears.'

And certainly the landing on that squalid shore was an occasion
quite unlike the arrival in Greece of any of the earlier Philhellenes,
who had all met either indifference or hostility. The raucous cheers,
the salutes of guns and musketry, the obsequious greetings of the
President of the Senate, of the picturesque guerilla leaders, the
bishop in his robes and the dozen or so of foreign officers in the
remnants of their garish uniforms – all this created a climax of
hope that something heroic was about to be accomplished. Of the
thousands of people who were there, Stanhope and Byron himself
were the only two who may have been half aware of the underlying
anomaly; for the Greeks were quite sincere in their welcome,
although they were cheering not because Byron was Byron but
because he was rich.

The town was swarming with guerillas who had followed their captains in from far and wide to attend a conference Mavrocordato had summoned, and then had stayed to see the fabulous visitor. Most conspicuous were nearly a thousand Suliotes, or men pretending to be Suliotes, who were terrorizing the town. The death of Marco Botzaris had left these unruly warriors with six leaders all of equal status and equal family pride. None of the six would serve under any of the others, but all had told Mavrocordato they would be happy to serve the English lord – for it was months since any of the Suliotes had been paid. Byron had already paid the fleet, and Mavrocordato's next plan was to persuade him to pay the Suliotes in order to keep them quiet, and to offer him as an inducement the rank of Archistrategos or Commander-in-Chief. And Byron willingly agreed. In spite of the trouble in Cephalonia, he still had his old romantic affection for men in Albanian dress, and he still, half ashamed, had the vision of himself as military leader. He took five hundred Suliotes into his pay, and Mavrocordato said he would pay a hundred more and add them to his command. Soon Byron was to be seen on his daily ride, accompanied by Gamba and Loukas and sometimes by Dr Bruno, Tita and the negro groom, all in their uniforms and liveries, and preceded and followed by packs of Suliotes loping along on foot as bodyguard.

Within the dank, ill-furnished house allotted to him, Byron decorated a reception room with friezes of swords and muskets, pistols, carbines, daggers, helmets and trumpets. Here, from the very beginning, he was besieged by tumultuous brigand leaders, all accompanied by their retainers, all shouting, hurling invective and shaking their fists in each other's faces and expecting him – a man who hated argument – to settle their quarrels although he could not understand what they were shouting about. And here, according to Gamba, most of the talk between these irruptions was of sieges, weapons and tactics.

Since the Turkish army had vanished from the district, there was only one possible objective for military plans. But it was one that had peculiar attractions: the fortified town of Lepanto, which had been in Turkish hands, like Patras, since the war began. Lepanto is called Nafpaktos now, and it lies just inside the entrance of the Gulf of Corinth on the northern shore: the battle of 1571, which was fought some fifty miles farther west, was named after the town because its minute and beautiful medieval harbour was the base for the Turkish galleys. Mavrocordato had a strategic theory that to capture Lepanto would give the Greeks control of the whole of the Gulf and might even force the Turks to leave Patras. Moreover, it would raise his prestige, which had not recovered from the disaster of Peta. For Byron, the attraction was possibly more historical. Lepanto was a famous name: to fight and win the second Battle of Lepanto would be a resounding start for his military career. And for both, it must have been pleasant to know that the capture would be easy – easier than subsequent accounts might make it seem. For the town was garrisoned mainly by Albanians, who had already said they would gladly surrender for a reasonable fee. All they asked was that somebody should make a token attack, so that they could save their honour by a token defence.

In the first month at Missalonghi, Byron threw himself into this project with an access of energy, and to point out its rather ludicrous attractions is not to sneer at him: nobody could or should have missed such a chance. His own ambiguous attitude to it emerges from what he said and wrote. To Gamba he made jokes about his title of Archistrategos, but he revealed, 'unawares perhaps,' that 'the romance and peril of the undertaking were great allurements to him.' And the famous poem that he wrote and showed to Stanhope on his birthday, 22 January, spoke openly of military glory, contrasting it with the frustration of love that he secretly suffered from his unresponsive page:

> '. . . The Sword, the Banner, and the Field,
> Glory and Greece, around me see!
> The Spartan, borne upon his shield,
>   Was not more free.

Byron's house at Missalonghi. *Below* The walls of Missalonghi
Overleaf Byron lands at Missalonghi

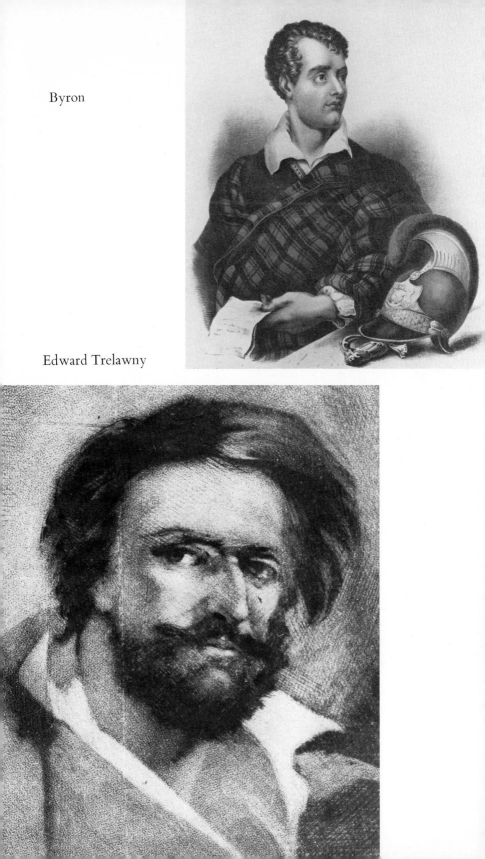

Byron

Edward Trelawny

Awake! (not Greece – she is awake!)
Awake, my spirit! Think through *whom*
Thy life-blood tracks its parent lake,
    And then strike home!

Tread those reviving passions down,
Unworthy manhood! – unto thee
Indifferent should the smile or frown
    Of Beauty be.

If thou regret'st thy youth, why live?
The land of honourable death
Is here: – up to the Field, and give
    Away thy breath!

Seek out – less often sought than found –
A soldier's grave, for thee the best;
Then look around, and choose thy ground,
    And take thy Rest.'

Yet in letters, fearful as ever that he might be laughed at, he took refuge in laughing at himself. 'Well, it seems that I am to be Commander-in-Chief, and the post is by no means a sinecure... between Suliote chiefs, German barons, English volunteers, and adventurers of all nations, we are likely to form as goodly an allied army as ever quarrelled beneath the same banner.' And again: 'If we are not taken off with the sword, we are likely to march off with an ague in this mud-basket; and to conclude with a very bad pun, to the ear rather than to the eye, better *martially* than *marsh-ally*: – the situation of Missalonghi is not unknown to you. The dykes of Holland when broken down are the deserts of Arabia for dryness, in comparison.'

Late in January, the third of the London Committee's expeditions reached Dragomestre: William Parry with his arsenal and the Benthamites' educational stores. The cargo was transferred to boats for the final passage to Missalonghi. Stanhope insisted the printing presses should be unloaded first, but by the end of the month the gear for the arsenal was installed in the empty and derelict Turkish seraglio, which was the largest building in Missalonghi; and Parry came to call on Byron to ask like everyone else for money – the London Committee had not provided enough to pay the artificers' wages.

Parry was what used to be called a rough diamond. He had not much education, and an accent and manners that stamped him at once among the rest of the English as being no gentleman. He quarrelled with his own artificers, and with the Greeks and Stanhope and everyone in Byron's entourage, and most of all with the foreign officers: between them, in their writings, they called him an officious, pompous, ignorant, presumptuous pot-house buffoon who was never quite sober. And he suffered from the over-enthusiastic build-up the London Committee had given him. Their letters had said he was a master of all the latest improvements in gunnery, and in particular that he had been the right-hand man of General Congreve, the inventor of the Congreve rocket, a weapon more alarming than dangerous which had been used against the French invasion fleet before Trafalgar and also at Waterloo. He was expected to manufacture these rockets in Missalonghi, and explosives and weapons of every kind. But it soon turned out he was unable to do it, partly at least because the functions of his arsenal needed coal, and it had not occurred to anyone in London that there was no coal in Greece.

Technically, therefore, Parry was a bitter disappointment. But Byron took a liking to him. He enjoyed the earthy sense of humour that affronted everyone else. He liked to hear Parry's rude imitations of Jeremy Bentham, and his scurrilous descriptions of the Crown and Anchor Committee. He could understand his belief in brandy as a cure for every evil. Parry had a crude, straight-forward common sense which Byron evidently found a happy relief from the neurotic affectations of the foreign officers, the charming incompetence of Pietro Gamba, the tortuous subtlety of the Greeks and the maddening self-assurance of Colonel Stanhope. This dockyard clerk came nearer than anyone else to being a friend. Byron appointed him commander of a new artillery corps, but that was a mistake. Parry, who had never been a soldier, began to call himself Major, and most of the mixed bag of officers adamantly refused to serve under his command. But before that difficulty had to be resolved, it was overtaken by others that were worse.

Half way through February, everything seemed to be as ready as it could be for the great attack. Five o'clock on the 14th was agreed as the time when an advance guard of Suliotes should march out of town for Lepanto, commanded by Pietro Gamba as Byron's lieutenant. And at that exact moment, the dream of glory suddenly started to turn to a terrible nightmare.

Assembled for the march, the Suliotes refused to move. They demanded more pay. And they requested that the government should appoint from among them two generals, two colonels, two captains, and about one hundred and fifty junior officers, with officers' pay, from the force of three or four hundred. When Byron was told of this crippling ultimatum, he 'burst into a violent passion' and wrote a furious note to Mavrocordato, saying he would have nothing more to do with the Suliotes. And it was the following evening, after a day of futile argument, that he had the fit that everyone thought was epileptic. Half an hour after it struck him, there was an alarm that the Suliotes had rebelled. Everyone rushed out, leaving him half-conscious, and two drunken Germans forced their way into his bedroom shouting that the arsenal had been stormed and they had come to protect him from the mob. It was all untrue; but three days later, when he was still weak from the fit and the leeches Dr Bruno had prescribed, the Suliotes did start a fight, a Swedish officer was killed and the arsenal was besieged. Byron was no coward. At the height of the riot, he summoned the Suliote chieftains, struggled into his full dress uniform to receive them, and sent them away apparently repentant. But then the primates of the town marched in upon him with a demand for 3000 dollars to bribe the Suliotes to go away and leave Missalonghi in peace. He paid it. Six of Parry's eight artificers took fright and demanded to be sent home: he paid their passages too. The few remaining Spetsiote ships, which he had already paid, went back to their island and left the town unguarded. Before that awful week was out, there was a serious earthquake; and all the time, the rain was pouring down.

Afterwards, Colocotrones was blamed for the Suliotes' defection. It was said he had rounded up more Suliotes in the Peloponnese and sent them across to infiltrate Byron's gang and sow dissension. Perhaps he did; he would have done anything to stop a victory that might have brought credit to Mavrocordato. But there was no need; the seeds of dissension were there all the time. Of all the bands of happy ruffians in Greece, the Suliotes were most proud of their brigandish habits, and least amenable to any kind of organization but their own. Mavrocordato had handed them over to Byron because he could not control them; Byron had been deceived by his own romantic memory of Ali Pasha's world; the Suliotes had been glad to be paid good money to follow him around Missalonghi, but had probably never intended to follow him into battle – especially in an assault on a walled town, which was the very opposite of their own ideas of tactics. And perhaps, after all, they had an arguing point: there was no explicable reason why all the foreigners should be officers, and hardly a single Greek. The revolt was bound to come: it was lucky it came at the gates of Missalonghi, not at the gates of Lepanto.

But it could hardly have been a worse humiliation: to have day-dreamed of leading the troops into battle, and even to a glorious death – and then to have failed to lead them out of their barracks. Any intelligent Greek could have warned him. For he had tried to do precisely what the earlier Philhellenes had tried and failed to do: Baleste, Tarella, Dania, the men of the German Legion, and General Normann, who died in his despair at this very place. He tried as a foreigner to command a native army, he tried to turn brigands or guerillas into a disciplined force, and he tried to combine them with a much smaller force of miscellaneous Europeans. He did not know that all this had been conclusively proved to be impossible, that it had always inevitably ended in disaster; and the people who did know, most notably Mavrocordato, were so blinded by their own self-interest that they did not tell him, but simply watched him putting his head in the noose.

After the fit, Byron never recovered his health, and after the crushing blow to his military hope, he never recovered his spirits. To Gamba, he said he feared he had done nothing but lose time, money, patience and health. Parry remarked that he had no friend in Greece, but was surrounded by people he neither loved nor trusted. Everyone noticed that he grew more irritable, especially over trifles – what Parry called peevish and little-minded. His mood began to vary from gloom to the playing of practical jokes which were often unkind. Many people tried to persuade him to go back to Cephalonia to recuperate. But he would not go. 'I cannot quit Greece,' he wrote in a letter, 'while there is still a chance of my being of any (even supposed) utility. There is a stake worth millions such as I am, and while I can stand at all I must stand by the cause.' Yet he also knew, and said, that there was nothing more he could do in Missalonghi.

Such determination may either be called heroic or stubbornly proud; it does not make much difference. For myself, I prefer to think of it as pride. He must have felt his hope of heroism had been made ridiculous, and he was exceedingly sensitive to ridicule. 'The Sword, the Banner, and the Field, Glory and Greece around me see!' The words he had written must have mocked him. He must have hated the thought of going back to the world he had left, branded with such a folly, laughed at by his enemies and pitied by his friends. Better to stay buried in Missalonghi, to hope that perhaps something useful might turn up to hide the shame and failure, or at least – for he felt he would not live long – that he might die there, not gloriously but honourably and obscurely. That was how General Normann died. And in Byron that attitude of mind, I think, is more probable and also more deserving of respect than the conscious heroism tradition ascribes to him.

*

On the day of the earthquake, one prime source of irritation removed itself: Colonel Stanhope decided he had finished his task in Missalonghi, and he bustled off towards the Peloponnese and Athens. 'Lord Byron is much shaken by his fit,' he wrote to the

London Committee, scarcely trying to hide his satisfaction, 'and will probably be obliged to retire from Greece.'

The Committee's two representatives had had only one stand-up quarrel, in which Stanhope called Byron a Turk and Byron said Stanhope should leave the army. Nothing but Byron's patience had averted more and kept them on speaking terms. Stanhope's conceit and pedantry were very nearly insufferable, and it was just as well that Byron never saw the daily reports he wrote and dispatched to London. All of them praised his own achievements, contrasting them, sometimes explicitly, with Byron's laziness. They included copies of written questionnaires he had given to Byron, requesting him to answer, yes or no, whether he would pay for establishing newspapers, whether he approved this or that action that Stanhope proposed, whether he sincerely favoured a free uncensored press. They even included his own verbatim version of the quarrel.

The trouble was that most of his questions could not be answered without reservation. Byron did believe in the freedom of the press, but he did not believe Greece was ready for it, or that Stanhope was fit to have a monopoly of it; for Stanhope's idea of freedom was that all newspapers should be edited by Benthamites he appointed. That could not have done much harm in Greece, because not many Greeks could read; but it might have harmed the cause of Greece abroad, if it gave the impression the war was being fought for Stanhope's extremely radical brand of political thought.

And Byron, forced into a corner by Stanhope's refusal to listen, could never resist poking fun at him and, which was worse, poking fun at the seer whom Stanhope called 'the finest genius of the most enlightened age, the immortal Bentham.' But Byron could not, or did not, stop him founding his newspapers. The first was called The Greek Chronicle, and it began to appear in January with the famous slogan under its title – 'The Greatest Good of the Greatest Number.' It published selections of the thoughts of the master, and news which was inevitably biased and sometimes untrue. Its circulation in Greece was said to be forty copies, though it sold rather better in the Ionian

Islands. To improve this figure, Stanhope soon started a second paper, which was printed partly in Italian. Its title was The Greek Telegraph, and its slogan 'The World our Country, and Doing Good our Religion.' And having founded them and written the first few numbers, Stanhope handed them over to a Swiss volunteer named Meyer who had impressed him on a short acquaintance with the purity of his political ideals.

As ever, one has to admit that this offensive and boring man did get things done. In the six weeks he spent at Missalonghi he founded not only the papers but also a school and a dispensary, using Byron's and the Committee's medical stores. And he also lectured everyone who would listen, and wrote long letters to everyone who would not, telling them in the utmost detail how they ought to run their own affairs. There was heartfelt relief in Missalonghi when he took himself off to do the same things in Athens.

But in Athens something very surprising happened: Stanhope was instantly and completely captivated by Odysseus, the brigand leader installed in the Acropolis. It is easy to see why Trelawny admired Odysseus: he was the kind of romantic swashbuckler Trelawny wanted to be. But Stanhope saw him as an untutored but instinctive Benthamite. It was on four days' acquaintance that he wrote to Byron, 'He has a very strong mind, a good heart, and is brave as his sword.' Odysseus, he added, was the only man in Greece who could keep order; he favoured strong government, constitutional rights and vigorous efforts against the enemy; he liked good foreigners and courted instruction; he spoke 'in the most undisguised manner' of the factions of Mavrocordato, Hypsilantes, Colocotrones and the primates; he had established two schools and given his enlightened support to the founding of newspapers. In short, he was a 'most *extraordinary man.*'

Stanhope might have said the same of any warlord he had happened to meet: they were all in a mood to flatter an Englishman, and he was no match for the kind of diplomacy Ali Pasha had taught. Odysseus, like everyone else, certainly wanted some if not all of the English gold, and therefore he wanted Byron; and as a first step, he welcomed Stanhope. Evidently, his technique was simply to agree with every single thing that Stanhope said. It is bizarre and pleasant to imagine their long conversations, Stanhope declaiming his non-stop convoluted Benthamite rigmarole, an interpreter hopelessly bemused but doing his best, and the elegant ignorant bandit wondering what on earth the man could be talking about, smiling, nodding his head and hiding his yawns. In a letter that Odysseus sent to Stanhope, there is a hint that he had had as much lecturing as he could stand: 'Do not ask my opinion about anything. I cannot give you advice. You know what is necessary much better than I do. Therefore do not hesitate to do everything you think desirable for Greece, or likely to advance her freedom.' Nothing could have pleased Stanhope more. But to be just, one must admit that in spite of his martial pride, Odysseus may have felt some intellectual humility. Certainly he had never in his life met anyone remotely like Colonel Stanhope.

The object of his patient listening came at the end of Stanhope's letter to Byron: 'Odysseus is most anxious to unite the interests of Eastern and Western Greece, for which purpose he is desirous of immediately forming a congress at Salona.* He solicits your Lordship's and Mavrocordato's presence. I implore your Lordship and the President, as you love Greece and her sacred cause, to attend . . . All delays, even that of a day, will, in the opinion of Odysseus, be injurious.'

Trelawny, in the memoirs he wrote afterwards, said it was Stanhope who first proposed this meeting and Odysseus, or Ulysses as he called him, who agreed. Trelawny was often wrong, but this time he may have been right. It looks more like one of Stanhope's sudden ideas. If it was, Odysseus had been more successful than he could have hoped. Trelawny added his own persuasion in a covering letter to Byron: 'I can assure you that Ulysses is perfectly sincere . . . the only man I have found in Greece that I think worthy of your confidence and co-operation. You do not know him, Lord Byron,

*Now called Amphissa. It is near Delphi, about a hundred miles from Missalonghi and rather more from Athens.

or we should have had you at Athens – nor do I despair (if you give us this meeting) of your making Athens your final destination.'

*

These letters, with an added request for gunpowder from Parry's stores, reached Byron about 10 March, some three weeks after his fit. They revived all the doubts that had worried him in Cephalonia. It was extremely awkward that Stanhope was backing a man who, whatever he said, was Mavrocordato's mortal enemy. It divided the committee's policy into two. And Byron could hardly believe Trelawny's assurance: he knew Odysseus was, or recently had been, in league with the Turks. And Odysseus was not the only one who was trying to win him away from Mavrocordato: Colocotrones and Petrobey were writing to him too. He distrusted the meeting at Salona, and Mavrocordato distrusted it even more; naturally, Mavrocordato produced a rumour that Odysseus meant to kill him at the conference, and rumours like that could never quite be discounted.

And yet, if Byron refused to go, it would perpetuate a division in the committee's work. It was hopeless to try to argue Stanhope out of his new enthusiasm. And he was doing no good in Missalonghi. It would at least be an expedition, a break from that awful town, a long ride through the mountains, royally escorted. And there was perhaps just a possibility it might be something useful, a road to the achievement he needed to mitigate his failure.

He agreed to go, and wrote that he would be at Salona on 28 March. He took it for granted that if he went, Mavrocordato would have to go too. As if to assert his independence, he refused to send any gunpowder.

Yet it seems likely that Mavrocordato had no intention of going, or of letting Byron go while he could find any way of stopping him. It was almost spring, but the rain was still teeming down. Byron was told the river crossings were impassable and an escort could not be provided. This was certainly no more than partly true. The journey was difficult and might be a little risky, but the messengers from

Athens had made it, and any determined horseman could have done the same. But Byron had no means of finding out for himself, and he accepted the story. So the 28th was allowed to pass. And in the first week of April there was a crisis that took everyone's attention.

What seemed to be a minor quarrel suddenly blew up into rebellion. One of the Suliote captains who had been exiled from the town attacked and captured the fort of Vasiladi which guarded the sea entrance. Another local captain in league with him marched on the town and put it in a panic. And the Turkish fleet appeared in the offing again. The town authorities, such as they were, rushed round the place arresting people indiscriminately. Among their captures was a man who was actually living in Byron's house, because he was related to the owner; and he confessed it was an organized plot to surrender the town to the Turks, overthrow the government, and seize Mavrocordato and Byron and Byron's money chest.

In the midst of the panic, Byron gave a display of Nordic coolness: he ordered his horses as usual and took his ceremonial daily ride, some miles out into the country. He also offered Parry's stores to the town's defence. The guns the committee had sent had never yet been used against the Turks, and they never were; but now they were used to threaten the very men that Byron had tried to lead. Next day, news came that the other Suliote chiefs had not been offered a part in the plot and were marching towards the town to fight the rebels. And as suddenly as it had started, the whole thing collapsed. The rebels abandoned Vasiladi, the ringleaders were rounded up and the Turkish fleet retired. But Mavrocordato's prestige had taken another blow, and he had not even the power to punish the traitors.

That was on 7 April. On the 9th, a mail arrived from London. Among other news, Byron learned that the loan on the Stock Exchange was going well. The first instalment would soon be delivered to Greece, and he and Stanhope were confirmed as joint commissioners to supervise the use and distribution of it.

So it was all the more urgent to go to Salona, to meet Stanhope again and at least to agree on a common policy. That afternoon, he went for a ride with Gamba. While they were out, they were soaked by a downpour of rain. As usual, they returned by being rowed across the marsh in an open boat; and two hours later, he began to shiver and said he had shooting pains in his back and limbs.

*

Odysseus was taking the meeting very seriously. He had already made the longer journey from Athens to Salona, with Stanhope and Trelawny and a crowd of representatives of the regions of his domain. They waited patiently. On the 17th, Stanhope wrote another letter: 'My dear Lord Byron, We are all assembled here with the exception of your Lordship and Monsieur Mavrocordato. I hope you will both join us . . . You are a sort of Wilberforce, a saint whom all parties are endeavouring to seduce; it's a pity you are not divisible . . . I implore you to quit Missalonghi, and not to sacrifice your health and perhaps your life in that Bog. I am your most devoted Leicester Stanhope.' Trelawny was sent to carry this fresh plea to Missalonghi. He rode off with an escort. Two days on the way, as he was fording one of the rivers, he met a messenger coming in the opposite direction, who told him Byron was dead.

It was exactly, tragically and pathetically the death he had told Lady Blessington he hoped would not be his fate – 'not on the field of glory but on the bed of disease.' The death-bed scene, of which he had said he had a horror, was appallingly prolonged. The doctors, relentlessly overpowering his revulsion, bled him without mercy. Even when they had bled him to death they flouted his wishes. 'One request let me make,' he had said to them. 'Let not my body be hacked, or be sent to England.' But they hacked it to bits in an amateurish and inconclusive autopsy, and when they had put it together again as well as they could they sent it to the Ionian Islands, after presenting the lungs to the people of Missalonghi to be buried there as a relic.

Byron died on Easter Monday, the 19th of April. On the 21st, a brig called the *Florida* reached the Ionian Islands from London, bringing Edward Blaquiere, 30,000 gold sovereigns and 50,000 Spanish dollars. The first instalment of the deluge of British money had arrived. A few days later, Stanhope arrived there too, having left Odysseus in Salona; for complaints of his political deeds had been made to the War Office, and he had received an immediate order to report back to London for army duties. Byron's body was put aboard the *Florida* and the ship which had brought the committee's gold returned to England with both the commissioners, one living and one dead. No provision had been made for appointing substitutes, and the money was therefore deposited in a British bank in Zante, the southernmost of the islands, to wait until orders could come from London telling somebody what to do with it.

*

Byron's death has often been called a death for Greece, as if it had been a deliberate sacrifice. But there is only the faintest suggestion that any such thought came into his mind in the days when he knew he was dying. 'I do not lament,' he was reported to have said in his weakness, 'for to terminate my wearisome existence I came to Greece. My wealth, my abilities, I devoted to her cause. Well, there is my life to her.' It does not seem to me a claim of hopeful sacrifice; rather a negation of hope, an acknowledgement that all he had done had been useless and dying was useless too. It was natural, as the news spread through Europe and America, that people wanted to mitigate the wasteful tragedy with the comforting thought that his death achieved something in the cause he had wanted to fight for. That belief has lasted ever since, and grown to a legend: the rest of this story will show what truth there is in it. My own belief is that Byron would firmly have said it was cant, his favourite word for a kind of muddled thinking he detested. If I have understood him at all, he would much have preferred to admit that his only success was to rescue a couple of dozen Moslem prisoners from the Greeks.

For the rest, his brave intention had ended in total failure, and that was the kind of fact he thought should be honestly faced. It undervalues him to make him a story-book hero.

PART THREE

The British Stratagem

1824-1827

CHAPTER NINE

Cargoes of Gold
February—December 1824

John Bowring · Joseph Hume · George Finlay

In the story of this curious war I am writing a disproportionate amount about the Europeans who mixed themselves up in it. My only excuse is that they were more literate than the Greeks and wrote more about it themselves, so that their characters are more comprehensible and their adventures more vivid. To keep the whole thing in proportion, I must say again that the Greeks did most of the fighting: for each European involved, there were several hundred Greeks. And they suffered most from it too. The Europeans had nothing to lose but their health and lives, while the Greeks could lose their families and their homes.

But during the summer and winter after Byron's death in 1824, the Sultan made no serious invasion and there were no Turks to fight, except the sad garrisons of the remaining fortresses – and they had been there so long that nobody took any notice of them. That year, for better or worse, the greatest influence on events in Greece was European. It came from Britain, and the centre of the story moves from Greece to the London Stock Exchange, which was the source of the sovereigns and dollars the *Florida* landed in Zante.

When the Greek deputies Louriottes and Orlandos came to London after calling on Byron in Cephalonia, of course they were innocent about the workings of the City. But the financier members of the Crown and Anchor Committee – especially the secretary, whose name was John Bowring – were eager to help them to float a loan for the government of Greece, and indeed to do it for them. Since there was so much idle capital in Britain, it was not at all a difficult operation. To give it a send-off the deputies were entertained by the Lord Mayor of London at a banquet in Guildhall, and when the loan was opened in February 1824 it was oversubscribed. The nominal value was £800,000, but it was issued at a discount of 41%, so that the sale of a £100 bond only realized £59. Interest was to be 5% on the nominal value, and for this the Greek government pledged the whole of the national property. In theory, after the deduction of commission and expenses for the city bank which was the contractor for the loan, and other administrative costs, including a personal commission of no less than £11,000 for Bowring, the Greeks should have received rather less than half the £800,000, while they had to pay interest on the whole of it. Perhaps that was a reasonable bargain. But buyers of the £100 bonds were required to pay only a first instalment of £10, with the rest spread over a period of months, and before those months were up the loan was in difficulties.

Several members of the committee invested in the bonds. That may have been legitimate enough, if they could afford it. But at least two of them, and probably more, made a gamble of it, not caring whether they helped the Greeks, but hoping to make a quick profit for themselves. These two were Bowring and another member named Joseph Hume. To increase the value of their stock they set to work to publish or invent the most encouraging news from Greece, successful battles and enlightened acts of government. Stanhope's crazily optimistic letters came in useful. For a time they succeeded, and the bonds rose above par. But in March, when the first enthusiasm began to wear off, they drifted down again; and when the news of Byron's death reached London in May they slumped to 45 against the issue price of 59. Bowring and Hume were both caught short, unable to pay the next instalment on their holdings. They told the deputies future instalments should be postponed until the situation in Greece was clearer. Perhaps they were right, but the deputies disagreed: after all, it was their job to collect the money.

Bowring and Hume both knew or suspected that the deputies had been gambling too, and using the fund for their own expensive tastes in London life. They threatened the deputies with hints of exposure, and forced them to use more money from the fund to get them out of their trouble. The deputies bought the holdings of Bowring and Hume at prices far above the current market value. Disputes between them grew to something like mutual blackmail, and the hush money either way came out of the fund. Tens of thousands of pounds disappeared in shady transactions, which grew until everybody involved in them knew there would be a first-rate scandal if they were ever discovered.

But still, as cash was collected it was dispatched to Greece. In May, just before the news of Byron's death, a second ship left London for Zante with £40,000. It arrived in June, and this money also was impounded in the British bank. And soon after the *Florida* reached London with Byron's body, she went out again with another £50,000. All of it was in gold or silver coinage.

In August, the committee succeeded in finding two men who were willing to go to Greece as commissioners, to supervise the use of the money in place of Byron and Stanhope. Several responsible men, including Colonel Gordon and Hobhouse, had been asked to go but had refused, because they heard rumours of the incipient scandal and of confusion amounting to civil war in Greece. The two who accepted were both young men of little standing or experience. One was named Hamilton Brown: he had been dismissed from government service in the Ionian Islands, and then as a volunteer had been given a passage by Byron in the *Hercules*, and he had travelled through Greece with Trelawny before he returned to London. The other was Henry Lytton Bulwer, who did win distinction when he was older, as British ambassador in Constantinople.

When these two reached Zante, they had an unpleasant surprise. The knowledge that such riches were so near had driven the Greeks to a frenzy of frustration, and with the help of the Philhellenes they had overcome the scruples of the bankers in Zante, who had released the money. All of it was already in the hands of the unstable clique who claimed to be the government.

Mavrocordato was still President of the Senate, although it was nearly a year since he had fled from that perilous post, first to Hydra and then to Missalonghi. The President and Vice-President of the Executive, at that particular moment, were both Albanians, one from Hydra and the other from Spetsai. These two, Conduriottes and Botazi, were both said to be jovial and good-humoured men, but in public affairs they were ignorant and narrow partisans who did not even speak Greek with any fluency. Colocotrones and many other leaders of his kind were fiercely opposed to them, and the opposition flared up into fighting from time to time.

One of their first acts when they suddenly found they were incredibly rich was to buy back the town of Nauplia from Panos, one of the sons of Colocotrones, who had occupied it and successfully fought the government when they tried to enter it. This young man had recently married the daughter of Bouboulina, and his formidable mother-in-law was living in Nauplia too. There were always good stories told about Bouboulina, so improbable that they almost had to be true: she was said now to be spending her time, since there were no Turks to fight, in stealing brass guns from the fortresses and making counterfeit money with the help of an ex-employee of the Sultan's mint. After buying off this picturesque family, the government moved to the town, and for some time afterwards Nauplia was the nominal capital of Greece.

The government also bought for cash the allegiance of captains of armed bands from north of Corinth, men who had been armatoli under the Turkish regime, and they brought them into the Peloponnese to fight against Colocotrones. They captured him, and the great old brigand was imprisoned in a monastery on the island of Hydra, where he lived morosely predicting that Greece would soon need him again. But shortly after, the primates of the Peloponnese, intent on a share of the money, formed a military party and rose in a new rebellion. Thus there were four separate sets of armed bands roaming round the Peloponnese, vaguely controlled by the armatoli, the primates, the government and the sons and allies of Coloco-trones. They did little harm to each other; the enmity was between the leaders, not the soldiery, and when they met in battle there was a general mutual understanding that guns should be fired safely in the air. But all of them perforce had to live by plundering peasant families, and the poorest people suffered more from these other Greeks than they ever had from the Turks.

Directly and indirectly, this state of anarchy had been caused by the British gold, and the anarchy caused the gold to vanish quickly. What happened to it was best described by George Finlay, who was in Nauplia all the time, and as it inspired some of his most felicitous prose I cannot do better than quote him:*

'No inconsiderable amount was divided among the members of the legislative assembly, and among a large body of useless partisans, who were characterized as public officials. Every man of any consideration in his own imagination wanted to place himself at the head of a band of armed men, and hundreds of civilians paraded the streets of Nauplia with trains of kilted followers, like Scottish chieftains. Phanariots and doctors in medicine, who, in the month of April 1824, were clad in ragged coats, and who lived on scanty rations, threw off that patriotic chrysalis before summer was past, and emerged in all the splendour of brigand life, fluttering about in rich Albanian habiliments, refulgent with brilliant and unused arms, and followed by diminutive pipe-bearers and tall henchmen. The small stature, voluble tongues, turnspit legs, and Hebrew physiog-nomies of these Byzantine emigrants, excited the contempt, as much as their sudden and superfluous splendour awakened the envy, of the native Hellenes. Nauplia certainly offered a splendid spectacle to anyone who could forget that it was the capital of an impoverished nation struggling through starvation to establish its liberty . . .

'Military commands were distributed with a bountiful hand . . . Chiefs were allowed to enrol under their private banners upwards of thirty thousand men, and pay was actually issued for this number

*History of Greece, Vol. 6, p. 338 *et seq.*, published 1877.

of troops from the proceeds of the English loans. But over these troops the government exercised no direct control. No measure was taken even to verify the numbers of the men for whom pay and rations were furnished. Everything was left to the chiefs, who contracted to furnish a certain number of men for a certain amount of pay and a fixed number of daily rations . . .'

An age-old practice of armed forces grew in Greece to proportions that were laughable. Among all the chiefs, Finlay mentioned a few he happened to know: 'Katzaro, the captain of the bodyguard of Mavrocordato, drew fifty rations, and did duty with only seven armed followers; General Vlachopulos, who pretended to be the leader of four hundred soldiers, was said to be unable to muster more than about eighty. These abuses were universal. The veteran Anagnostaras marched against the enemy with only seventeen armed peasants, though he was paid by the Greek government to enrol seven hundred men. Ghoura subsequently drew twelve thousand rations, when he commanded only from three to four thousand men.

'The waste of money on the navy was even greater than on the army. Ill-equipped and dull-sailing vessels were hired to take their place in the Greek fleet, because their owners belonged to the faction of Conduriottes. Fire-ships were purchased and fitted out at unnecessary expense, because their proprietors wished to dispose of useless vessels. The sailors, who were spectators of the jobs of the primates and captains, became every month more insolent and disorderly . . .

'The illegal gains made by drawing pay and rations for troops who were never mustered, quite as much as the commissions of colonel given to apothecaries, and of captain to grooms and pipe-bearers, demoralized the military forces of Greece. The war with the Sultan seemed to be forgotten by the soldiers, who thought only of indulging in the luxury of embroidered dresses and splendid arms. This is the dominant passion of every military class in Turkey, whether Greeks, Albanians or Turks. The money poured into Greece by the loans suddenly created a demand for Albanian equipments.

The bazaars of Tripolitsa, Nauplia, Missalonghi, and Athens were filled with gold-embroidered jackets, gilded yataghans, and silver-mounted pistols. Tailors came flocking to Greece from Joannina and Saloniki. Sabres, pistols, and long guns, richly mounted, were constantly passing through the Ionian Islands . . . The complaint that Greece was in danger of being ruined by this extravagant expenditure was general, yet everybody seemed to do his utmost to increase the evil by spending as much money as possible in idle parade . . . It is not to be supposed that military anarchy was established without some opposition on the part of many patriotic Greeks. But its opponents were civilians, and men generally without either practical experience or local influence.'

So the money that escaped the frauds in London finished up as gold embroidery and decorative weapons, or was hidden in men's cartridge belts or under their mattresses, and none of it was honestly spent to defend the precarious freedom Greece had won. The committee's young commissioners could not do anything. They went to Nauplia, hung around the town for a while, found nobody who would take the slightest notice of them, both fell seriously ill and had to beg a passage out of the country in a British warship. Lytton Bulwer wrote afterwards, with perhaps a slight air of surprise: 'We (the British) have generally busied ourselves about the government of Greece, which was really no business of ours; while the management of our money, in which we might be thought concerned, has been left entirely in the hands of the Greeks.' General Gordon, who knew the Greeks much better, was more forthright. With perhaps one exception, he wrote, 'the members of the executive are no better than public robbers.' It was true, but once again it was a judgement by European standards, while Eastern standards were the only ones the Greeks so far had known. Finlay, who loved the Greeks but hated their leaders, saw the thing in rather better perspective. He knew that any ruler of any race in the middle east, being suddenly handed a fortune in actual coinage, would have used it in much the same way. He put the blame where it belonged, in England. 'Foreigners,' he wrote, 'were amazed at this display of financial insanity on the London Stock Exchange. Future years have proved that the disease returns in periodical fits, which can only be cured by copious bleeding.'

*

One man who unexpectedly suffered from the British loan was Byron's friend Trelawny. His story is a small side-issue, but it is worth re-telling.

In Missalonghi after Byron died, Trelawny laid claim to the guns and gunpowder in Parry's stores, and he carried them off to the hide-out of Odysseus in the cave on Mount Parnassus; so that was the end of the committee's arsenal. Parry went home, wrote a good book on Byron's last days, and drank himself to death. But a few of the Europeans in Missalonghi threw in their lot with Trelawny when their pay from Byron's money chest suddenly came to an end; and among them was a Scotsman called Robert Fenton. Trelawny's swashbuckling claims made Mavrocordato very angry, and the quarrels between them must have been a curious spectacle, the Greek in his rusty frock-coat and his glasses, and the Englishman dressed up in imitation of his brigand hero.

When Odysseus was in Athens or travelling in his domain, Trelawny was often left in charge of the cave, and here in the summer of 1824 this life-long romancer devised a setting which perfectly suited his taste. The cave was impregnable, 150 feet up a cliff, approached by a series of ladders and a trap-door and guarded by battlements, the committee's guns, half a dozen retainers and a ferocious dog. At the foot of the cliff, a larger guard of armed men was installed in a camp surrounded by walls, and Trelawny put Fenton in charge of them. Within the main cave, which made Trelawny think of cathedrals, smaller caves were walled off as separate dwellings and as stores for weapons, powder and shot enough to defend the place for years. It was stocked with all the necessities of life and some of the luxuries, and a permanent spring of ice-water flowed into a cistern. Here under his protection were the family of Odysseus and his treasures, the booty of many conquests.

And here, to complete the warped romantic picture, Trelawny, who was 32, married the brigand's half-sister Tersitza, who was twelve or thirteen.

The committee's powder and guns were the only profit Odysseus made from the charm he had exercised on Stanhope. When the money arrived, he went to Nauplia like everyone else to lay claim to a share of it. But the government so distrusted him that they would not even bribe him. On the contrary, they started to bribe his followers to leave him; and such was the power of the money that Odysseus, the ruler of most of eastern Greece, could soon muster only two or three hundred men. So he went to the Turks again, and renewed the truce he had made the year before.

Trelawny claimed afterwards that he argued against this truce, but he was certainly present at some of the parleys with the Turks, and the arguments he wrote in his memoirs seem rather in its favour. Odysseus believed, like Colocotrones, that he had a perfect right to rule his part of Greece because he had won it from the Turks and successfully held it against them; and it was certainly an arguable point that he had a better right than Mavrocordato or Conduriottes, who had never been in it at all. If the government, he said, seduced away his troops, he could not fight the Turks; so the only hope was to keep them away by a temporary truce. He believed that when the government had spent its money and the Turks attacked again, he would have to be recalled to fight them off. Perhaps the reasoning was muddled, but it seems to have been sincere.

But in the meantime, Odysseus was branded a traitor in the government's eyes, and Trelawny with him. And Trelawny's idyll was shattered when he and Fenton and another Englishman were at pistol practice on the terrace in front of the cave, and Fenton suddenly shot him twice in the back.

Immediately, one of the guards shot Fenton dead, so he never had a chance to say why he had done it. The other Englishman, who was described as a crack-brained young man, seems to have thought the cave was Fenton's by right, and Trelawny was an impostor.

Trelawny survived, by sitting in the cave without moving for forty days (so he said) before he let anyone touch him. There was probably only one man in Greece who could have saved him, and would have taken the trouble. That was Commodore Hamilton, who was still patrolling in his frigate and always heard of everything that happened. He managed to send an English doctor to the cave – presumably his own ship's surgeon – brought Trelawny down to the coast and took him, with Tersitza his infant wife, to Cephalonia. Trelawny recovered, but quarrelled with and parted from Tersitza.

Trelawny always believed that Fenton had been bribed by Mavrocordato to kill him, and so did many more trustworthy Philhellenes. It was and still is the likeliest explanation, and if it was true it was yet another use for the English gold.

And it was certainly Mavrocordato, or the government as a body, who had Odysseus pursued and seized and imprisoned in the Acropolis where he had ruled; and without much doubt their agents who strangled him there and threw the corpse off the top of a tower and down to the foot of the walls, and then tried to spread a story, which nobody for a moment believed, that he had fallen over while he was trying to escape.

*

Of course one wonders what Byron could have done if he had lived a little longer. He would have had the advantage over the new commissioners of controlling the money before the government got it, instead of trying to control it afterwards. That would have put him in a position of power, and also of danger. He might have been able to stop the worst of the civil war by cutting off the cash. But however carefully he doled it out, it is hard to see how he could have stopped it going into the pockets of the leaders and whatever men they thought they ought to bribe. Greed for the money was a violent passion; disposing of hundreds of thousands of sovereigns and dollars, he could not have trusted anyone in Greece to protect him. He might have retreated to Zante or Cephalonia, or accepted Trelawny's plan of moving around in a ship with a

British flag. If he had not, he could hardly have escaped being murdered and robbed, or at least made captive and held to ransom by one faction or another.

Perhaps he would have kept his own faith in the people of Greece, like Finlay and Hastings and a few other Philhellenes and honest Greeks who saw it all. But with his sense of justice, there was one thing he would certainly have done. He would have made sure, by some means or other, that the British public knew what had happened to its money, which nobody who survived him dared or was able to do until many years after.

It is a useless speculation like any other. But I conclude that the committee's besotted naïvety in sending cash to Greece condemned any man who really tried to control it to something near a certainty of death, not to mention failure. If that man had been Byron, he would have made sure that the truth about the money came out. That would have discredited the cause of Greece, but he would still have done it. He of all men would not have kept quiet and watched the next of the City's follies: the second and larger loan which was successfully floated when the first, in the course of rather less than a year, had been totally squandered.

That second loan was to be a thunderous scandal. But before it broke, Greece had suffered the worst disaster of all.

CHAPTER TEN

The Pasha of Egypt
July 1824—April 1826

Mehemet Ali : Ibrahim Pasha

All the leaders of Greece knew the threat that hung over them. So did the Philhellenes: Hastings wrote to Byron to warn him, and Trelawny told Odysseus. The Egyptians, who also were vassals of the Sultan, were arming for an invasion of Greece.

The ruler of Egypt was Mehemet Ali, and in his way he was the most remarkable man who comes into this story. He was not an Arab, he was yet another Albanian, and he had been a tobacconist in his native town until he was thirty. He first went to Egypt as a volunteer to fight for the Sultan against Napoleon, and it is recorded that after Napoleon's victory at Aboukir in 1799, Mehemet Ali was rescued from drowning in the sea by the gig of the British admiral Sir Sidney Smith. That gentlemanly act had important results. Six years later, by methods like those of his countryman Ali of Joannina, Mehemet Ali was chosen as Pasha of Egypt by the assembled sheiks and confirmed in his rule by the Sultan. And in 1807, when the British tried an expedition in Egypt, he was able to decorate an avenue in Cairo with the heads of British sailors on stakes.

Ali of Joannina had never fought against European troops, but Mehemet Ali had; and from the beginning of his career, unlike the Greeks or Turks, he recognized that European methods of war were more effective than any in the Moslem world. So he built up his army and navy with European instructors. A few were Philhellenes who had been disgusted with Greece and had gone to find a place where their services were welcome. The majority were French, and the most senior was a romantic colonel called Sève. He was one of the very few men who claimed to have fought both at Trafalgar and Waterloo, and in Egypt he became a Moslem and took the name of Suleiman Pasha. Under Mehemet Ali's despotic power, these men did what the Philhellenes had never succeeded in doing: they drilled the native army and navy into something like Napoleonic forces. With the army, by 1824, Mehemet Ali had extended his dominion to Mecca and Khartoum. His navy had scarcely been tested, but it looked much more efficient than the Sultan's. And to follow his history beyond the scope of this, in 1838 he so rivalled the Sultan himself in power that he brought the whole of Europe to the edge of war, some countries supporting him and others the Sultan.

Yet he was illiterate. He never learned to read or write, and only began to learn to speak Arabic when he was old. In 1824, when Egyptian forces were ready to fall upon Greece, the President of Greece and the Pasha of Egypt were both Albanians: the President of Greece did not speak Greek and the Pasha of Egypt did not speak Arabic. The habits of Albanians were repulsive, but one has to admit their success.

Early that year, it was common knowledge in Greece that new warships were being built for Mehemet Ali in Marseilles and that he was gathering transports in Alexandria. A little later there was news of his armies being ready to embark, and it was no secret that they were bound for Greece. The Philhellenes were greatly alarmed, but not the Greeks. In the euphoria of the English money and their victories the year before, they told themselves they had beaten the Turks and could beat the Egyptians too. And besides, they would not believe Mehemet Ali would really fight for the Sultan. They persuaded themselves he would fight for his own independence, rather than rob them of theirs.

But what they did not know and nobody knew was the price Mehemet Ali had extorted from the Sultan for his help. He had been promised at once the island of Crete, and if he succeeded in

beating the Greeks, Syria and Damascus were also to go to him as
Pasha, and the Peloponnese to his son Ibrahim. Ibrahim took after
his father, and there is not much doubt he expected from the
beginning to kill off the men of the Peloponnese and enslave the
women and children, and populate the country afresh with his Arab
followers.

With this irresistible prize before him, Ibrahim embarked in
Alexandria in July 1824, and swore he would not set foot ashore
again until he landed in the Peloponnese. He kept the oath, but it
took him seven months to cross the Mediterranean, and that long
delay was mainly to the credit of Admiral Miaoulis and the sailors
of Hydra and Spetsai.

*

Those islanders had been roused from their strikes and money-
making by two catastrophes. Two other islands, competitors with
them in privateering, had been suddenly sacked and destroyed by
the enemy. The victims were Psara and the little island of Kasos,
which lies off the east end of Crete. Both of them had fleets and had
made a habit of raiding the Turkish coast, and both had suffered
from over-confidence and neglected their own defences. Psara fell
to an enormous Turkish fleet which was said to have landed an
army of 8000 men; and Kasos, more ominously, to an Egyptian
fleet which carried an army of Albanians. The populations of both
were almost wiped out by slaughter and enslavement.

These seemed to be acts of revenge, and Hydra and Spetsai
feared their turns were coming next. They both hired troops from
the mainland to protect their homes, and sent their fleets to sea to
intercept whatever enemies were coming. They were too late to
rescue Psara or Kasos, but their ships were cruising off Turkey when
Ibrahim's enormous fleet came into sight.

It was a stroke of luck for the Greeks. If Ibrahim had sailed straight
to Greece there would have been nobody there to oppose him.
But he had gone to Turkey first to join up with the Sultan's fleet.
Between them, in the port of Bodrun on the Turkish mainland close

to the island of Kos, they assembled 85 warships: frigates, corvettes, armed schooners and brigs, and one ship of the line which wore the flag of the Turkish admiral. Under their protection was a convoy of nearly three hundred transports, which were said to be carrying twenty thousand soldiers and one thousand horses. Most of these transports were European merchantmen which had traded into Alexandria and had been chartered by Mehemet Ali, and they were still flying their national flags: Austrians, French, Italians, British ships from Malta and even one American. For sheer numbers of sail, so large a fleet had seldom been seen in any part of Europe.

Early in September, Miaoulis appeared off the port with seventy or eighty brigs, and the Turkish and Egyptian navies put to sea to meet him.

It must be admitted the battle that followed was a slightly ludicrous affair, but it was very gallant of the Greeks to offer battle at all. They were vastly outnumbered and outgunned. However, they still despised their enemy, and indeed that particular Turkish admiral had the reputation of always contriving some accident that kept him personally out of danger. This time, in the only battleship, he missed stays before the battle began and carried away his main topsail and topgallant yard, and prudently ran back to harbour for repairs. For a whole day the fleets cannonaded each other with a minimum of damage. As usual, the Greeks did not close within range of their pirate cannon, and it was said of the Turks that they never altered the elevation of their guns, so that when they fired a broadside to windward the shot went sky-high and when they fired to leeward it plunged straight into the sea. The Greeks still put their faith in fireships, although those were really only a weapon against a fleet at anchor. That day they used several, which burned without setting any of the enemy on fire. But they had an indirect effect. In their anxiety to avoid them, the Turks were always running aboard each other, and several were seen retiring from battle with broken jib booms and spars.

A few days later, an almost identical battle was fought in the same place. That time, the Greeks burned six of their fireships, and succeeded in blowing up a Turkish corvette and a 44-gun Tunisian frigate. From the frigate they captured an admiral, whom they killed.

On the whole, the fighting had gone against the Greeks, which was only to be expected. They had used a large proportion of their fireships and only destroyed a minute proportion of the enemy fleet. But they made Ibrahim change his plans. He had never fought a naval battle before, and he concluded it was too risky to take his convoy to sea against opposition. His troops were beginning to die of disease; so were the horses stabled in the transports. So he landed them at Bodrun and put to sea without them. The Turkish admiral went to Constantinople. About the end of September, the first of the winter gales scattered Egyptians as far as the islands of Naxos and Mykonos, where they landed and planted their flags without doing any damage. When they assembled again, Miaoulis was still dogging them with his brigs and a new supply of fireships. And their troops were still no nearer their destination.

For Miaoulis it was a great achievement, the more so because his fleet was still commanded by capricious independent captains, while Ibrahim's was perhaps the most strictly disciplined that ever put to sea. When his own flagship dragged its anchor off Rhodes, Ibrahim had his captain bastinadoed on his quarterdeck. Several others suffered that very unpleasant and ignominious fate for clumsy manoeuvres in battle. Eleven of them after one voyage were degraded from their commands for failing to keep to windward of the transports. One was strangled for abandoning his ship too soon when it was set on fire, and Ibrahim in person beat another to death with a cudgel for some fancied fault of seamanship. When captains were treated like that, no doubt the same ferocity or worse extended right down through the ranks.

Greek captains, on the other hand, were still only bound by the rules of medieval merchantmen and were proud to be free to carry out the admiral's orders if they liked them and if their crews approved, or to neglect them if they felt they knew better, or to depose the admiral and elect another. Ibrahim, to say the least, carried discipline too far. But if Miaoulis had had a hundredth part of the same authority, his task would have been easier and its result more certain. As it was, when winter began, his ships began to exercise their ancient right to go home. The Spetsiotes went first, and then the Hydriotes started to slip away, and in November he was left off Bodrun, beating about among the islands in heavy weather, with only twenty-five of his eighty sail.

Seeing him weakened, Ibrahim embarked all his troops again and made a bid to reach the safety of Crete. It was a desperate voyage. He could not maintain his army on the Turkish coast all winter, and his contract with the chartered transports had already been renewed. On the other hand, no navy of that era could have kept such a convoy together in winter weather. Miaoulis watched it come out, hundreds after hundreds of sail spreading from one horizon to the other. And he hung on to it, picked up a lagging transport here and there, and even made short-range attacks, for the first time in the war, on escorting frigates. He found the Egyptians were indeed much better seamen than the Turks, but were just as bad at gunnery. Between his threats and a series of northerly gales, the convoy was scattered. Part of it reached the lee of Crete, part put back to Turkey, some ships entirely disappeared and others ran for the coast of Syria. Eight transports went back to Alexandria, where Mehemet Ali had the captains nailed to the masts by their ears and sent them to sea again.

Miaoulis had done all he could. For almost four months, he had kept the sea. No seaman in those days expected comfort, but the small Greek ships, which were built and fitted for warm summer seas, must have been exceptionally bleak in winter. And probably he thought his success was final. Nobody he knew had ever fought in winter in the Aegean, and he believed the Egyptians would wait until the spring. So he came home. But after all his efforts, that was a fatal mistake. Ibrahim collected his fleet again, and in mid-winter, without any opposition, he took it to Suda Bay in Crete. He put the troops ashore again to recuperate and paid off the hired transports. And on February 24th 1825, when he was least expected, he approached the western coast of the Peloponnese and landed at the fortress of Modon. Without transports, he had brought a first contingent of the army in his warships, and he sent the ships back at once to fetch more from Crete. A month later, ten thousand Egyptian soldiers on foot and a thousand horse surrounded the town of Navarino.

*

It would be cruel to say this new turn in the war was good for the Greeks: it was the cause of misery. But it made them grow up as a nation and put an end to most of their clownish boasting. Against a new enemy more ruthless and efficient than the Turks, they found a strain of genuine bravery on land as they had at sea. Reading about them, they seem like a different people.

It began absurdly enough. The government which had been issuing pay and rations for thirty thousand troops discovered that less than a third of them really existed, but it did not have the power to complain. The President Conduriottes, like Mavrocordato two years before, appointed himself commander-in-chief. If possible, he was less qualified. He was large and fat, and in General Gordon's words 'averse to locomotion.' After a month's consideration, he decided it was his duty to take the field. He was hoisted on to a handsome Arab mare, richly caparisoned and led by six grooms; and followed by a train of secretaries, guards, pipe-bearers and advisers, including Mavrocordato, he departed from Nauplia to the salute of cannon from the ramparts, the fortress above and the ships in the harbour. But an eye-witness spoiled this picture by adding that he hung over the saddle like a sack of hay, and two of the grooms were there to hold him in place. He found the exercise trying, and the ride to Tripolitsa, which is forty miles, took him three days. A fortnight later he was still nowhere near the enemy, and he seemed to have repented of his boldness. He turned off the Navarino road and went to Kalamata, and took a ship back in comfort to Nauplia.

But farce was turning to tragedy. While the President was making his leisurely circular tour, several Greek armies did meet the Egyptians round Navarino. The Greeks built their little walls of stones and prepared to fight in the way they had always fought. But the Egyptians, taught by the French, advanced in Napoleonic ranks, fired in volleys on words of command and charged with bayonets, while their cavalry waited the moment to charge and complete the rout of the enemy. The Greeks could not contend with this text-book manoeuvre. Every time it happened, they scattered and ran and the cavalry caught them. In the years before against the Turks, when a dozen men had been hurt in a battle it could be called a second Marathon. But now they began to count their dead in hundreds, and soon in thousands.

People who knew their ancient history remembered an earlier fight at Navarino. It is described in some graphic chapters in Book Four of Thucydides. When the Athenians and Spartans were at war in 425 BC, there was fighting by land and sea in this district, and both sides observed that the key to the defence of the Bay of Navarino was the island of Sphacteria which shelters it from the open sea. Four hundred and twenty Spartans occupied the island, and the Athenians commanded by Demosthenes besieged it for 72 days by rowing round and round it in their triremes.

In 1825, for the same reason, just about the same number of Greeks were posted in Sphacteria, some soldiers and some sailors from the ships that were in the bay. Mavrocordato had one of his moments of genuine gallantry. He left the President's circus and hurried to Navarino. When he arrived he saw over fifty Egyptian warships in the offing, but he insisted on being rowed to the island. He was one man who certainly knew Thucydides, and he probably hoped to resist an equally famous siege.

But the Greeks were up against strength they could not resist. One day went by, while the Egyptian ships fought another long-range battle with Miaoulis, who had come up astern of them. On the next, both fleets were becalmed. The Egyptians turned their guns on the island and sent scores of boats ashore under cover of the smoke. The defence lasted not for 72 days, but about that number of minutes. Half the Greeks were killed and half were captured. An off-shore breeze came up and the Greek ships in the bay made their escape, all except one which waited for its captain who had gone to fight ashore. Mavrocordato and three or four other survivors rowed out to this solitary ship, a brig of 18 guns. They told the crew their captain was dead, and the crew cut their cable and prepared to run the gauntlet of the whole of the enemy fleet. They succeeded. The breeze fell light, and the brig was under fire from dozens of enemy ships for the whole of the six remaining hours of daylight. But she had no crippling damage, and that was a measure of the state of naval gunnery in this war.

No European who knew Mavrocordato and wrote about him afterwards could resist making fun of him, even when he did something really brave. 'During six hours of mortal agony,' Colonel Gordon wrote, 'Mavrocordato sat in the cabin, holding a pistol, which might save him the ignominy of being sent in bonds to Constantinople: he uttered no word, except now and then a sentence expressive of the vanity of ambition, and a resolution, if he survived, to retire to private life; a sentiment as fleeting as the peril.'

A week later, Navarino surrendered. Ibrahim offered the Greeks the same terms they had offered the Turks in the same town: they had to give up their arms, and ships would take them away and land them on a friendly shore. Perhaps the Greeks marched down to the harbour with apprehension, remembering their own broken promise and the massacre they had committed there. But Ibrahim kept his word.

That was in May. In that summer of 1825, more and more Greeks sallied out against the new enemy, and all were defeated. There was an outcry to bring back Colocotrones, and he was released, as he had predicted, from his captivity in Hydra and made Commander-in-Chief again. But his old guerilla tactics and strategy were as useless as everyone else's. The Greek forces dwindled into the scattered bands lurking in mountain hide-outs that they had been before the war began. Ibrahim's army marched all over the western Peloponnese, devastating the country and burning the villages when and where it wished. Worst of all, it was widely believed the Egyptians were cutting down the olive trees which were an almost sacred symbol of the stability of peasant life. It may not have been true, but the belief was enough. Nothing else could so clearly have told the Greeks the alternatives they were offered, to submit or starve.

Before the end of June, Ibrahim had captured Argos and was in sight of Nauplia, where the government was cowering. In person he observed the town from the opposite side of the gulf; and he certainly saw, among the small Greek brigs that were clustered in the anchorage, two frigates and a sloop that were flying the British flag. It was Commodore Hamilton again. He had heard, as he always did, that a crisis was coming, sailed in with what ships he could muster, and landed with some of his officers in the beleaguered town. He had a private conference with the government, and he moored his ships in positions that made the Greeks and Egyptians believe he was going to help the defence. And he started a rumour – or at least he allowed it to spread – that in case of attack the Greeks were authorized to hoist the British flag and put their country under British protection.

It could not have been true: he had no authority to say it, or to fight the Egyptians. But neither had Ibrahim authority to fight the British: the countries were not at war. It was all a tremendous bluff, and also a tremendous risk. But he brought it off. Ibrahim, whether he believed the rumour or not, drew back his victorious army and left Nauplia to breathe again. And Hamilton sailed away.

Nobody knows what Hamilton said to the government. The idea of hoisting the British flag could only have been a ruse to save the Greeks in a desperate situation. But they seem to have seized the idea as a permanent way out of all their difficulties. In July, they met in secret session. It was a meeting of despair. They drafted a new act, and immediately passed it into law. After a long preamble, there was only a single operative clause: 'In virtue of the present Act, the Greek Nation places the sacred deposit of its liberty, independence, and political existence under the absolute protection of Great Britain.'

This forlorn, naïve submission was signed by the Vice-President and members of the Executive, by Mavrocordato and members of the Senate, and by the bishops and most of the prominent people of Nauplia. It was the nearest they had ever come to unanimity, and the President himself refused to sign it only because it was signed by so many of his rivals. Demetrius Miaoulis the eldest son of the admiral was sent in a ship of his own to London to present the plea to the Foreign Office. But the Foreign Office, so to speak, smiled benignly and shrugged its shoulders. No European power yet had recognized the political existence or the independence of Greece. They could not protect a freedom that did not officially exist.

*

The Egyptians confined themselves to the Peloponnese, the country the Sultan had promised to Ibrahim. North of the Gulf of Corinth, Turkish armies were on the march again that summer. Their pashas were less energetic than Ibrahim, but in one way they were more successful. In the Peloponnese, nobody of any consequence tried to make peace with the Egyptians, but farther north most of the local captains came to terms with the Turks and accepted some kind of command under their regime. Up there, in the country that had been Ali Pasha's, the idea of loyalty to Greece had not made much impression. The only freedom people understood or wanted was the freedom to plant their crops and herd their goats without being ravaged too often by rival armies.

The exception was Missalonghi. On the very day when Navarino fell, a Turkish army appeared again outside the wall of that miserable town, and it found itself besieged for the second time.

The second siege of Missalonghi was quite different from the first. In fact, it was not like any other episode in the war. It lasted a whole year, and the people of the town agreed they would rather die than surrender.

I must admit this is a mystery to me. I cannot imagine either how or why twelve thousand people could make a decision like that and stick to it while their companions were slaughtered and their families starved and their town was reduced to rubble. They had no inspiring leader, no orator to rouse them. Their military plans were made by a council of nine minor captains, and civil affairs were run by a municipal committee. They cannot have had any special love for the town. It had no history, no beauty, no symbolic value, and by that time no strategic importance. For two thirds of them, it was not even home. They had no reason to think that defending it to the death would do any worthwhile good to their country or their countrymen. Yet that is what they did.

Historians of the nineteenth century were content with such words as heroism and love of liberty to explain this kind of deed. 'Even after the lapse of seventy years,' one of them wrote in 1897, 'it is impossible to read the account of the heroic defence of the town, and of its terrible fate, without emotion.' Heroism, I feel, is only a semantic explanation, but I cannot do much better. Perhaps it was not exactly a deliberate decision, but something like the communal stubbornness of London and most other towns that were bombed in the second world war. Whatever the reason, these are the facts.

When the siege began, the town was much better equipped for defence than it had been the time before. The five foot mud wall on the landward side had been built up to three times the height and faced with stone, and about fifty guns were installed on it. The other three sides were still defended, as ever, by mud and water. There was plenty of powder and shot, and food enough for the summer. Of the twelve thousand people inside the wall, four or five thousand were the original inhabitants. The rest were men the captains had brought with them, and refugees who had drifted in because life in the surrounding countryside was too precarious for farming.

They began with the confidence of the earlier siege, when they had outwitted the Turks in trickery. But this time, trickery was not among the weapons that were used. It was evident the Turkish Pasha had different orders from Constantinople – not to try to talk the place into a more or less willing submission, but to take it by force or suffer the fatal displeasure of the Sultan. And he began not by building barracks but by digging trenches to approach the wall, setting up batteries to breach it, and making fascines to fill the defenders' ditches – all the conventional preparations for an active attack.

The busy digging went on most of the summer, covered by an artillery bombardment better aimed than before, which ruined most of the town but injured few of the people, who lived and slept in cellars, dug-outs and ditches. The first serious attack was not made until August, when the Turks exploded a mine under one of the batteries on the wall and rushed the breach in such numbers that twenty of their standards were planted inside the defences. The Greeks fought back with new ferocity and drove them out again. And soon after, they counter-attacked: a thousand of them sallied out at night, armed only with swords and knives, and assaulted the Turks in their trenches and batteries. Everything had changed since the other siege, when the Greeks had been happy shouting insults and firing scrap-iron at the enemy, and had thought there was no need to keep watch at night. For better or worse, it had become a real war.

Both sides were being supplied by ships, and their fortunes depended on which of the fleets had the upper hand beyond the marshes in the Ionian Sea. And that depended largely on whether the government or anyone else could raise the money to pay the sailors of Hydra and Spetsai. Miaoulis and perhaps a dozen un-mercenary captains were at sea nearly all the time, but the rest still refused to leave harbour without a month's pay in advance; and after all, one cannot entirely blame them – no doubt most of them had families, and families have to eat. The government tried to raise money by offering land for sale, but that was a failure: nobody believed the government had any valid title to the land. So they organized collections in Nauplia. It became a patriotic fashion to subscribe, and even those whose greed outweighed their patriotism were forced by public opinion to disgorge a few sovereigns from the private hoards they had saved from the British loan. By these precarious means, Miaoulis was sometimes given enough ships to fight a battle. But it was a week's voyage, more or less, from Hydra to the Ionian Sea, and the sailors made sure of being back at Hydra when the month was up. So on each voyage, they were only about a fortnight on duty off Missalonghi.

However, when there were enough ships they always got the better of the Turks, who retreated beyond the forts that guarded the Gulf of Corinth and left the Greeks free to send boats ashore with supplies for Missalonghi. And in the early autumn, Miaoulis won a notable moral victory. The whole of the Turkish fleet came out of the Gulf. The Turks had improved their tactics, and they formed the line ahead that all other navies had used in battle for centuries. Miaoulis got to windward of it and engaged it in the middle of the Ionian Sea. The line was a brave display, and proof against the gunnery of the Greeks. But Miaoulis sent three fireships straight at the Turkish admiral's flagship. Bearing down from windward, they could outsail the Turkish line and in theory, given the courage, their crews could overhaul the flagship, grapple her, light their fuses and escape in boats. Against any other navy they would have been shot to pieces, and even against the Turks it was a gallant gesture. The effect was dramatic. The admiral set all sail, broke out of his own line and bore away to the southward to escape. All the rest of the fleet abandoned its warlike formation and fled after him, and they did not bring up again until they came to Alexandria, where the admiral claimed a victory on the rather flimsy ground that none of his ships had been lost. Perhaps it was true he had meant to go there anyway, for the next thing he did was to join Mehemet Ali's fleet and bring reinforcements up to Navarino. But the Greeks were left rejoicing.

That admiral took the news to Alexandria that the siege was going slowly, and a few weeks later Ibrahim was ordered to help the Turks at Missalonghi. In mid-winter he left Navarino by land, marched across the mountains to Patras burning towns and villages as he went, and crossed the narrows of the Gulf of Corinth with a formidable army.

Ibrahim is said to have laughed at the Turkish Pasha when he saw the feeble wall of Missalonghi. But by then, not only the wall was keeping the Turks at bay; so was the mud. Fierce fighting was still going on, but every movement on either side was clogged with mud. For Ibrahim's army, it was hard enough even to reach the place. It landed at the village called Krioneri, which stands where the mountains of Acarnania rise above the plain. From there to Missalonghi is twelve miles, skirting the marsh and crossing the river Evinos, which of course was in flood. There was no road, and Ibrahim had brought no transport across with him. Everything, the food, the guns, the powder, shot and shell, had to be carried by soldiers through the slough: long lines of them were seen, each trying to balance a cannon ball on his head. Born and bred in an arid climate, they suffered acutely from the cold and wet, and before they began to fight, a convoy went back to Navarino packed with invalids.

And when they were ready, after six weeks of labour, they made no more impression on Missalonghi than the Turks alone. Both armies together bombarded the place for three days, firing precisely nine round shot, twelve bombs and three howitzer shells every quarter of an hour. The remains of the houses were blown into smaller fragments but the people crouched in their dug-outs still survived. Then the infantry stormed the wall again, urged on by Ibrahim in person. But the result was the same as it had been for the past ten months. The Greeks with their new-found skill repulsed the attack and carried the battle back to the Turkish trenches.

That was the last attack that was ever made on the wall of Missalonghi. But Ibrahim had an idea that nobody else had ever seriously thought about: to attack through the marsh. In the spring of 1826, a new and uniquely macabre kind of war began, fought mainly by men who were floundering up to the waist in the evil bog. Ibrahim collected a fleet of local punts, and had five rafts built at Patras. The rafts were towed across by a paddle steamer, the first that had ever been seen in Greece: she was a Margate packet Mehemet Ali's agents had bought in London. Each raft was armed with a 36-pounder gun, and each punt was crammed with thirty musketeers.

There are several islands in the marshes, distinguished by being solid enough to put a building on. Some round about Missalonghi had small garrisons on them, whose job was to keep an eye on the boat-channels into the town. The most important was Vasiladi, which had a small fort or blockhouse with a dozen guns to guard the main channel from the sea. The man in charge was an elderly Italian artillery captain, and his men were a gang of local fishermen. So far, it had been an easy post. The island was out of range from the solid shore and from the open sea, and nobody had troubled it.

One afternoon in early March, the men of the garrison saw the rafts. They were being towed or poled very slowly along the channel. That evening, they bombarded Vasiladi for several hours. The garrison fired back as well as they could, but the rafts were not much of a target and their nerves were badly shaken. Early next morning, they saw the fleet of punts approaching, crammed with men. They were a sitting target for grape-shot, and the slaughter was great. But there were so many they could not stop them all: some reached the island and grounded in the mud, and the Egyptians jumped overboard and struggled ashore. The garrison fled in boats of their own, leaving only the Italian commander. Without a boat, he waded into the mud, and he floundered through it all the way to Missalonghi, where he crawled out, four or five hours afterwards, more dead than alive.

Ibrahim expected to capture the fortified islands one by one, and he had a second costly success a few days later. But towards the end of March, Missalonghi had its most gruesome day when he tried to take the convent of the Holy Trinity, a solitary tower which stood on a mud-bank of its own half a mile from the town. The rafts bombarded it, and the soldiers came in their punts and also waded out from the shore. They tore down a palisade that surrounded the island but they could not get into the tower, and the Greeks inside it mowed them down with grape and musketry.

Seeing them fail, Ibrahim seems to have suffered one of those fits of furious obstinacy that sometimes overwhelm a military mind. He sent out more and more men to struggle through the swamp, to do what the first had shown was impossible. They could not drag themselves out of the mud in face of the guns in the tower. Towards the evening, they gave up trying, and simply stood waiting, seeing death ahead of them and Ibrahim behind. When darkness fell he admitted the failure by sounding a retreat, and the garrison sallied out to take what booty they could find. It was said a thousand bodies were floating in that fetid water, but that was a figure of speech – who counted them? A possibly more exact idea of the suffering round this utterly unimportant island was given by the trophy the Greeks erected: not of heads, but, so they claimed, of 1200 European muskets.

In spite of that defeat, the Egyptians controlled the marsh, and Missalonghi was cut off from the sea. For a week or two more, there remained one secret creek as the last connection with the world outside. Hidden by reeds, it led to the bay of Petala, which is on the west coast thirty miles away. They used canoes in it to bring in a little food, but not nearly enough for the town. It was said they used divers in it too, but the report did not say what they did; perhaps, in the stretches of open water, they revived the stratagem of the Spartans in Sphacteria, who were relieved by men who swam under water towing bladders with grain in them. They also sent out a despairing letter that way, and it reached Miaoulis at his station off shore. He resolved to fight his way in past Vasiladi. But the Turks discovered the creek before he could answer, and in face of starvation the Missalonghiotes knew they could not survive.

They still refused to surrender. All the time, the Turks and then the Egyptians had offered them terms and promised to spare their lives, and the offer was still open. Perhaps the defenders did not believe the promise, but if so they undervalued their enemies: the Greeks themselves had always broken such promises, but the Turks and Egyptians had always kept them.

Whatever the reason, they decided to fight their way out: three thousand men under arms to clear a way, and some five or six thousand women and children and other non-combatants who would follow behind. It is said they all agreed in the decision, but not all of them could go: there were people too old, or too sick, or too badly wounded to move, and there were some who refused to leave their homes. So families were divided. Many who might have gone elected to stay behind with their friends or relations.

On the evening of 22 April, three years under a day since the siege began, word was sent round the town that this was the night. Women put on men's clothes and armed themselves, and weapons were given to children big enough to pull a trigger or hold a knife. Precarious bridges of planks were laid over the ditches, and thousands of people crossed them in silence and lay down in the dark outside the wall. The moon rose and somebody shouted an order, and they rushed forward away from the town and towards the enemy's camp. But among the townspeople themselves there was a sudden confusion and panic, and while some were still crossing the bridges others tried to fight their way back again.

A Bulgarian deserter, it was said afterwards, warned Ibrahim what had been planned. His whole army was deployed and ready, the trenches occupied and the cavalry mounted behind them. Only statistics remain to describe the despair on the sodden plain that night, the families pursued and sabred by horsemen, the women who carried their babies, the children lagging and lost; or in the town, when the Moslems sacked it and groups of Greeks blew themselves up in the powder magazines rather than wait for the slaughter. Ibrahim claimed three thousand heads; six hundred starved in the mountains; three or four thousand women and children were enslaved, but Philhellenic funds bought back the freedom of some. About 1800 escaped to safety, but only two hundred were women.

CHAPTER ELEVEN

The Steamship
February 1825—December 1826

Captain Lord Cochrane · Stratford Canning
Dr Samuel Gridley Howe · Colonel Charles Fabvier

During that year of 1825, when Missalonghi was fighting for life and the Peloponnese was grieving for its new enslavement, events of a different calibre occurred in England and America. In February, at exactly the time when Ibrahim landed in the Peloponnese, the second loan for Greece was opened on the London Stock Exchange.

This second loan was not organized by the London Committee: on the contrary, they were carefully excluded from it, and it served them right. In the course of the blackmailing quarrel between the Committee and the two Greek deputies, the Committee wrote formally to the Greek government to complain about the deputies' behaviour and to say that no further loan would be possible in England unless they were dismissed. Bowring then went to Paris and made a contract with a French banker to float a loan in France, for which he certainly expected another huge commission. When he came back, the deputies thanked him and said he was too late. They had learned how it was done, and they themselves had arranged an exclusive loan in London.

So the second loan, which realised nearly a million pounds, was entirely in the hands of the two deputies. The Committee faded away; it stopped its regular meetings and took no more active part in Greek affairs, though some individual members of it helped to spend the money. As a beginning, they and the deputies spent over £100,000 of the new loan to buy up bonds of the old one in the hope of pushing the price up and selling at a profit. And a sum which was never disclosed but was probably even larger vanished for ever in even simpler swindles.

It was nearly a year before the bondholders woke up and began to demand an enquiry. In the files of *The Times* for 1826 there are dozens of letters, of a length and pomposity that would be inconceivable nowadays, in which the deputies and the committee members hurled furious accusations at each other. William Cobbett, the scourge of knaves and fools, took up the cause in the astonishing weekly *Register* that he wrote and printed and published year after year; and here among the original instalments of his Rural Rides are his involved, repetitive, sarcastic commentaries on 'that theatre of Westminster Rump humbug, the Crown and Anchor Tavern in the Strand.' Leigh Hunt's *Examiner*, which had invented so many Greek victories in the past, entered the battle against him; cartoonists drew slanderous pictures and satirists wrote verses. For two or three months, the British public must have delighted in the series of revelations. Bowring and Hume and a good many other financiers were plainly shown up as rogues, and it was perhaps even more entertaining that the Benthamites and do-gooders on the committee were made to seem gullible and stupid. Several commissions of investigation were appointed, and Bowring had the nerve to get himself appointed secretary of one and a member of the others, so it is not surprising that none of them made any headway. And then suddenly, everyone grew bored with it all. The subject was dropped in the papers and nobody was prosecuted. But everyone knew what had happened. Shrewd men in Nauplia had embezzled small fortunes, but shrewder men with less excuse in London had embezzled large ones.

It was forgotten, but it was far from the end of the story of money-making at the expense of Greece. There was still quite a lot to spend. This time, very little was sent to Greece in cash. The government had a better plan: it had begun at last to listen to Frank Hastings. That patient Philhellene was still arguing that the only place to defend the freedom of Greece was on the sea. Since the

Egyptian invasion, the failures on land and the successes of Miaoulis had gone some way to prove that he was right. And when the second loan was launched, he was on the spot in London armed at last with a letter from the government to the deputies which proposed they should spend some money on a steamship. The deputies released £10,000. But it was not given to Hastings, it was given to a member of the committee named Elliss. Elliss, with no sense of urgency, put the money into his own account and ordered a ship to be built at Deptford on the Thames. Its machinery was a separate contract, given to a London engineer called Alexander Galloway. Hastings agreed to supply its guns at his own expense, and the ship was named in advance the *Perseverance*. That was the quality Hastings had needed all the time and he needed it still, for he had to wait a year in England before she was ready for sea.

Once they had grasped the idea of building a navy, the Greeks went at it with enthusiasm, but without discretion. Their next decision was to build two frigates. The British government would not have allowed a warship, as opposed to a harmless steamer, to be built in England, and the frigates were therefore ordered in America. As their agent to supervise the building, the deputies made the unusual choice of a French cavalry officer who, so far as anyone could discover, knew nothing either of ships, finance or America.

Next, they decided they needed an admiral. It seems bad luck on Miaoulis who had done so well, but they were setting their sights much higher. Their choice fell on the most famous, eccentric, flamboyant maverick of the age at sea, Captain Lord Cochrane, heir of the Earl of Dundonald.

Cochrane in every way was a man who seems larger than life – in his massive figure, red hair and ponderous features, and also in his astonishing exploits at sea and his sordid quarrels ashore. He was fifty when he offered to go to Greece: when he was in his twenties, before Trafalgar, he had won a tremendous reputation as a frigate captain and made a naval record in prize-money: he sailed in to Plymouth after a three months' cruise with three silver candlesticks lashed to his mastheads and a personal claim for £75,000. He also

achieved a particular kind of fame because one of his midshipmen was
Frederick Marryat, and Cochrane was the prototype of the infallibly
heroic captains of Marryat's novels who inspired the later generations of Victorian seamen. But at the same time he offended his
seniors by chronic lack of respect, and by forcing a court-martial of
his commander-in-chief, and perhaps most of all by becoming a
Radical member of parliament – which almost anyone could do in
those days if he could afford to bribe enough voters. His business in
parliament was to attack the corruption of the navy; as he was still
a serving officer it made him a national figure, immensely popular
with the mobs around Westminster and immensely unpopular with
the Admiralty. Both his careers, in the navy and in politics, came to
a sudden end in the year before Waterloo. A courier landed at Dover
and breathlessly posted to London with news that Napoleon was
beaten; shares rocketed up on the Stock Exchange, and Cochrane
was one man who sold out at a profit before the hoax was discovered.
Rightly or wrongly, he was charged with being a party to the plot,
convicted, sent to prison, dismissed from the navy and expelled
from the House of Commons. He escaped from prison and marched
into the House again shouting that his trial had been rigged, and he
had to be carried out by force.

By the time he had served his sentence the war was over and he
left England, morbidly convinced of a plot to persecute him. For
the next ten years he was an admiral in South America, commander-
in-chief of the navy of Chile, then of Peru and finally of Brazil.
For each of them he did legendary deeds at sea, and sometimes on
shore, against the Spaniards and Portuguese. But he also quarrelled
with each of them, mainly over money. In 1825 he turned up in
Portsmouth in a Brazilian frigate, requested a salute of guns from
the harbour captain, left the frigate there and went home to Scotland.
He said the Brazilians owed him a hundred thousand pounds, and he
was welcomed home as a hero.

All this was done in defiance of British law: the Foreign Enlistment Act prohibited British officers from serving foreign powers.
The government turned a blind eye when people did it from

conviction, but Cochrane was a mercenary; he often talked about fighting for freedom, but he fought strictly for cash. Although he laughed at laws he was liable to be put in prison again; so he had every reason to listen when he heard the Greeks had need of an admiral, and had plenty of money.

Cochrane was one of those splendidly confident men who set such an astronomical value on their own ability that their clients are shocked into paying whatever they ask. The fee he demanded from Greece was £57,000, a respectable fortune by anyone's standards and a perfectly outrageous amount to ask from a starving country. £30,000 was payable in advance and the rest, he insisted, must be put in a trust account at once and handed over when Greek independence was won. Apart from that, he wanted £97,000 for an expense account, and he claimed a right to all the prize money the navy might win under his command, the proceeds of the sale of any ships they captured. The fleet he required was also grandiose. He agreed with Hastings' ideas and told the deputies to order five more steamers with 68-pounder guns. He needed two yachts for himself and his staff, and two old ships of the line with the upper decks cut down and extra heavy guns mounted on the lower decks. He would also take under command the two new frigates and whatever useful ships the Greeks already possessed. With these forces, he said he would rout the enemy navies and burn Constantinople.

His fee alone was just about the entire national revenue of Greece for a year – a revenue which had already been pledged for payment of interest on the first of the loans. But the deputies, dazed into submission, agreed with everything. The £30,000 was paid, the £27,000 was put irrevocably into trust, the yachts were bought and five more steamers were ordered on the Thames at a price half as much again as Hastings' modest design, with five more sets of machinery from Alexander Galloway. Delivery of them was promised within three months, to coincide with the date, November 1825, when the frigates would be ready in America. The only part of the plan they seem not to have started was the two old battleships.

The furore over Cochrane's appointment alarmed the British government, which decided to prosecute him, for this was the fourth time he had defied the Foreign Enlistment Act. He rushed off to Brussels to avoid arrest, and waited there for his fleet to be provided.

Then everything started to go wrong. The three months' delivery date had been only a salesman's story: after six months nothing was anywhere near being ready. Galloway in particular scarcely seemed to be trying, and Cochrane came back in disguise from Brussels to see him. He confessed he was also working for Mehemet Ali. Indeed, his son was in Egypt with a new engine for the Pasha's Margate packet, and was hoping for a well-paid permanent job. Galloway was afraid to offend the Pasha by doing too much for the Greeks.

And worse news came from America. The French cavalry man had made an appalling muddle. The deputies had agreed to spend $500,000 on the frigates, which should have been enough. But he had chosen a firm of bankers who professed to be Philhellenes, and had given them the impression that speed was important and money was no object. They gave the same message to two shipbuilders in New York and told them to go ahead on a 'cost-plus' basis. The bankers themselves expected commission of 10% of the cost of the ships. So it was in everyone's interest to spend as much money as possible, and another separate swindle grew like a snowball. It was a shipbuilder's dream. The ships were designed for 64 guns, the largest that could possibly be classed as frigates. The most expensive materials were used, and the fittings were the last word in naval elegance. In November, when the ships were due to be finished, the deputies were told there were four more months of work to be done, and the cost was already $750,000. When they tried to protest, they were also told the whole project was illegal and if they did not pay up the ships were liable to be seized by the United States government.

This was the crisis: the deputies had met their match. There was simply not enough money left in the fund to finish the frigates. Something had to be cancelled to cut the losses. If it had been the steamships, Cochrane would have resigned, so it had to be a frigate. Other Americans, ashamed of what had happened, persuaded their government not to foreclose but to take over one of the unfinished ships at a price that was not much more than half what it had already cost. That brought in just enough cash to finish the other, and in November 1826 the Greeks took possession of her: one resplendent ship, a year overdue, which had cost about £200,000 – a price that in honest and competent hands could have bought a whole fleet of the kind of ships they really needed. They named her the Hellas.

What then had the Greeks to show for their million pounds? One admiral, who could not come to England for fear of arrest and would not go to Greece without his fleet; two yachts, one frigate, and five steamers in various states of unreadiness. Of these, two ultimately made the voyage to Greece, but too late to take part in the war; for the other three, Galloway never finished the engines, and the hulls were left to rot away in the Thames.

And they also had the *Perseverance*. She had cost £10,000 out of the million, and in the early autumn of 1826, eighteen months after the loan was opened, she was the only product of it that had arrived in Greece.

*

Hastings and Cochrane represent the extremes of the Europeans who purported to fight for the Greeks: Cochrane who agreed to do it for an exorbitant fee, and Hastings who did it year after year for nothing, and spent his own modest fortune on it simply because he thought the Greeks were worth it. And the difference showed in their eagerness to get there. Cochrane spent more than a year living on board the yachts the Greeks had bought him, first in Ireland and then in Italy and the south of France. But the moment the *Perseverance* had got up steam in the Thames, Hastings manned her with a few of his friends as officers and a transit crew who were mostly British, and he took her out of the estuary, down the Channel and across the Bay of Biscay. When he was clear of England, he changed her name and her flag. *Perseverance* had been a pseudonym, adopted in case the British authorities made a fuss about a ship being built for a country they did not recognize. Henceforth she had a Greek name, *Karteria*, and she wore the flag of Greece. For the same reason, she sailed unarmed. The great guns he had bought had been shipped in advance to America, to be forwarded to Greece from there.

The voyage itself was a novel adventure. Not many steamers in 1826 had been so far, and whoever had taken Mehemet Ali's packet to Egypt deserved a place in the history of the sea. The American *Savannah* had crossed the Atlantic in 1819, and Cochrane himself had taken a steamer to the Pacific, the first that ever went there. But both those had retractable paddles that were stowed on deck, and they made nine tenths of their voyages under sail. The year before, in 1825, the British *Enterprise* had reached Calcutta using steam for two thirds of the way, but that was a record unbeaten for many years.

And no ship built of iron had ever been thoroughly tested in the open sea. From the very beginning, Hastings had wanted an iron ship because he reasoned it was less likely to be crippled in battle, or to catch fire – either from enemy shells or from accidents with the red-hot shot he meant to use. But the novelty of it would have daunted most men. The first recorded ship of iron, apart from barges on canals, was only completed in 1820: she was wrought in sections in a Staffordshire ironworks and put together in London, and was used on the cross-channel run. If the *Karteria*'s engine broke down in the Bay of Biscay she could sail; but if her plates cracked or her rivets burst she would sink, and there was no past experience to go on; only faith.

As for Hastings' intention to fight in his steamer, most naval opinion at the time would have been appalled or derisive. The British Admiralty in the past five years had used a few tugs to tow ships out of harbour in contrary winds, but that was the only use they would admit for the new invention. Two years after Hastings' expedition, in 1828, the First Lord of the Admiralty, Lord Melville, made his memorable statement that 'their Lordships feel it their bounden duty to discourage to the utmost of their ability the use of steam vessels, because they consider the introduction of Steam is calculated to strike a fatal blow at the supremacy of the Empire.'

Steaming down Channel in May 1826, Hastings had therefore set himself an adventure nobody else had even begun to attempt. After four solid years of trying, he had exactly the ship he wanted, and he was about to test the tactical theories he thought might revolutionize war at sea. He was still only just over thirty: young enough to enjoy the excitement of it.

The *Karteria* was rigged as a four-masted schooner, with a long ungainly bowsprit and an immense but spindly funnel as tall as the mainmast. Her engine, at that date, must have been a sighing monster that turned incredibly slowly – sixteen revolutions a minute was a usual figure. For her time, she was very successful. Design of engines and boilers then was empirical, and nobody could be sure a new ship would raise enough steam to make any headway until she ran her trials. The *Karteria* did; but that is not to say she was free of trouble. In the Mediterranean, her boiler burst, which was a common mishap, if not a disaster, when boilers were made of riveted iron. Hastings put in to Sardinia, and fretted there for three months while people hammered at it in the engine room. It was September before the triumphant day when he steamed up the Gulf of Argos. He anchored off Nauplia in the middle of the night, but the thrashing of his paddles woke the town and thousands of people came down to the harbour to celebrate. The Greeks were as proud as he was to have a steamship, and the expectations of some were even higher: one peasant in from the country swore he had seen the ship start its engine and fly to the top of the fort of Palamedes – which after all was not much harder to believe than the miracle of moving against the wind.

But when Hastings went ashore and asked where his guns were nobody knew. They had disappeared in America.

*

For all he had known on his voyage, the Greeks might already have lost the war. They were very near it. After the fall of Missalonghi the whole of the country north of the Gulf of Corinth had gone back to Turkish rule. Turkish armies had marched towards Athens again, and just before Hastings arrived the town had fallen and the Acropolis was besieged again, this time with Greeks inside and Turks without. The Egyptians possessed nine tenths of the Peloponnese. The only part of Greece that could call itself free was Argolis, the peninsula to the east of Nauplia, some fifty miles long and twenty wide, and the islands which border it, Hydra and Spetsai in the south and Poros, Egina and Salamis in the east. Most of the other Aegean islands were still free of invaders, but they had little connection with the rest of Greece and subsisted in their poverty alone. The government moved from place to place in this shrivelling domain. Sometimes it was in Nauplia, which was within a day's march of Ibrahim's outposts, sometimes in Salamis which was even closer to the Turks, and sometimes in Egina. The peasants were in the depths of destitution and the towns were often ravaged again by plagues.

A great many local captains had given up altogether, yet none of the prominent leaders had deserted. Colocotrones was still at large, and Petrobey was secure in his mountains of Maina. It was more remarkable, and more admirable, that Mavrocordato and Hypsilantes and most of the men who had come with them to Greece were still there after five years of it, although they might easily have left the country on any excuse and lived in safety and comfort somewhere else.

But they had lost all hope of complete independence and freedom. In the winter of 1825, the British appointed a new ambassador to the Sultan's court, Stratford Canning. On his way to take up the post, in a British man-of-war, he put in to the sound between Hydra and the mainland, and Mavrocordato went out to meet him there. Canning told him the British could not guarantee the freedom of Greece, as the Greeks had requested, but he had instructions to mediate with the Sultan. The Greeks, he believed, would have to acknowledge the Sultan's supremacy; if they did, they might get in return some kind of autonomy. Mavrocordato accepted that advice.

Just as they separated, a sudden storm nearly put an end to them both. Canning's ship lost her canvas, a brig-of-war foundered and Mavrocordato was shipwrecked. But they survived.

These terms seem exactly the same that Odysseus had accepted, the terms for which in more hopeful times he had suffered a traitor's death. But the government now endorsed what Mavrocordato had done. In April 1826 they held another assembly – again in an orange grove for lack of a roof to hold it under – and they formally wrote to Canning to ask him to sue for peace. They acknowledged they should pay tribute to the Sultan, as they had in all the centuries past, and they listed their requests. Most were humble enough: the Greeks should have a flag of their own, and be allowed to coin money and keep a sufficient army for domestic security and a navy to protect their trade; the Sultan's authority should not extend to internal administration or the Church. Some, on the other hand, were impossible, especially their definition of Greece: it included all the Aegean islands, and all the mainland where Greeks had taken to arms. The crux of it was Article One, which said with stark simplicity: 'That no Turk shall be allowed to inhabit, or hold property in the territory of Greece, on account of its being impossible for the two nations to live together.'

It was a sad and slender remnant of what they had fought for. Yet in proposing any terms at all they were deceiving themselves. They thought Canning was willing to argue their case on its merits. But in that era – perhaps in any – diplomatic decisions had little to do with merit; they were based on expediency, the self-interest of the major powers and the perpetual need to preserve the balance of power. And when the Greeks so painfully wrote out the list of their terms, they did not know that other terms had already been decided – not in a Grecian grove, or even in Constantinople, but thousands of miles away in St Petersburg, which is Leningrad now, where no less a personage than the Duke of Wellington, a fortnight before they met, had signed a protocol.

*

It would be impossible now exactly to weigh the events that had
tilted the balance of power. The death of Czar Alexander had something to do with it; so did the impatience of a Russian army encamped on the borders of Turkey with nothing to do; so did the
ambitions of the French, who had made a plan to put a Bourbon
duke on the throne of Greece; so did the grumbles of British merchants whose trade had been interrupted. From such causes as these,
the statesmen of Russia and Britain had each begun to fear that one
country, not their own, might win an unhealthy dominance in
Greece. In their delicate judgement it had seemed advisable to bring
the affair to an end, and the British had thought it important enough
to send their most distinguished citizen on the tedious journey to
Russia. The protocol he signed recorded that His Britannic Majesty
and His Imperial Majesty were agreed in their intention to seek a
settlement of the matter, and would invite the co-operation of the
Courts of Vienna, Paris and Berlin. The terms they proposed for
their mediation were that Greece would have liberty of conscience
and freedom of trade, but would remain a dependency of the Sultan's empire paying an annual tribute, and would be governed by
native authorities in whose nomination the Sultan would have a
voice.

It was vaguely worded, no doubt by intention, and it might have
meant the Greeks had fought for nothing. But it was on this basis,
and not on the Greeks' requests, that the diplomats of Europe went
to work in guarded, long and secret discussions in 1826.

The Greeks waited month after month for an answer from
Canning, but nothing came. Since they had met Ibrahim's army all
of them, even Colocotrones, had begun to see the advantage of
employing European experts, not perhaps as commanders but as
instructors; and the lingering hope they still had was kept alive that
year by the numbers of foreigners, some old hands and some new,
who were converging on Greece for the final acts of the drama.
Lord Cochrane, eagerly awaited, was hovering in the wings and
waiting to make a prima donna's entrance. So was an Irish general,
Sir Richard Church, the latest and last of the men who thought they

ought to be commander-in-chief. Among the conspicuous characters already at work was a French Bonapartist colonel named Charles Fabvier. Colonel Gordon also had uprooted himself from Aberdeen and hurried to Nauplia, not intending to fight but hoping to help to salvage something from the wreckage. And when Hastings steamed in he found several old friends still alive and made a new one: the American Dr Samuel Gridley Howe, who was 25 and joined the *Karteria* as surgeon – and survived to become a world-famous philanthropist.

Gordon found Greece in gloom and Nauplia its capital a scene of disorder and chaos: 'the streets heaped up with filth, the buildings dilapidated, the square and coffee-houses full of idle military men and gay loungers, the lanes crowded with sick and hungry paupers; everywhere the contrast of vanity and riot, with beggary, disease, and death.' The fortress of Palamedes above the town was held by one brigand gang and the town itself by another, and a body of Suliotes was in mutiny for its pay. The government had fled in fear to the other fortress of Bourdzi on the island in the harbour, and had locked itself in. Everyone was expecting the Turks to land in the island of Hydra and lay it waste, and for lack of money the fleet was on strike again. And the national treasury contained the sum of sixteen piastres, which was worth rather less than one dollar – or would have been if the coins had not been forgeries.

In that situation, Gordon had the pleasant experience of saving Greece single-handed, at least for a while. The deputies in London had given him what he called the last sweepings of the second loan, and had told him to use it however he thought best. It was £14,000. To keep the cash safely he had chartered a schooner under the British flag. He paid off the Suliotes to stop their mutiny, then sailed to Hydra to pay the fleet so that the threat to the island should be opposed.

Other pittances of European money kept Greece alive that year. The rest were not loans but charity, organized by an efficient benevolent Swiss named Eynard. Eynard had learned the lessons of the British loans and he sent his own agents to Greece, half a dozen sober and incorruptible men. He only sent money for specific uses: one of them was to buy back women and children who had been enslaved at Missalonghi. Mostly, he sent corn or flour, gunpowder, lead and clothes. In spite of the agents, some of it was garnered by Greeks who sold it, but at least the food fed somebody and the clothes kept somebody warm; and every bullet the soldiery fired that year was a European gift.

Into this scene of beggary, just before Christmas 1826, came the frigate *Hellas*, absurdly and tragically elegant and pretentious. She had cost nearly three times the sum that the Swiss contributed and Eynard disbursed so carefully – enough to supply the whole of the essential needs of Greece for at least another two years – and she was almost useless. Most of the men who brought her across the Atlantic were American, and they went home again. Greek sailors had to learn to handle a ship much bigger than they had ever owned or needed. The government could not agree who should have the honour of manning her and they prescribed a mixed crew from Hydra and Spetsai, with some survivors of Psara. That was disastrous. There were fights on board, she was twice nearly wrecked in Egina and she drifted ashore in Poros, luckily on the muddy side of the harbour. So they handed her over to Miaoulis, who picked a crew of his own. But all alone, she had no possible place in the kind of naval war the Greeks could fight.

However, she brought a useful cargo from America: Hastings' guns. At the turn of the year, the *Karteria* was ready to fight, and nothing was going to stop him trying her.

One other foreigner was ready too, and that was Colonel Fabvier. Fabvier seems a thoroughly worthy man, like General Normann who died in despair after the rout of Peta. He was one of those Frenchmen who had never forgotten or forgiven Waterloo, and he detested the English. But he detested even more the Royalists of France, and for the past ten years he had fought in revolutions in Italy and Spain, and travelled all over Europe in disguises and under *noms-de-guerre* promoting Bonapartist plots. He had collected a band of admiring followers and brought a good many of them with him when he came to Greece. He was proud, immensely tall, aloof, excessively sensitive to insults and often extremely rude, especially to members of the government.

In his history, he was typical of the roaming officers who had flocked to Greece in the early days and formed the Regiment; but unlike most of them he was a very capable soldier and his pride had some solid foundation. Most of them, if they had been colonels, would have called themselves generals, but not Fabvier: he stuck to his Napoleonic rank. He arrived at the very moment when the Greeks had been beaten by Ibrahim and begun to change their minds about European tactics. Like Baleste, Tarella, Normann and all the rest, he offered to train an army; and in the desperate days when Ibrahim was in sight of Nauplia, his offer was thankfully accepted.

It had all happened before. But this time, Greek soldiers were eager to learn, and Fabvier was just the man they needed: tough, dangerous when anyone opposed him, indifferent to comfort or money – he refused any pay – and completely the master of his trade. He would not accept volunteers, who he said would be the dregs of the population, and the government decreed a peculiar kind of conscription by lottery, in which one out of every hundred men in the country would have to join Fabvier's army. It is hard to imagine how this was organized, but it did produce some men. He gathered three thousand, nearly ten times the number of the Regiment at its best, and he started a course of training as strict as any in Napoleon's armies.

Nevertheless, his first two expeditions were failures, for the same old reasons. He tried to co-operate with guerilla forces and they deserted him at the most important moments. And when his own men were threatened by Turkish cavalry the new kind of training broke and the old tradition took over: they ran away. In disgust he offered to resign, but the government begged him to try again. So he did, with longer and stricter training. He decided to cut off his men from other Greeks and take them to a place where they could not easily desert whatever he made them do. He chose the bare volcanic peninsula of Methana, which sticks out towards Egina from the eastern side of Argolis. He fortified the narrow isthmus that joins it to the mainland and entrenched himself in the only sizeable village, which he renamed Tacticopolis. He seems to have thought of this stark retreat as a final fortress that he still might hold when everything else had fallen; and there all alone he laboured to hammer out a Napoleonic corps from the gang of cheerful and wayward ruffians he had been given. Gordon found him there depressed and on the point of giving up for lack of money. He knew a good thing when he saw it, and he gave him the rest of his funds. It was £3500, and it set the corps on its feet again.

In that desolate winter, when total defeat was in sight, the thoughts of most of the leading Greeks and all the Europeans turned towards a single remaining citadel: the Acropolis of Athens.

CHAPTER TWELVE

The Last Siege of the Acropolis
January—June 1827

Sir Richard Church · Karaiskaki

For six months the Acropolis had been besieged. It had little strategic value, if any: the Turks possessed all the rest of Attica and could have left it to starve. But it had a symbolic value – not perhaps for ordinary Greeks, but certainly for the Philhellenes in Greece and all over Europe and America. Everywhere, people felt without any logical reason that if the Acropolis fell Greece would be finished. It was typical of this European sentiment that Stratford Canning, in a whole year in Constantinople, only won a single concession from the Sultan's ministers: to refrain from shelling the Parthenon. It made no difference; their soldiers shelled it but missed, and they also drove mines underneath the outer walls, but those either did not explode or were countermined by the Greeks. The Parthenon is not standing there now through the Turks' forbearance but through their incompetence.

During the winter the garrison began to run short of gunpowder, and an enterprising chieftain escaped through the Turkish lines on horseback to ask the government for more. The government appealed to Fabvier in his private redoubt at Methana, and he agreed to try to run powder in by night.

Fabvier was the only man in Greece who could have organized such a delicate adventure. He landed some hundreds of men on the coast south-east of Piraeus, each carrying a sack of powder and his musket and nothing else, and he carried a sack himself. The essence of the thing was quiet and speed, and he knew that excited Greeks always let off their muskets, so he took away all their flints before they started. They crossed the country between Piraeus and Athens without being seen. Outside the ring of Turkish besiegers they sounded drums, a signal to the garrison for a sortie. In the confusion it caused they rushed through the Turkish posts. A few men were killed, but the rest reached the gates in safety and scrambled inside.

The government had agreed that Fabvier and his force should come out again; there were plenty of men to defend the place, and his own would only have meant more mouths to feed. He intended to escape the following night. But as anyone might have foreseen, the men of the garrison thought they had done their stint: they should be the ones to leave, and Fabvier's men should stay. Whenever he tried to go they started shooting and roused the Turks so that nobody could get out. Fabvier and the men he had trained so carefully were shut in for a tedious unnecessary defensive chore that anyone could have done.

He was furious – and all the more furious when he came to believe it was a government plot. Improbable though it seems, many men who ought to have known believed it too – that the government had sent secret orders to the garrison to keep their only reliable general out of the way. While he was impotently shut in the Acropolis, he heard they had appointed another man over his head – and not only another man but a man who seemed the enemy of the ideals he had fought for all his life. It was Richard Church. The government had already appointed Cochrane over Miaoulis, which was ungrateful enough; but Miaoulis was a placid honest man they could rely on to take it calmly. They may well have foreseen that appointing Church over Fabvier would provoke an explosion.

Church's history was equivocal. Sixteen years before, when Britain took over the Ionian Islands from the French, Church was one of the officers who fought there and formed the regiment of Greeks in British pay – the regiment Colocotrones had joined when he was in exile. Perhaps the Greek and Irish temperaments are rather similar – several people said so at the time – and Church got on very well with the Greeks he commanded. When he left the islands in 1812 he was given testimonials full of praise and gratitude by his men, and among the signatures on them was Colocotrones'. Ever after that, he felt a proprietary affection for Greece, as people often do for foreign countries where they were happy or successful when they were young.

But since then, his life had taken a different turn. He was only a lieutenant-colonel in the British army. His generalship was conferred by the King of Naples, whose army he commanded for thirteen years: his knighthood likewise was Hanoverian. The King of Naples, or more correctly the King of the Two Sicilies, was among the most despotic of European rulers, and Church's mission with him was to put down his political opponents, who were all classed together as bandits and criminals. He did it ruthlessly, cruelly and successfully. But these opponents were the very men who had come in such numbers to Greece. They had fought for political freedom at home and been beaten, and then, in their own eyes at least, had consistently come to fight for freedom in Greece. No Philhellene could have trusted Church, and to Fabvier he seemed doubly villainous: he had fought for tyranny, and against Napoleon.

Church seems not to have seen any contradiction in suppressing freedom in Italy and supporting it in Greece. On the contrary, as soon as the war began he felt sure, like so many other people, that he ought to be leading the Greeks to glory in the field. But he did not go. Nothing less than the rank of commander-in-chief would do for him, and nothing less than a letter from the government which begged him to save the country.

He waited five years for an invitation that was flattering enough, and he got it early in 1827 – and with it a letter from Colocotrones, who had resigned himself to having a foreign commander and preferred to have one he knew. 'My soul has never been absent from you,' the crafty old fellow wrote. 'Come! Come! and take up arms for Greece, or assist us with your talents, your virtues and your abilities, that you may claim her eternal gratitude.'

With that assurance of the respect he thought was his due, Sir Richard Church left England, and in March he sailed into the

Bay of Portocheli, which is opposite Spetsai. A portrait at that time of his life shows a wiry little man in all the panoply of Albanian costume, dagger and sword, and holding a monster helmet with a plume: he has a shock of hair, a fierce moustache, and an expression of animal wildness in his eyes. But in Portocheli he announced he had not come as a general: he was only a travelling gentleman. He was not committing himself until he saw how the land lay.

He had chosen that obscure but beautiful landing place because he had heard that Colocotrones and the government were in the nearby village of Hermione. And at sunrise next morning Colocotrones arrived to greet him with a guard of honour. They embraced as old comrades-in-arms, and Colocotrones presented Church to the guard with the words: 'Our father is come at last – we have only to obey him and our freedom is sure.' In Hermione there was joy and feasting, but Church's caution was wise. This, it turned out, was only one government of Greece; there was another, equally claiming to be the sole authority, thirty miles away in the island of Egina. The first was Colocotrones' government and the other was Mavrocordato's, and they refused to meet. Neither could legally govern, because the constitution provided that two thirds of the elected delegates, 120 men, had to be present to form an Assembly. Mavrocordato could only muster 70, and Colocotrones 26 – though he had proclaimed a new election to bring his numbers up. Church said he was going home unless they settled their quarrels, and he sailed to Egina to see what he could do about it. Mavrocordato's welcome was rather more muted; he was offended that Church had gone to Hermione first.

Three days later, three strange ships were sighted off the island. By pure coincidence, Lord Cochrane had arrived, with his two yachts and a second-hand brig, the *Sauveur*, that the French Phil-hellenes had given him. None of the warships he had ordered were ready; he had come because he had heard the news, three months late, that the *Hellas* was already in Greece. Everyone had given up expecting ever to see him, and his sudden breezy apparition caused a sensation. Deputations hurried out to his yacht to pay their homage, and Church for a moment had to take second place.

Thus both governments within a week had acquired a promising saviour of the country. Luckily, both saviours agreed that one government was enough. Even more luckily, the only man that everyone would listen to came sailing in: the ubiquitous Commodore Hamilton. One suspects he would not have dreamed of missing such a party. Socially, it must have been a strange encounter – Cochrane the famous renegade, an admiral in the Brazilian navy; Church the ex-lieutenant-colonel, now a general in the army of Naples; and Hamilton the only genuine lawful officer. But Hamilton used his diplomacy, as he so often had before, in sorting out the problem of the Greeks. 'Mavrocordato is detested by all parties,' he wrote in a letter at the time, 'but still useful to me. I also put no confidence in him, but rather use him as a spy, it being very convenient to have one who is not paid.' In spite of such a partisan opinion, he persuaded both governments to meet at Poros, half-way between the rival capitals.

They formed an Assembly there, but there was nobody among them they could agree to recognize as President, and they nominated a Corfiote Greek called Count John Capodistrias, who had been high in the service of the Czar of Russia and was well-known in Europe – and had the particular merit of never having been to Greece in his life. In the hope that he would accpet, they appointed a vice-governing commission of three men who had not made enemies simply because they had not held any position of authority before. So, from having two governments, the country had no practical government at all. But before they all dispersed they confirmed the appointments of Cochrane as Admiral of the Fleet and Church as Commander-in-Chief of the Army. And each of these arrogant men, apprised of the situation, saw in a moment the world-wide fame he would win if he saved the Acropolis.

*

The Acropolis is five miles or so from the port of Piraeus – and the country between, where the Greeks were to fight their final battle, is the only part of Greece that has changed so much it can hardly be recognized. Athens and Piraeus are one continuous mass of buildings now, and the coast of Phaleron Bay south-east of Piraeus is a solid line of hotels and apartment houses leading down to the international airport. But in those days Athens was small and Piraeus was not much more than a cluster of hamlets, with a monastery and some ancient fortifications, scattered on the steep hills round the harbour. The road from Athens was a country lane and the shore of Phaleron Bay was as wild as any other.

Before Cochrane and Church arrived in Greece, Colonel Gordon was already on this shore, encamped with some Greek artillery on one of the hills of Piraeus; he had been persuaded to take an active part in the fighting, and the Greeks had made him a General. A large crowd of guerillas was also waiting a few miles farther east, opposite the narrows of Salamis. And Hastings had been there too. He had steamed the *Karteria* into the harbour and cannonaded a fort the Turks were holding. It was not the sort of thing he wanted to do, but of course it surprised the Turks to see the steamer and the size of the shot it fired. Their Pasha salvaged one of the monstrous 68-pound balls and sent it to the Sultan, with a note to explain that that was what he was up against.

Hastings wanted to fight against ships, not forts, and he got his first chance in April. The supplies for the Turkish armies round Athens were coming in by sea on the other side of the peninsula of Attica, and Hastings was sent to interrupt them. The port they were using was Volo, at the head of the Gulf of Volo. That gulf has a narrow entrance and mountainous shores, and the port was defended by batteries of guns. Hastings steamed into the gulf with two Greek brigs and two schooners astern of him; and there on the afternoon of 20 April 1827, a steamship first entered the history of warfare, with devastating success. As Hastings approached the port, he sighted eight ships moored close inshore below the batteries. Perhaps the battle was won before it started, by the mere sight of a ship which lashed its way across the gulf with a plume of smoke, for the defenders had never seen such a thing before or probably even heard it was possible. Hastings anchored, and quickly drove the Turks out of their batteries with shellfire, and out of the ships with grape. The Greeks boarded five of the ships and towed them away. They burned two which had no sails on board, and the eighth, which the Turks had managed to run ashore within musket shot of their fort, was destroyed with shells. As darkness fell and the night breeze began to blow off the land, the Greeks made sail with their prizes and took them back in triumph to Egina.

Hastings stayed another couple of days, searching the creeks for anything more he could capture, and he found a large brig-of-war. It was well armed, and moored head and stern to the rocks below another pair of batteries, and a large detachment of infantry seemed to be there to guard it. He tried to board it by rowing in with muffled oars at night, but his boat was heard or seen and he had to escape under gunfire. Next morning, he tested his theory of long-range red-hot shot. The Greek crew he had trained heated seven shot in the boiler furnace, and carried them up on deck and loaded the guns with an instrument he had invented. He steamed round in circles a mile away from the brig, sighting and firing each of the guns in turn, and when the seven shot were away he waited to see what happened. The crew of the brig abandoned her. After a while flames burst out of her deck, her guns still loaded on the shoreward side went off and fired their shot among the rocks, some mortars on deck discharged themselves high in the sky, she burnt down to the waterline and her magazine exploded. The *Karteria* had been damaged in her rigging, but not in her iron hull. On her way home she found another two ships that were loaded with wheat, and she took them to Egina: seven ships captured and four destroyed. All his theories had worked.

In Egina he found that Cochrane and Church, after three weeks in Greece, had left for the frontal attack on Athens.

Between these two men, the division of command was unusual. Church, as army commander, chartered an armed schooner and lived aboard it. From the comfort and safety of this unmilitary post he proposed to conduct the fighting on land, and in the battles that followed he was seldom seen ashore. On the other hand Cochrane as Admiral enrolled a thousand soldiers of his own, put a young relation of his in command of them and sometimes appeared on shore in his admiral's hat to urge them into battle with his telescope. He hoisted his flag in the *Hellas* and invited Miaoulis to stay as his flag captain. Most men might have taken this as a studied insult, but not Miaoulis: he was pleased to reveal that he spoke a little Spanish, so that he could speak to his admiral without an interpreter. But Cochrane did not move to the flagship, he stayed in his yacht, which still flew the British flag.

According to Church, ten thousand men assembled at Piraeus. If it was true, this was much the biggest single force the Greeks had put in the field. It was certainly true that it was commanded by two self-centred rivals, each jealous of his own reputation, each cruising around in a yacht, each ignorant of the people, the language and the events of the past five years, and each determined to be the first to reach the Acropolis. On shore under their command was Gordon, who had not meant to fight and felt he ought not to be there at all, and an outstanding Greek captain named Karaiskaki who had only lately risen to eminence. And inside the Acropolis was the unlucky Fabvier, who hated being there, and hated even more the prospect of being rescued by Englishmen, and hated most of all Sir Richard Church.

The mass of men came from all parts of Greece, each band of them under a captain of its own. Of course there was no formal chain of command: every captain could claim a right to his own opinion, and a right to express it to the commander-in-chief. Like Byron at Missalonghi, Church in his yacht was besieged by men who argued angrily in words he could not understand. The only man they respected was Karaiskaki. Oddly enough, this was the man who had led the abortive plot at Missalonghi to overthrow Mavrocordato and Byron and take the money chest. But since then he had earned a better reputation and won an influence over the other captains, because he had the qualities they most admired: bravery, eloquence, cunning and humour. Of course he was involved in all kinds of intrigues – nobody could survive if they were not – and he had a healthy dislike of Europeans. Yet he always gave Church and Cochrane sound advice whether they took it or not, and he rescued Church from the worst of the arguments by sorting out the captains' demands and presenting them coherently.

Each of the bands set up its own camp when it landed at Piraeus, and the Turks already had small stockaded strongpoints scattered among the hills and along the shores; so the outposts of the armies were mixed up together without a dividing line, and in the first few days there were skirmishes that never lasted long. A major fight blew up on 25 April, and it was Cochrane who started it. Some ships came to anchor in the mouth of the harbour and landed a party from Spetsai, and Cochrane went ashore from his yacht to have a look round. With a more practised eye than most, he noticed that the Turks had withdrawn some guns along the north side of the harbour, and he attracted the Spetsiotes' notice with shouts and hurrahs. A red-haired Brazilian admiral waving a telescope was not what they expected to see on the enemy shore, and they took up the shout and followed him in a charge which drove out the Turks from a series of their stockades. Some of the enemy fled for the hills and some, who were mostly Albanians, took refuge in the monastery, which stood at the end of the harbour close to the quays where nowadays the ferries to the islands come and go.

Next day, Miaoulis warped the *Hellas* into the harbour and bombarded the monastery, and Gordon joined in with the Greek artillery on the hill. Two days of shooting demolished the upper floors of the building but did little harm to the men inside, who sheltered in trenches and vaults.

Then they asked for a truce. It was granted by Cochrane: Church had been excluded from the whole affair. But Cochrane misunderstood the customs of the war. The Albanians were willing to surrender their post, but they expected to be allowed to retreat with their arms and rejoin the body of their army. Cochrane insisted they must be taken on board his ships as prisoners of war. That was a concept no one had ever heard of: to the Albanians, it only meant that they would be sold as slaves or tortured to death. So the talks broke down and the shooting started again.

Cochrane seems to have been obsessed by impatience to march in triumph to Athens. He was furious at the delay. The Greeks themselves and everyone who knew them tried to explain, if they dared, that a Greek battle could only be fought in the way the Greeks understood. But he would not listen: there was nothing, he insisted, to stop the army advancing. If the monastery was an obstacle, it must be taken at once by assault, and the barbarians inside it put to the sword. If something decisive was not done at once, he would withdraw the navy and his own thousand soldiers. In his rage he accused the Greek captains of cowardice.

He could not have done anything worse to affront their philotimo, their self-esteem: he might have accused them of almost any sin without upsetting them, but not of cowardice. They were not afraid of assaulting the monastery, it would have been easy. But they could not see any point in it, or in the noisy expensive bombardment he had ordered. The men inside had no food and hardly any water: they would have to surrender. Why go and get killed? they argued; why not wait a few days? Karaiskaki went to Church, but Church felt he had to agree with Cochrane. He ordered the assault to be made the next morning, and he ordered Gordon to support it with artillery.

During that night, surrounded by other advisers, Church changed his mind. Perhaps he had understood that his order would not be obeyed. He did not tell Cochrane or Gordon, but he decided to accept the request which Cochrane had rejected, and let the Albanian troop march away to Athens. He told Karaiskaki to offer them safe conduct. Anyone who had been in Greece for the past few years would have known what was likely to happen. Karaiskaki knew, and he offered himself as hostage, with several other captains, to march inside the retreating column. But Church took no precautions to protect the march and did not even come ashore from his yacht when it was due to begin.

In the morning, Gordon came down to the harbour to take his

part in the assault, and with him was George Finlay; at this moment, the two most reliable historians of the war were together. Both of them saw with astonishment that messengers were passing in and out of the monastery. Church's yacht was nowhere to be seen, but Cochrane's was in the harbour, and they rowed out to it to ask what was going on. He knew no more than they did, but said he feared that Church had agreed a capitulation. Finlay was the youngest of these three; while his seniors were talking, he stood respectfully aside, and he saw the Albanians open the monastery gate and begin to march out. 'All those men will be murdered,' he called in distress. 'Do you hear what he says?' Cochrane said to Gordon; and Gordon answered, 'I fear, my Lord, it is too true.' All of them watched the massacre begin.

Two hundred and seventy men marched out: two hundred were slaughtered 'in an instant.' The rest ran for the hills while the Greeks stopped to strip the dead and fight over the spoils. Karaiskaki, in the middle of the column, did his best. He was said to have shouted to the Albanians, 'Forgive me as I forgive you – I can do no more for you.' None of them paused to kill their hostage, which was their right.

That episode threw the army into chaos. Church was suitably horrified: he said he would resign, but changed his mind again. Gordon actually did so, either in disgust at the massacre or more probably at Church's lack of command. Greek captains blamed each other, but they were not really to blame; it was the lowest of the soldiery who did it. The European officers – there were twenty or thirty of different nationalities – were united among themselves in blaming Church for doing nothing to protect the men whose safety he had promised, and especially for staying on his yacht. Cochrane's thousand soldiers mutinied because he had moved them away from the monastery and they had not had a chance of booty; his own views, such as they were, were only revealed in the message he sent to pacify these men. He had withdrawn them, he said, to preserve the honour of the navy unsullied and to secure an equal distribution of the prize-money. Nobody knew what he meant. As for the enemy,

The Acropolis of Athens, 1798

Admiral Andreas Miaoulis

Bouboulina attacking Nauplia

it was said that when the Turkish Pasha was told what had happened, he rose very solemnly to his feet and exclaimed, 'God will not leave this faithlessness unpunished.'

The Pasha had no military comfort. Looking out towards the coast from the hills of Athens, his assessment was much the same as Cochrane's: he could see nothing to stop the Greek army advancing. The road from Piraeus ran most of the way through olive groves, and they were a perfect terrain for an army on foot: the ground below the trees was always kept clear so that the olives could be gathered, the canopy above would hide the troops from artillery, and cavalry could not attack them under the spreading branches. He could not defend that route when he had lost Piraeus. He expected soon to be surrounded, and was prepared to retreat and raise the siege.

Yet Cochrane and Church at that moment made a new decision: to abandon the direct route and make a new landing with part of the army at the other end of Phaleron Bay. Everyone else was dumbfounded. Gordon plainly said it was lunacy, and put it down to Cochrane's impatience to dine in the Acropolis. Karaiskaki agreed with him. For neither Church nor Cochrane had reconnoitred the country or even seen it, but everyone else knew there were no olives on the route they had chosen. It was open heathland, cavalry country – and the Turks had the cavalry.

Karaiskaki predicted disaster, and a disaster came – but not the one he expected. A few soldiers having a drinking party sallied out in their courage to attack the remaining Turkish stockades without anyone's orders. Karaiskaki was sick, and was lying down in a tent. He heard the noise and got up, and went out to take charge and was hit by a stray shot. They carried him out to Church's yacht and he died the next day – the only Greek that all the rest respected, and the only one with the strength to stand up to Church and Cochrane. Bereft of his leadership, the captains and Philhellenes who were picked to make the new landing consulted together and agreed that although it seemed foolish they were bound to try it.

Church's account of all these events, as might be expected,

differed from everyone else's, but no positive explanation of this move was ever given; it seems most likely that he and Cochrane wanted to get away from what seemed to them an insoluble chaos, and start again with a smaller more manageable army. But if the scheme was foolish, its execution was pitiable. On the night of 5 May, two and a half thousand men were embarked at Piraeus and landed again five miles away and still the same distance from Athens. Church issued a written disposition to the captains: he had not yet understood that a good guerilla captain did not have to be able to read. And he stubbornly stayed on his yacht. The landing was not completed until it was nearly dawn. The captains, all on an equal footing, did what seemed best to them and halted where they chose when daylight came. Those who had landed first were nearly at Athens, and the rest spread all the way back to the sea. Their instinct was to dig themselves in and build their little walls of stones, but they had nothing except their daggers to dig with. As the sun rose the whole operation on the naked heath was visible from the Pasha's headquarters. He deployed his cavalry and opened fire with a single howitzer. At the eighteenth shot of the howitzer the Turks chanted a prayer in chorus, and at the twentieth shot the cavalry charged.

Church came ashore with confidence as the day began. Cochrane landed a few minutes after him, with the expressed intention of congratulating him on victory, and also without any doubt of being the first to reach the Acropolis. Both of them were just in time to meet the routed army racing back for the shore with the cavalry overtaking them. Cochrane and Church escaped by wading up to their necks to reach their boats, which were then rowed off to the ships. Some thousand survivors were left on the beach. A hundred or two plunged into the sea in panic and were drowned, and the rest would have died if the Turks had ever been able to complete a victory. But as soon as the cavalry reached the shore it galloped back towards Athens to hunt for booty, and the demoralized remnant of Greeks was rescued by boats when darkness fell again.

It was by far the worst single disaster the Greeks had suffered in battle. The last of their armies was destroyed, their best men killed and the rest dissolved away in desertion. It was and still is beyond question that Cochrane and Church were to blame. They had not waited to learn what a Greek guerilla army could do, and had insisted on putting it in a position where it could not do anything, not even save itself. Cochrane sailed away to Hydra. Church remained for three weeks on one of the hills of Piraeus with a dwindling band of angry men, and from there he ordered the Acropolis to capitulate. The garrison answered with the words expected on such occasions; 'We are Greeks, determined to live or die free. If the Pasha wants our arms, he may come and fetch them.' But when Church abandoned Piraeus they lost their theatrical heroism. They said it was Fabvier's fault, and one can easily believe he did not want to prolong a useless defence which had no end in sight. By good luck, the French naval commander-in-chief of the eastern Mediterranean came sailing in to Piraeus, and he arranged the terms of capitulation. The Acropolis surrendered on the fifth of June.

CHAPTER THIRTEEN

The Battle of Navarino
June—October 1827

Admiral Sir Edward Codrington

The Pasha at Athens left the punishment to his God. When the garrison marched down from the Acropolis, within a month of the massacre at Piraeus, he might have been forgiven for taking a human revenge; but he did everything Church had omitted to do. He moved his own troops away from the line of march and provided horses to carry the garrison's baggage, and in person he patrolled the road to Piraeus with a force of cavalry. The French admiral and his officers marched at the head of the dismal column, and Turks of eminent rank as hostages in the middle of it. The whole of it, with Fabvier and his men, was delivered in safety and taken in neutral ships to Salamis, where the men disbanded and made their own ways home. In a black rage, Fabvier went back to his fastness at Methana. He said he would never take orders from Church, and Church had the sense not to give him any.

It must be said for Church that he learned his lesson. Without any money and without a government, the title of commander-in-chief was an empty honour, and he never assembled another army or fought another battle. But on the other hand he never surrendered. Separated from Cochrane, he made friends among the Greeks and became a guerilla captain. He gathered a faithful band of a few hundred men, as hungry, tattered and disorganized as any other band, and installed himself on the Isthmus of Corinth. He and a few other captains continued to march here and there and fight occasional skirmishes from the hills, and just by existing they kept up a symbol of the existence of Greece.

It was only by chance that a thin strip of land could still be called free, the strip from Corinth to Nauplia and the off-lying islands. It was part of the Peloponnese, which was the Sultan's gift to Ibrahim. The Turkish Pasha who had reconquered the north had no wish to fight the battles of the Egyptian Pasha, and the Egyptian Pasha, in winter quarters at Navarino, was in no great hurry to tidy up the last corner of his domain. He saw the final move as a naval operation; rather than march through Argolis, he intended to come from the sea and take Hydra first and then the other islands, and let the mainland perish in isolation. A new fleet was fitting in Alexandria to finish the job before the summer was out.

Until it was ready, men like Mavrocordato still had a perilous habitation where they could claim to speak for Greece, and Cochrane, Hastings and the remains of the fleet still had some harbours as bases.

The size of the fleet that Cochrane commanded depended as ever on how much money could be scraped together to pay the wages. Soon after the defeat at Athens, there was another of the moments of farce that distinguish this war in retrospect. Cochrane decreed a naval review in Poros. He had left his yacht and taken command of the *Hellas*, replacing Miaoulis with an English flag captain who called himself St George. In the outer harbour of Poros, Cochrane watched from the great cabin of the flagship as ship after ship of the fleets of Hydra and Spetsai sailed past him in a semblance of naval splendour. An eye-witness said it was a most impressive sight, against the sun descending over the mountains of the Peloponnese. But that harbour has a second narrow exit, and instead of coming to anchor in serried ranks the fleet vanished out of the harbour at the other end and went home. Cochrane had run short of money and had only offered a fortnight's pay in advance, in place of the customary month's. Most of the departing crews intended to take to piracy, which seemed to them the only way they could support their families. There were plenty of men with access to government paper and seals who were willing to give them letters of marque in return for a share of the profits. Piracy grew that year in the eastern Mediterranean to become an international menace, and when the pirates were caught they could always produce an official-looking document which seemed to give them the government's authority to act as privateers.

But still, Cochrane had the *Hellas*, the *Karteria* and the French brig *Sauveur* which was now commanded by a Scotsman named Roberts, and from time to time he was able to raise a dozen or so of brigs. He cruised around, once all the way to Alexandria. He seldom found any enemies, but when he did he introduced the Greeks and Turks to his own brand of naval warfare. There were no more gunnery battles fought safely out of range; he horrified friend and foe by sailing in to pistol-shot and blasting opponents to bits with the broadside of the *Hellas*. The younger Greeks in his crew stood up to these trials well, but – in his own words – 'the oldest, and ugliest, and fiercest-looking bravoes of Hydra ran to the other side of the deck, roaring like market bulls.' And the commander-in-chief in the midst of battle was apt to charge down to the gundecks, himself roaring orders in English that nobody understood, to lay his own guns and knock out with his fists any man who seemed to him to deserve it.

Hastings also cruised about under sail, hoarding his coal for the moment he longed for: a meeting with an enemy fleet at sea, the bigger the better, in calm weather when he could manoeuvre and they could not. He had none of Cochrane's buccaneering manners: he was formal and correct, his crew was picked and trained and disciplined, and he gave his orders in Greek. But he never got his perfect opportunity. All his fights were close inshore. The only time he met a major fleet in the open he was alone half-way to Alexandria and his engine had broken down, and the enemy sheered off in alarm and left him there.

While Cochrane and Hastings kept the sea, sometimes alone and sometimes with a dozen ships, Mehemet Ali's new fleet was completed in Alexandria, and late in July that summer it sailed for

Navarino, to join the ships already there for the final attack on Hydra. It was a fleet of nearly a hundred sail, and fifty-one of them were men-of-war. Greece could not hope to resist it, and the country seemed doomed.

*

In that same month, two ships of the line were sighted beating up the Gulf of Argos and approaching Nauplia. It was nothing new for foreign warships to put in there: Hamilton's frigate had often done so. But these were very large, and the sight of them silenced for a moment the guns of the fortresses, which as usual were in the hands of rival brigands who were shelling each other to the detriment of the town that lay between. The ships were the *Asia*, 84, and the *Sirène*, 60, the flagships of the commanders-in-chief of the Mediterranean fleets of Britain and France. The admirals, Sir Edward Codrington and Comte Henri de Rigny, requested representatives of Greece at a conference on board the *Asia*. Greece still had no President; it was the indestructible Mavrocordato who led the delegation. The admirals informed him that an alliance had been made between the governments of Britain, France and Russia; in accordance with it, the Greek and Turkish governments were invited to observe an armistice. The Greeks agreed – they had no choice. But when the news was known there was not much rejoicing, and some of them, encouraged by Cochrane, Church and Fabvier, still persuaded themselves they could go on fighting and win good terms for themselves without the intervention of foreign governments.

The new alliance was called the Treaty of London, and its name emphasizes how little it had to do with the hopes or hatreds of either the Greeks, the Turks or the Egyptians. It was the development of the protocol the Duke of Wellington had signed in St Petersburg: fifteen months of diplomatic labour had caused the French to join it and given it the status of a treaty. The powers had hesitated to interfere in what had seemed to be an internal affair of the Turkish empire; the cause of their action at last was the story that Ibrahim hoped to wipe out the Greeks in the Peloponnese and make it an Arab country – a hope that seemed to go beyond domestic politics – and their interest in a settlement was increased by the menace of Greek piracy. They were prepared to insist on an armistice while terms were discussed; and to give point to their insistence squadrons of the British and French navies had been ordered into the area and a Russian squadron was on its way from the Baltic.

It was not very clear what the governments meant to do if either side in the war rejected their intervention, and that is what happened. The Greeks accepted the armistice, but the Sultan refused it. So did Mehemet Ali, who denied the story of wiping out the Greeks – although he agreed the rebellion would be put down by whatever methods were needed, which seemed to mean much the same thing. The admirals, especially Codrington who was the senior, were left to interpret a difficult set of orders.

Any British admiral was used to making his own decisions on foreign stations, where if he asked for an explanation of orders he might have to wait for months. Codrington was a man in his middle fifties with long experience and ample common sense. Like most British officers he had joined the navy as a small boy, and his 45 years of service had included the whole of the Napoleonic Wars: he had fought under Howe at the 'Glorious First of June' in 1794, and under Nelson as the youngest of the captains at Trafalgar, where he commanded the *Orion*. Yet even he, in this novel situation, found it hard to translate his orders into coherent instructions for his captains. Since Greece had agreed to the armistice and Turkey had not, it was their duty to intercept supplies of men or materials intended for use against Greece. The interception must be carried out with caution, and must not degenerate into fighting unless the Turks or Egyptians persisted in forcing passages denied to them. Firmness was to be used, and if absolutely necessary the policy was to be enforced by arms.

Nothing in the orders was straightforward, everything depended on the admirals' judgement, or in their absence on each captain's judgement. So started a chain of cause, effect and chance which, in the course of a single month, brought the six years of war to its climax: a chain that was misunderstood at the time and often distorted afterwards.

Since Ibrahim and the Turkish and Egyptian fleets were already in Navarino, Codrington went there as soon as the orders from London were confirmed. He had to explain to Ibrahim that he was obliged to enforce the armistice which the Sultan had refused. On 24 September the *Asia* and *Sirène* stood into the bay and sailed through the enormous fleet assembled there; the band of the *Asia* played on deck, and the crews gave a confident display of naval seamanship in coming precisely to anchor in front of Ibrahim's tents which were pitched on the shore. Codrington took five officers ashore with him, and one of them was his son who was a midshipman; and that very young man's account of the meeting, which he wrote in a letter to his sister, was more entertaining than his father's dispatch.

Inside the large tent, they found a smaller pavilion, the strings of which interfered very much with the midshipman's cocked hat, and beneath the pavilion Ibrahim reclined on a sofa: 'Father came to, on the said sofa, close alongside him; and the French Admiral brought up also, on the sofa, under father's lee.' All three were provided with jewelled hookahs ten feet long, and coffee was served while they talked about the weather. The young man was critical of Ibrahim's appearance – a man of about forty, not at all good-looking, but with heavy features very much marked by the smallpox, and as fat as a porpoise. But when business began, he was impressed by his intelligence, and apparently also by his father's: 'I must say I was very much surprised by the clearness and ability with which father's arguments were carried on, and the good sense which Ibrahim showed . . . I liked him pretty well.'

So did everyone else: there was an unexpected feeling of sympathy. Codrington expounded his orders and had the appropriate parts of them read out. Ibrahim said his duty was to obey the Sultan's orders, not to negotiate; those orders were to capture Hydra and so bring the war to an end; his troops were embarked, he was ready to sail, and sail he must whatever the consequences. Codrington argued that if the Turkish and Egyptian fleets put to sea to go anywhere except to their own home ports, he was obliged to destroy them; the Sultan had not known of this when he ordered them to Hydra, and he could not possibly want them to be destroyed. And after a long and reasonable discussion, Ibrahim agreed to report the changed situation to Constantinople and to do nothing until he had an answer, which would take 21 days.

But he added that it was unjust to restrict his fleet and let the Greeks fight on: Cochrane especially should be restrained. Codrington said that was quite a different matter, because the Greeks had accepted the armistice and the Sultan had refused it: until the Sultan accepted, the Greeks were justified in fighting. This perhaps was sound reasoning, but he can scarcely have hoped that Ibrahim would follow it. He agreed to see that Cochrane should not extend the fighting to any new area. And on that, the meeting turned to what the interpreter called joking talk, about life and affairs in general.

Codrington in fact had heard on the previous day that Cochrane was in the Ionian Sea with a plan to put Church and his men ashore somewhere north of Missalonghi. Ibrahim only heard of it after the meeting was over, and he sent his interpreter urgently out to the *Asia*: he requested permission to dispatch a fleet to intercept Cochrane and protect Patras. Codrington refused: he had promised to do it himself.

Since Ibrahim had undertaken to stay where he was and do nothing for 21 days, Codrington let his own fleet disperse. The French went off to the Aegean, and two of the major British ships to Malta. In the *Asia*, he stationed himself off the island of Zante with a frigate to watch Navarino, and he sent a sloop to find Cochrane and tell him to keep the peace. The sloop came up with the *Hellas* and delivered the order, and then went into the Gulf of Corinth, where Church was found encamped on the southern shore. Neither Cochrane nor Church had done anything effective, and both agreed to be 'guided by the spirit of the order.'

Four days later, Codrington had a report that the *Hellas* had been sighted off Cephalonia sailing south and towing a steamship. His mind was relieved: it was natural to suppose that the steamship was Hastings' *Karteria*, and that the whole of Cochrane's serviceable fleet had gone home. But in fact it was not. It was the first of the five steamers the deputies had ordered in London two years before, which had just staggered into Greek waters and had met the *Hellas* by the purest chance. Hastings was still at large. He had not received Codrington's order, but had steamed through the narrows beyond Patras and into the Gulf of Corinth in company with the brig *Sauveur* and two very small Greek gunboats; and nobody knew he was there, except the Turkish garrisons in the forts at the entrance who shot at him as he went past.

To say the least, it was bold to enter the Gulf with no way out and the whole of the enemy fleet between himself and home. But on 28 September, the day when the *Hellas* was sighted towing the steamer, Hastings was forty miles beyond the narrows, steaming past the village of Galaxidhi which had suffered the disaster of losing its fleet in the early days of the war. He had heard that an enemy fleet was sheltering near the village, and on the 29th he sighted it: a schooner mounting twenty guns, six brigs-of-war, one flying an admiral's flag, and two Austrian merchant ships which were loading a cargo of currants. It was lying at anchor in the small bay of Salona, which is close to the modern town of Itea where car ferries land below Delphi. The bay is a desolate place nowadays, disfigured by mining; but when Hastings approached it, it was an anchorage of some importance, defended by two batteries and hundreds of troops on shore.

The Turks who saw him coming are said to have held their fire for fear of scaring him away, because they expected to capture the whole of his insignificant squadron. He anchored five hundred yards off, and then the Turks opened such a fire that the *Sauveur* had to anchor three hundred yards astern of him. He fired a few ranging shots, then loaded his long guns with explosive shells and his 68-pounders with red-hot empty shells – a new idea, because he had found his 68–pound solid shot was likely to go right through a ship and out the other side.

Hastings' skill with the guns of that era remains as astonishing now as it must have been at the time. At 500 yards he fired one salvo each at the four largest ships, and all four of them burst into flames. The *Sauveur* took on the batteries, and they all advanced and boarded the schooner, whose crew had fled. But she was hard aground within musket-shot of the troops ashore. Hastings steamed right in and tried to tow her off but his hawsers broke, so they took her brass guns and set her on fire. That left two brigs which had also run immovably aground, and Hastings destroyed them with shells.

That completely successful battle, which lasted half an hour, had far more drastic results than Hastings could have foreseen. In naval history, it was the second that had ever been fought by a steamship, and it precipitated the last that was ever fought by fleets of sailing ships.

The first of its consequences was to destroy the tenuous trust between Codrington and Ibrahim. Ibrahim seems to have heard of it within three days, perhaps from other ships in the gulf, or even from people who saw the smoke and heard the explosions from the southern shore. Codrington, out in Zante, heard of it much later. To Ibrahim it appeared that Codrington had broken his promise to keep Cochrane under control. He felt absolved from his own promise, and immediately ordered a squadron to sea to catch Hastings and protect Patras. Codrington's frigate on watch outside reported the squadron coming out. And to Codrington, who believed that Cochrane had taken his fleet away, it appeared that Ibrahim was treacherously breaking the promise he had made.

In good faith, he had left himself with no other ships than the *Asia*, the frigate and two corvettes or sloops. With that meagre fleet he angrily put to sea in threatening weather, and intercepted thirty-six of Ibrahim's ships. He sent a peremptory letter to the Turkish admiral by boat, ordering him to reverse the course of his fleet, and he was flattered and rather surprised to see the admiral do so. But next day the fleet came on again, with another fifteen ships commanded by Ibrahim in person. Again he opposed them and fired some warning shots. There was no limit to the confidence of the British navy, but Codrington was surprised to find himself issuing orders to a fleet of fifty ships from a fleet of four. This time, the weather helped him. The wind was rising from the north-east, and Ibrahim's fleet came to anchor under the lee of the land. Night came down with thunder, rain and squalls, and in the next dawn it blew a hurricane. The *Asia* put before the wind under bare poles for the shelter of Zante. And when the weather cleared, Ibrahim's fleet was seen to be scattered to leeward, and all of it heading back to Navarino.

It had been a delicate moment, and Codrington was extremely glad in the next few days when his fleet began to assemble again. His own ships came back from Malta, and the French from wherever they had been. And the Russian squadron joined them, commanded by Count Heiden, whom Codrington found 'a plain-sailing, open-hearted man', an easier colleague than de Rigny, who hardly seemed to him to be a seaman.

Thwarted at sea by an opposition he thought was unjust, Ibrahim seems to have made up his mind to pursue the war on land with such ferocity that he would annihilate the Greeks in the Peloponnese before the foreign powers could stop him. Refugees began to come over to Zante with new and terrible tales of massacres and armies on the march. From anywhere off the coast, the smoke of burning villages could be seen. And among the ships that joined Codrington's fleet was the frigate *Cambrian*, still commanded by Gawen Hamilton – now promoted captain – the man who had faithfully watched the war for the past five years and always unofficially helped the Greeks. He must have been hardened to atrocities, but he had just put in to Kalamata in the south of the Peloponnese, and even he was shocked by what he had seen. He reported to Codrington that the Pasha's soldiers now were laying the country utterly to waste. They were not only burning villages; now, if they had not done it before, they were uprooting the vineyards and orange and lemon groves, and setting the olive and fig trees on fire. The surviving Greeks had taken to the hills and were trying to hide in caves and keep themselves and their children alive on boiled leaves and grass. It all seemed to confirm that the Egyptians, in spite of their denial, did intend to wipe out the Greeks and might soon succeed. The three admirals wrote a joint letter to Ibrahim requesting him to stop, and they sent a frigate to take it in to Navarino. But his staff said he had gone inland and they did not know where he was.

Codrington, one must add, was almost equally angry at the piracy of the Greeks which was still increasing in the Aegean, and he sent an equally adamant letter to the secretary of the government at Egina: while British officers like Hastings, he said, seemed to be the only people fighting the war for the Greeks, the Greeks themselves were spending their time and energy seizing British merchant ships and condemning them as prizes of war in illegal courts. Of course that letter also went unanswered.

To put an end to both these urgent evils, the devastation on land and the piracy at sea, the admirals had to do something more than wait. Winter was coming on. Blockading Navarino would soon have been difficult and dangerous and probably would have been useless; storms would certainly have driven them off station and given Ibrahim chances to slip out undetected – one day was all he needed – and finally win the war by laying Hydra in ruins. And a blockade would do nothing to stop the annihilation of the Greeks in the Peloponnese. The only alternative was to enter the bay and anchor there in shelter, compel the fleet to stay where it was and try again to make Ibrahim come to terms.

On 18 October the admirals met at sea off Navarino and signed a protocol recording their agreement that this was the only positive action they could take. They hoped it would 'without the effusion of blood and without hostilities, but simply by the imposing presence of the squadrons, produce a determination leading to the desired object.' None of the powers was at war with Turkey, Egypt or Greece, and there was no definable reason why the squadrons should not shelter in the bay, where there was plenty of room for themselves and Ibrahim's fleet. But of course they knew they were running a risk of battle.

The frigate that had taken their letter reported the fleets inside were anchored in a defensive three-quarter circle facing the entrance, 89 warships in all, the largest in front and the smallest disposed behind, with fireships ready on each flank and batteries on each shore. Farther inside the bay were forty or fifty transports. It was a kind of trap arranged by the French advisers with the Egyptian fleet: in theory, ships which came in with a following wind would be caught by fire all round before they could hope to beat out again. Codrington could have sailed through the ring and anchored behind it, but he reckoned that would look like a hostile act. He therefore chose to anchor inside the trap they had set.

On 19 October there was not enough wind to go in. On the 20th, early in the afternoon, he led the combined fleet into the harbour, not in line of battle but in the peaceful double line of the sailing order: ten ships of the line, ten frigates, four brigs and three small cutters. The ships were cleared for action, but the lower deck gunports were only half open, the usual position for sailing in fine weather. All this, to a naval eye, was a plain indication of the orders he had given the ships: not to fire unless they were fired upon. But his order had ended: 'In case of a regular battle ensuing, it is to be observed that, in the words of Lord Nelson, "No captain can do very wrong who places his ship alongside that of an enemy."'

They entered slowly with a gentle breeze astern, passed the shore batteries in a tense silence, into the waiting circle. The *Asia* anchored within a ship's length of the Turkish and Egyptian admirals, whose gun crews stood ready with the guns run out and loaded almost to the muzzles with shot and scrap iron. The band of the *Asia* was ordered on deck to start an entertainment. Two by two the ships astern took station each within pistol shot of a chosen opponent. A British frigate sent a boat to request the fireships to move. The boat was shot at by musketry and an officer was hit: the frigate fired muskets in retaliation: an Egyptian ship fired one cannon shot at the *Sirène* and the *Sirène* fired back. And so it began. Before the sternmost ships were in the bay it was so thick with gunsmoke they could not find their stations. The 'bloody and destructive battle,' Codrington wrote in his dispatch, 'was continued with unabated fury for four hours; and the scene of wreck and devastation which presented itself at its termination was such as has been seldom before witnessed.'

To the survivors in the allied fleet it seemed a glorious and splendid victory: glory was always the comfort of men in war, and they needed comfort. Four hundred and fifty of them were killed or wounded. They lost no ships, but nearly all were damaged, most of all the *Asia*: she was dismasted, and at one moment Codrington, with two bullet holes in his coat and one in his hat, was the only man on his feet on the upper deck. But in retrospect this final battle of all the centuries of navies under sail seems a sordid slaughter. It was fought at anchor, without the redeeming skill of handling ships and canvas in the open ocean. And it was fought at ranges that needed no skill in gun-laying. It only proved that the efficient drill of a European fleet could devastate an eastern fleet at any odds. Codrington reported: 'As each ship of our opponents became effectually disabled, such of her crew as could escape from her endeavoured to set her on fire.' A wooden warship on fire was sure to blow up sooner or later when her magazines were hot enough. 'During the whole night,' he wrote more flippantly to a friend, 'we were entertained with most beautiful though awful explosions.' In one wardroom, the officers cheered at each shattering bang and opened another bottle. At dawn, the bay was seen to be full of corpses and floating planks and spars with thousands of men clinging on to them and calling for help, and at least sixty of the Sultan's warships were wrecked beyond repair.

Battle of Navarino

Mehemet Ali

Frank Abney Hastings

S.S. Karteria

Envoi

Greece was free – bankrupt, starving, diseased and ruined, but free. The Battle of Navarino did not end the war in a day: it took five years of diplomacy to wrest the formal concession of Greek independence from the Sultan, and all through those years the Greeks went on fighting, sometimes against the Turks and Egyptians and sometimes against each other. And one might almost say the war has never ended: on and off, the Greeks and Turks have been fighting ever since, and there is still no sign that they will ever stop. But the destruction of the Sultan's fleet that afternoon, as Hastings had always predicted, brought his rule over Greece to an end that was final: he could not maintain his armies in Greece, and they slowly faded away.

The news caused rejoicing in Europe and America, but the three governments whose fleets had won the battle took it in different ways. The Russians declared war on Turkey and fought in the Balkans and the Black Sea. The French government seemed content with an unexpected wave of popularity; but the British government, with more than a hint of hypocrisy, affected to be embarrassed at having demolished the fleet of a nominally friendly power, and in the speech from the throne at the subsequent opening of Parliament the battle was described as an untoward event. Codrington was recalled. He was not formally censured for fighting the battle, but he was unfairly blamed for something else. The remnants of Ibrahim's fleet went back to Alexandria laden with wounded; also, stowed in its holds, it carried two thousand Greeks into slavery. There was a strong opinion in England that Codrington somehow ought to have stopped that happening, although nothing in his orders gave him authority to search a fleet that was leaving Greece.

It took a French army, in 1828, to oust the last Egyptians from the Peloponnese. By that time, Count Capodistrias had accepted the offer of the Presidency and arrived in Nauplia. But he was an auto-cratic unpopular ruler. In 1831 he wanted to use the frigate *Hellas* against his political critics; but the honest and gallant old Admiral Miaoulis could not bear the idea, and to stop it he blew up and sank his own expensive elegant flagship in the harbour of Poros. And later that year, Capodistrias made a final mistake: he insulted and im-prisoned Petrobey, so that a son and a brother of the chieftain felt compelled by their family pride and their Mainote sense of honour to assassinate the President on the steps of a church in Nauplia. After that, a king was chosen. He was Prince Otho, who was 17 years old, the son of Ludwig of Bavaria, one of the more liberal of con-temporary monarchs. Otho reigned for thirty years, but government continued chaotic and corrupt, and he was deposed by a revolution in 1862.

In the year after Navarino, Frank Hastings fired what may have been the last effective gunshot of the war. It was back in the marsh of Missalonghi, and it must be the most astonishing shot that was ever fired with a round ball from a smooth-bored cannon on a ship. He anchored the *Karteria* as close as he could to the shallow shore and raised one of his guns to an elevation of 28 degrees; and after two ranging shots he landed one plumb on the tiny fort of Vasiladi and blew up its magazine at a range of a mile and a quarter. Later, he led an attack in boats through that detestable marsh, and was shot in the arm and died of blood-poisoning at the age of 33, the most faithful and useful of all the Philhellenes. It was 25 years before the British navy adopted his revolutionary tactics and began to use steam gunboats in the Crimean War.

Hamilton, after four years of sailing in Greece, and after fighting at Navarino, lost his frigate *Cambrian* by shipwreck. He had cleared up a well-known nest of pirates in the island of Grabusa, off the west end of Crete: the *Cambrian* fell foul of another English frigate in the narrow sound, paid off on the wrong tack and drove on a reef.

Hypsilantes died young, but Mavrocordato survived it all, and was prime minister under Capodistrias and the King. Colocotrones was growing rather old, by the time the fighting was over, for an active brigand's life, but he had plenty of successors, and brigandage flourished in Greece for most of the rest of the century. Church lived to a very old age in Athens, in and out of office as general and senator. So did George Finlay, writing his seven-volume history of Greece. Fabvier led an expedition to Chios with no success, and resigned his command unhappy and dissatisfied. Cochrane left the country soon after Navarino in a fury with everyone and everything. He had done almost nothing for his exorbitant fee, but with some justice he blamed the lack of ships and discipline. He continued his stormy career, and after some years was forgiven his many transgressions and received back into the British navy. When the Crimean War began he was Commander-in-Chief in the West Indies, and he applied for the more active war command of the Black Sea. He was 79, and his request was rejected: not because he was old, but because the Admiralty 'feared his adventurous spirit might lead to some desperate enterprise.'

For two or three years after Navarino, the most important man in Greece was the young American who had been Hastings' surgeon in the *Karteria*, Dr Samuel Howe. Very few Americans had been active in the fighting, but they took the lead in patching up the suffering afterwards. Howe was shocked at the poverty and degradation the war had left behind, the thousands and thousands of homeless people dying of neglect, the children stunted by want and the maimed beggars crawling in the streets. He was still only 27, but he and a couple of friends began a tremendous campaign in America for food and clothes and medicines, and when the gifts began to arrive he travelled round the country in constant risk of his life to make sure they reached the people who needed them most. Men from most of the countries of Europe had tried to help the Greeks to win their war; Britain, France and Russia, in an almost casual gesture, had won it for them when it was almost lost; America rescued them in its awful aftermath.

Outside Greece, I suppose, the death of Byron will always be remembered as the main event of the war. In retrospect the Greeks made a hero of him. But try as I may, I cannot find that his expedition or his death did any tangible good to the cause of Greece. While he was there, they scrambled for his money, but when he was dead and the money was gone they never (so far as I can discover) gave him another thought until after the war; there was too much else to do. Certainly, in Europe and America the news of his death brought the plight of the Greeks to the notice of many people who had scarcely heard of it before. Perhaps as a consequence – though even this is hypothesis – it brought in a little more money, but very nearly all the money was wasted. And perhaps it brought a few more romantic volunteers, but very nearly all of them were useless. Dr Howe, I think, was the only important exception; he said that Byron's death was one of the events that made him go to Greece – the other was that he had been crossed in love.

Nevertheless, the legend of Byron's heroism grew, and inspired generations of people who in one way or another believed they were fighting for freedom against oppression: the legend of Byron the poet of freedom, who fought for freedom and died for it. It was a noble legend. But as for the facts, I am sure that Byron of all people, if he had kept his health, would have insisted on putting them in their just proportion. There were many heroes in Greece: he would have refused to count himself among them – because he never fought, and when he tried it was a ludicrous fiasco. He had told Lady Blessington that if he survived his adventure he would write two poems, one an epic and the other a burlesque. Well, he wrote a few epic verses; if he had lived to write the other, he would have kept his promise to spare nobody, and least of all himself – and what a superb burlesque it might have been.

*

In the summer of 1974 I sailed my same small boat out of Greece again, through the Ionian Sea and up the Adriatic on the way to Venice. The last anchorage in Greece as you head that way is the little island of Othoni north-west of Corfu, and we rested there one evening. A boat load of small boys rowed shakily out to see

who we were, people were singing discordant songs ashore, and
we heard the wet slaps of a fisherman pounding an octopus on the
rocks. The sea in the sandy bay was its unbelievable turquoise, and
as it grew dark the scent of the herbs came down from the hills of
the island and a small herd of goats wandered home through the
olive trees ringing their bells, urged along by a girl who was not
much taller than they were.

> '. . . This shall go onward the same,
> Though Dynasties pass.'

We sailed sadly by night with the light of Othoni astern and
Albania safely far to starboard; for the Albanians are still peculiar
people, allied to nobody now except communist China, and they
are said to arrest inoffensive boats within the twelve-mile limit of
their coast. When we were past them we sailed more slowly on,
among the friendly islands of Jugoslavia; and in the uniquely
dreamy detachment of a small boat on a foreign shore, we heard no
news of anything until we came to the north of Italy, where we
saw the word WAR in a headline in a newspaper kiosk. It was the
Greeks and Turks who were at it again: they had started the day
we left Othoni. And there yet again was the news I had read in
the papers of the 1820's. The Greek government had fallen, among
accusations of cruelty, corruption and conspiracy; another had
taken office, with promises of democracy. There were stories, now
from Cyprus, of improbable feats of arms, of massacres and villages
in flames and graves full of headless corpses. And there were state-
ments by leaders using exactly the phrase the Greeks had used when
they asked for terms in 1826: that it is impossible for Greeks and
Turks to live together.

It is no more precisely true now than it was then; I suppose it is
a remnant of the 'ethnic' truth. All through the centuries of Turkish
rule, there had been many Greeks and Turks and their families who
were kind and friendly neighbours. There were still many in Cyprus,
which was the only place where large numbers of them were still
mixed closely together. But ever since 1453, the mixture has exploded

from time to time in mutual rage. There is always some superficial reason, but they do not really seem to know why it happens. And there seems to be nothing anyone else can do; only wait till their rage has cooled, and then try to help to heal the wounds they inflict on each other and themselves.

Index

Index